D1713613

The Golden Age
of Liberalism

To the family, friends, and colleagues of Roméo LeBlanc
whose generous support made this work possible,
in the hope that they find it a fair likeness.

I am told that there is a proverbial phrase among the Inuit: "A long time ago in the future." Let the children see our history, and maybe it will help the future.

—**Roméo LeBlanc**

Contents

Foreword

Roméo LeBlanc was a great Acadian whose life showed the best qualities of Canadians and was proof of what is possible for our people.

He was born in a small settlement on the banks of the beautiful Memramcook River, which flows into the Bay of Fundy, the youngest surviving son of a family of farmers. He was born a French Canadian and had great pride in this heritage in a province where the majority of the population is English speaking. It was the financial support of his sisters that enabled him to go to college, where he achieved a brilliant scholarly record.

I first noticed Roméo when he was one of the foreign correspondents for Radio-Canada. His reports from London and Washington were clear, informative, precise and well documented. These characteristics marked his work when he became press secretary, first to Prime Minister Pearson in 1967 and later for Prime Minister Trudeau. Roméo faced a press gallery that was none too kind at this time and a caucus that was even less well tempered, but he always remained calm, well prepared and often spoke with a smile.

In 1972, he joined us as a member of Parliament and later on became a Cabinet minister. I never met anyone in Parliament who did not like him. I dealt with a colleague who was polite, knew what he was about, was determined and incredibly persistent. Certainly, he had an enormous success as the minister of fisheries. Even decades after he left the ministry, he was fondly remembered. Recently, I met fishermen from Prince Edward Island who told me that Roméo LeBlanc was the best fisheries minister ever. They said he was the best because he had stayed in the job a long time and was really "one of us."

With the retirement of his friend, Prime Minister Trudeau, Roméo left the House of Commons for the Senate. During the election of 1993, Senator LeBlanc became the mentor to a number of young political assistants and campaign workers. Roméo ran the most efficient war room that I have ever known. It was perhaps the best the Liberal Party has ever had. In 1994, he became, for a short time, one of the most respected speakers of the Senate. However, the country had never had a governor general from the Atlantic Provinces, and it was also time to name a francophone.

And what kind of governor general was Roméo? Simple, affable, good humoured, intelligent, politically savvy, knowledgeable, a raconteur, a world traveller, all wrapped inside a great personality. I have never met an enemy of Roméo LeBlanc. Upon moving into Rideau Hall, Roméo decided to open the previously closed gates to the general public and make Rideau Hall welcome to as many Canadians as possible. He was as much at ease with the heads of state that came to visit Canada as he was with the most humble of us.

One of the most memorable moments of my life was when I returned to politics in 1993. Fernand Robichaud gave up his electoral district—which had been Roméo's riding for years—for me to run in. Throughout the campaign that followed, Roméo came with me to introduce me to his former constituents. It was an honour for me to be elected by these most courageous and worthy French North Americans, the Acadians.

During the three years when I represented this riding I came to know that my friend Roméo had earned the respect and love of the anglophones of Sackville as he had the francophones of Richibucto. He was the first Maritimer and the first Acadian to become governor general, and he made these people very proud of him.

Roméo well deserves to have a biography dedicated to his remarkable life.

—*The Right Honourable Jean Chrétien, P.C., O.M., C.C., Q.C.*

Introduction

A Gift of Friendship

Roméo LeBlanc had a talent for making and keeping friends. He liked people. He was curious about their experiences and genuinely interested in how they coped with the circumstances of their lives. I had the good fortune to enjoy his friendship for more than fifty years, and it was a friendship we both cherished.

We first met in February 1954. He was at the Sorbonne working towards a doctorate in the teaching of French. I was in my first year as an undergraduate at London University, and was only briefly visiting in Paris. I was not yet twenty; Roméo's twenty-sixth birthday had been the previous December. I expected this meeting to be short, because it had come about at the request of another Canadian, Winnifred Dionne, who asked me to pick up two books from him. Winnifred was studying at the Institute of Education in London and lived in the same university residence, Canterbury Hall. Her home was in northern New Brunswick, where Roméo had been a teacher the previous year. He had crossed the Atlantic with two of her books, and she wanted them back.

I have kept a diary, sporadically, for much of my life, so I can be precise about some details of our first meeting. It was on the seventh of the month, a Sunday afternoon, and took place at la Maison du Canada, which was part of the Cité Universitaire, a collection of residences built for international students by the Sorbonne in 1925. I remember it was a cold and grey day. I arrived at the Cité at dusk and, instead of a ten-minute book collection, the meeting turned into an evening meal at a local restaurant with Roméo and another friend of Winnifred's, Rhéal Gaudet. We spoke mostly in French, and I wrote that night that "I felt no edginess or embarrassment with them and we talked snobbery, conventions, the differences between the English and French." There was nothing more to the occasion than a pleasant conversation among university students, with no more than a thought that a future meeting was unlikely but would be welcome. We came from very different backgrounds, and our ideas about how and where our lives would unfold were, literally, an ocean apart. I was born and brought up in Sussex, UK. My family was middle-class, agnostic, socialist, with a mixture of Irish and Welsh in its heritage. His family was rural, French-speaking, Catholic, and Acadian—this last a heritage about which I knew nothing at the time. His future was clear: the teaching profession in New Brunswick. Mine was cloudy—in 1953 in the UK women made up less than 10 per cent of the undergraduate population, and a degree in medieval history, for which I was studying, had no obvious career path.

That meeting might very well have been it, if events had not brought us both by different paths to Fredericton, New Brunswick. In 1955, family circumstances forced Roméo to cut short his studies in Paris and return to his home province in order to help his family financially. He took a position that year as a teacher in the provincial Normal School in Fredericton. A year later I arrived in the city to study for an M.A. at the University of New Brunswick with Dr. Alfred Bailey. My choice of city and university were due to other Canadian friends who had introduced me to the scholarship of A.G. Bailey. I was intrigued by his ideas on the rise and fall of civilizations, and I wrote to him. He answered and offered me a $700 fellowship for graduate work if I could find the passage money to Canada, which I managed to do. If graduate work in Canada seemed unlikely, events there took an even more unforeseen turn. I came with the intention of working on Protestant-Catholic relations in New Brunswick, but I ended up writing about the historiography of the Acadians. Dr. Bailey steered me in this direction for a number of reasons. The first was that he considered the subject of the importance of religious differences in the political life of New Brunswick a particularly contentious issue in 1956. His choice of Acadian history for me sprang from his belief that, since 1785 when the University of New Brunswick was founded, no one had ever chosen to study Acadian history. Finally, I was competent in French.

Given that I had spent the last three years studying medieval history, with an emphasis on the Hussite movement in Czechoslovakia, I faced an unknown territory to explore. My ignorance of Acadian history at that time was matched by an equal ignorance about New Brunswick in general. My circumstances, however, were fortunate for learning about both. The parents of yet another friend, Mr. and Mrs. Sansom of 83 Shore Street, once the home of poet Bliss Carman, gave me bed and breakfast free. At the time, Mr. Sansom was the purchasing agent for the provincial government of Hugh John Flemming, and I came to know a fair amount about anglophone New Brunswick through this connection. At the same time, I spent at least one weekend every month in Edmundston, a town where over 90 per cent of the population was French-speaking, at the home of

Winnifred Dionne, whose borrowed books had been the cause of my meeting with Roméo in the first place. The perspective her family gave me on New Brunswick politics became the grounding for my knowledge of francophones in the province. Another important source of information was my occasional, increasingly comfortable, meetings with Roméo. I arrived in Fredericton in mid-July, and by mid-September I had some idea of the task before me. I discovered that the university library had more than two hundred articles, pamphlets, and books written about the "Deportation of the Acadians." Dr. Bailey was an outstanding supervisor, and he helped me to understand that my very ignorance of contemporary attitudes about the past was a strength. As a result, I was guided to frame three questions for investigation: Why had so much been written about the Deportation in 1755 of fewer than 10,000 French-speaking Catholics by the English from what was then known in international treaties as "Nova Scotia or Acadia—l'Acadie ou la Nouvelle Écosse"? What were the main interpretations of this event? And, to a lesser extent, what was the link between these writings and the sense of identity of twentieth-century Acadians in New Brunswick? The title of my thesis was "The Acadian Deportation: A Study in Historiography and Nationalism." It was examined in the spring of 1957.

At that time, the University of New Brunswick still held public orals for M.A. candidates in the humanities. Mine turned out to be lengthy. In addition to the appointed members of the examining board, members of the audience—many of whom were from the town—were allowed to question the candidate. Roméo was there and, looking back, I now think this was of major importance in the development of our friendship. The beginning of the examination was much as I expected, but then members of the audience began to participate. I concluded my introductory remarks on my work by saying that the Deportation took place as a result of the policies of the governments of both France and England, as well as the ambitions and fears of Quebec and Massachusetts. Then I went on to suggest that far more important than apportioning blame for the destruction of this original Acadian community was awareness of its immediate results: the breaking up of extended families, a high death toll on board the ships, and exile without end for many. That there was still an Acadian people in existence today, I concluded, was a totally unforeseen and undesired outcome for those who had carried out the Deportation. It was this judgment that raised the particular ire of a number of questioners. One man wished me to acknowledge that Acadians had brought the Deportation on themselves. Furthermore, he considered that I should admit that the Deportation had not inflicted all that much hardship and suffering. Finally, during the twenty minutes of his intervention, it seemed to me that he wanted me to agree that the present legal situation of the Acadians in New Brunswick was justified. In 1956, French was not recognized as a language for the purposes of court proceedings. Even if judge, prosecutor, defence lawyers, defendant, and jury members were all French-speaking, every word had to be translated into English for the proceedings to be legal. All provincial examinations for high-school graduation were in English, except for the French-language examination. His questioning was brought to a close by Dr. Desmond Pacey, who chaired the proceedings. As he sat down, however, the questioner remarked loudly that my conclusions were those of a "sentimental woman." Nonetheless, the official examining board saw fit to grant my M.A.

I planned to go to Columbia University in the fall of 1957 to study with Dr. John Brebner, but a bureaucratic tangle there meant that, instead, I went to teach at Collège Maillet, the small women's college attached to St. Louis University/Université Saint-Louis in Edmundston. It was this experience that cemented my interest in the Acadians as a people, that led to my career

studying their history, and that helped develop my lasting friendship with Roméo. Over the next year, I came to know the society
that had shaped him, a society that was completely different from
any I had encountered, and which I came to like very much.
It was based on rural life and the primary resource industries
of forestry and lumber mills and the fishery. Six to eight children in a family were common, and ten or more children were
not unusual. Life at a subsistence level was widespread in Kent
County. Yet at the same time, the county had a lively intellectual
and cultural élite.

If the transition from London, England, to Fredericton, New
Brunswick, was something of a culture shock, the move from
Fredericton, an English-speaking Loyalist city, to Edmundston, a
French-speaking town across the St. John River from the United
States, was equally so. However, during the nine months I lived
in this part of New Brunswick, I made lifelong Acadian friends
and learned a great deal about the Acadian communities of
the province, the people whose past history and present needs
formed the frame for Roméo's thoughts and feelings.

Edmundston, it should be noted, was an obvious stopping
place for anyone travelling from Fredericton and Moncton to
Quebec City and Montreal. It was a nexus for the continuing
social interaction among the Acadians who had been to college in
the 1940s and 1950s. The network of acquaintances and friends
made the professional and political lives of Acadians tight,
with an enduring structure of communication between them.
There were spaghetti parties with good wine (Pontet Carnet was
three dollars a bottle) on Friday nights at Winnifred's, bringing together three or four people from the town and whoever
was driving through. These were joyful occasions, with the talk
covering events across New Brunswick, as well as national and
international matters. I was caught up in the camaraderie of this
group, which included Léonard Forest, who later made his name

as a filmmaker and poet. Others, such as Paul-Émile Carrier and Rhéal Gaudet, also went on to work as commentators, reporters and producers for Radio Canada. It was an age when telephone calls were expensive but the postal service fast and cheap. Letters criss-crossed the group and carried gossip about who was where, doing what and, of course, with whom.

In 1957, New Brunswick had a population of 554,616, the majority of whom lived outside the cities. Over one-third of the population was French-speaking. Most people in rural New Brunswick, whether French or English, lived close to, or below, the poverty line. However, those who spoke French were most often found in the lowest economic stratum. They were clustered mainly in three areas: the northwest, where Edmundston was the principal town and about 98 per cent had French as their first language and the language of the home; the northeast, the area stretching from the Baie-des-Chaleurs to the Miramichi estuary, where the majority of the population were similarly French speaking; and the coast between the Miramichi and the border with Nova Scotia. The province has an area of 72,908 square kilometres, and in 1957 only the major highways were paved. Increasing numbers of families had cars, but the railways and long-distance buses were still crucially important. However far apart the Acadian settlements looked on a map, the connections between communities were strong. I learned quickly that any first encounter between two Acadians was always initiated with a discussion about how their families were related, by third, second, or first cousins, or by a marriage link between the in-law of a family relative with a similar connection through a marriage of another in-law. Only when this matter was settled would a conversation proceed. Such a structure of kin relationships is close to the connections acknowledged, even today, among many Welsh families, or those living in the Scottish Highlands.

I also came to understand that such connections in no way meant that the political opinions among the regions were identical. Of course there was considerable uniformity of opinion about major political questions: the need for the recognition of the legality of the French language; of the right to have children taught in their mother tongue throughout the school system; of the importance of having the French-speaking population of the province properly represented not only in the legislature but also in the civil service. There was also, in this period, a fair consensus that the way to achieve such goals was through the political pressure of the élites for better education. But the circumstances of their daily lives gave the communities very different temperaments. In broad brush strokes, Acadians living in Edmundston and the surrounding county of Madawaska, close to the United States and Quebec borders, who worked in the pulp mills and the forests, preferred direct political arguments. With the St. John River often sufficiently frozen during the winter months to be crossed safely by foot, many from the area considered a little smuggling a perfectly natural activity. The number of cross-border marriages helped to support this idea. Acadians of "la Péninsule," with the Gaspé a near neighbour and the people of the French islands of St. Pierre and Miquelon as familiar as fishermen from Newfoundland and Prince Edward Island, had a temperament that was slow to rise and even slower to defuse. It was in this region, especially around Caraquet and Bathurst, that explosive political action most often occurred. However, as with the fishermen of Newhaven and Dieppe, who faced each other across the English Channel, there was, and is, a tradition of help among fishing vessels, except when rights clashed. The people from further down the coast, from Bouctouche, Shediac, and Cap-Pélé, made their living from both the forest and the sea, and were considered the most even-tempered of the Acadian communities—if, perhaps, the most stubborn. The Quebec saying, "entêté [stubborn] comme un Acadien," voices an opinion about all Acadians.

My time in Edmundston was also when I saw, first hand, not only life in large families but also what an extended family meant. Winnifred Dionne was one of eight children. Her mother was a LeBlanc from Bouctouche, which linked her to a network of cousins who lived at the other end of the province, some of whom were fishermen in villages along the coast and some of whom lived in middle-class circumstances in Dieppe, on the outskirts of Moncton. I was once part of an unforgettable Christmas Day with a family of fifteen, the siblings ranging in age from their late teens to their early thirties, some back home with their own spouses and children. It was such Christmases that Roméo knew as a child, since he had a brother and two sisters married and settled in the neighbourhood. The women were involved throughout the whole day in cooking, cleaning, feeding, washing, and comforting a crowd of little ones. In my memory, it seems there were at least ten children under five. The men were occupied with work around the small holding, which was not a farm but more than just a garden. The heating was by wood stove, the chickens needed care, meat needed to be brought in, much of this from an animal shot during the fall. After more than fifty years, my strongest recollections are of the small ones being often in someone's arms, of coffee and buckwheat pancakes served throughout the day, and of the main meal served continuously from around three o'clock in the afternoon to well into the evening. It was common then, over the Christmas season, which went until New Year's Day, to seat twenty to thirty people for meals.

Acadian society at this time was on the brink of the massive transformation that took place in the 1960s and 1970s. This transformation touched every aspect of Acadian life. Reforms introduced by Louis Robichaud, who became the Liberal premier of the province in 1960, made New Brunswick the first, and still the only, officially bilingual province in Canada. He called his government policies an "Equal Opportunity Program," and they applied to the poor, anglophone and francophone alike, throughout the province. His major changes began with the abolition of county councils and the centralization of education and health care under provincial control. Since anglophones were just as poor as francophones in many areas of the province, Robichaud's support crossed linguistic barriers. At the same time, the Second Vatican Council, which met between October 1962 and December 1965, fostered the growing tide of secularism among Acadians. The influence of the Catholic clergy over the education and health policies of the government began to shrink. There was a parallel reduction of the church's direct control of schools, colleges, hospitals, and nursing homes. In the 1950s, the local school boards supported extracurricular duties for teachers, which included teaching catechism. Board members also monitored teachers' attendance at Sunday Mass. The reduction of their authority gave many in the teaching profession a liberty not previously enjoyed. This dwindling importance of faith did not take place only in New Brunswick, but was equally drastic in Quebec.

In 1958, I left northern New Brunswick for London University, thanks to a Lord Beaverbrook Overseas Scholarship, to begin work on a doctorate. Roméo left Fredericton to join Radio-Canada in Ottawa in 1959. Thanks to the social life of Edmundston, our friendship was now on a firm footing.

When I returned to Canada in December 1960, my Acadian friendships were intact. I joined Carleton University in 1961 as a sessional lecturer in the Department of History and in 1962 was given a tenure-track appointment as a lecturer. I spent the rest of my working life at that university and am still attached to Carleton as a "distinguished research professor" in its history department. As I adjusted to life in Ottawa and at Carleton, Roméo and other Acadians, such as Laurier Melanson who worked for the Dominion Drama Festival, helped me settle in. Over the next years their friendship was important to me and frequent visits to New Brunswick helped deepen my acquaintanceship with Acadian scholars. Roméo left Ottawa to become Radio-Canada's foreign correspondent in London in 1963. We met whenever we were on the same side of the Atlantic, usually for an evening meal, and once we had caught up on the lives of those mutual acquaintances we had seen, the conversation turned to the political life and times. My diary entries show telephone calls and the occasional letter over this period. Roméo was transferred to Washington in 1965, and in 1966 I was there, as I worked my way down the coast tracing the Deportation route of the Acadians. An evening at a dinner party in Roméo's apartment, where Knowlton Nash was one of the guests, brought a vigorous discussion on civil rights and Vietnam. Roméo returned to Ottawa in 1967 as press secretary to Prime Minister Pearson. He married Joslyn Carter at the end of 1966.

Over the next five years, our meetings were less frequent. We both had family responsibilities: his, a wife and growing family; mine, the last years of my father's life. Our careers were also in vastly different fields—mine in university and his in the political mainstream of the country. However, our friendship continued. By early 1972, life had become more organized, if not more tranquil, for both of us, and meetings became somewhat more frequent. Discussions about current events were a major component of such occasions, but Roméo was never a gossip. While I was to the left of Roméo politically, having worked for the Labour Party in London before I came to Canada, I enjoyed listening to him talk about the choices that federal politicians faced, finding him an astute and nonpartisan commentator. In turn, he found my writings about Acadian history interesting. In 1976, I obtained my doctorate ("The Acadian Deportation: Causes and Development," London University). By then I had published three books, two of them about Acadian history: *The Acadian Deportation: Deliberate Perfidy or Cruel Necessity?* (1969); *The Acadians: Creation of a People* (1973); and *Penelope's Web: Some Perceptions of Women in European and Canadian Society* (1976). The questions which occupied most of our discussions surrounded the issue of minority identities in a federal state: Where did different cultural traditions need to be given the opportunity to flourish? Where must assimilation to a majority culture be enforced? And how? What about minority rights? Collective rights? The Acadians were not our only interest here. What should be the rights of Mi'kmaq and Malecite, the First Nations people of the Maritimes? Even when Roméo was appointed to the Cabinet in 1974, he made time for our friendship. There were the occasional lunches in the parliamentary restaurant and a lecture on whatever problem of the fisheries obsessed him at the time. Almost always there was a meal between Christmas and New Year with him and his family. When he was appointed minister of public works, there was considerable discussion about what exactly the federal government should do about the housing market. When he was appointed to the Senate in 1984, I was dean of Arts at Carleton University. In 1985, I was delighted to welcome Roméo for a term as a visiting fellow in the Institute of Canadian Studies, which was one of the departments for which I had responsibility. Our friendship by this time had lasted more than thirty years and remained interesting to us both. In the last decade of the twentieth century, Roméo served from February 8, 1995, to October 7, 1999, as Canada's twenty-fifth governor general.

When he retired, I spoke to him about the necessity of him writing his autobiography. He flatly rejected the idea: nothing doing. I was aware that he had kept very few records, and almost no personal correspondence or personal diary. I was also aware that he had never sought personal publicity, and that he had a very strong sense of his right to privacy. As an historian, however, I felt that there should be a record of a life that had been, in my view, important for Canadians. I finally persuaded him to have a number of conversations with me about what he considered were the important times for him. These were to be conversations: no tape recorder, no notes made during the conversations. The aim was literally a memorandum to be used by a possible biographer. I had no intention of writing his biography because I wanted to write a concluding work to follow the publication of my book *From Migrant to Acadian: A North American Border People, 1604–1755,* with one dealing with the period 1755–1784. I thought it important, however, that at least some of Roméo's personal recollections about his life should be preserved. From 2000 to 2004, I visited him on a number of occasions. As the meetings progressed, he realized that he had been stricken with Alzheimer's disease. At the last of these meetings, in the summer of 2004, he said to me: "My mind is not going to be much use for this any more—but you will write it, won't you?"

What follows is my answer. I have not tried to write a conventional "life and times" biography. Instead, I have attempted to give in words a portrait of a very dear friend, an Acadian who was beloved by his people, a man much treasured by fishermen, a modest man, and a quintessential Canadian.

CHAPTER 1

From Memramcook to Rideau Hall

The installation of Roméo Adrien LeBlanc as the first governor general of Canada from the Maritimes, and the first Acadian, took place in the Senate chamber of the Parliament of Canada on February 8, 1995. His nomination and installation were the occasion for the usual array of public commentaries, both positive and negative.

Ever since 1952, when Vincent Massey was appointed the first Canadian-born governor general, questions have arisen about the possible partisan political loyalties of the individual chosen. The office, after all, is neither hereditary nor elective. As one political scientist has remarked, the governor general has been for a considerable time the "non-political representative of the people selected by their chief political officer."[1] Inevitably, such a paradoxical arrangement has meant that appointments to the position have almost never received universal approval. To what extent did the choice of the prime minister of the day represent nothing more than the wish of a partisan politician to reward past

Official photograph of Roméo as governor general, 1995

services to the political party in power? Furthermore, by 1995, the office itself was being questioned. For some, having a governor general was a waste of public money, and many considered it to be the final colonial tie to the United Kingdom, which badly needed cutting. For others, it was the process of selection that was flawed. If the governor general was supposed to be without political prejudice, then surely the selection procedures should be visibly non-partisan? All these views were expressed when, on November 22, 1994, Prime Minster Jean Chrétien announced Roméo LeBlanc as the successor to the Right Honourable Ramon Hnatyshyn as governor general of Canada.

There was a good deal of positive commentary on the nomination, made the stronger because of the reaction of Preston Manning, leader of the Reform Party, to the announcement. Manning immediately criticized the appointment on the floor of the Commons, calling it both "unwise and inappropriate." As Susan Delacourt pointed out in the next morning's *Globe and Mail*, "Never in the 44 years since Canadians have been appointed to the largely ceremonial position has the choice of the Queen's representative been opposed in such a manner in the Commons."[2] Since, by tradition, the representative of the Crown cannot speak in the House of Commons, it had always been considered that such an attack in that place of privilege would be unfair. Taken aback, the prime minister responded by noting that Manning's comment was "unprecedented," and remarked that LeBlanc had decided to forgo his parliamentary pension during his tenure as governor general. Lucien Bouchard, head of the Bloc Québécois and leader of the Opposition, welcomed the appointment, and said that it showed a general "open-mindedness towards francophones." Outside the Commons, Bouchard commented that Manning's remark was "cheap," and that the prime minister's choice was "a good appointment and shows that Mr. Chrétien is a true federalist, who has a sense of the country he lives in and defends, Canada."[3] Meanwhile senior Conservative senator Lowell Murray observed that anybody appointed to the position needed some background in public life, and thought that Roméo LeBlanc would "do just fine."[4]

As the *Globe and Mail* pointed out, much of the reaction sprang from the temper of the House of Commons, where the Progressive Conservative Party (Sir John A. Macdonald's legacy to the polity he helped found in 1867) held only two seats and the Bloc Québécois, whose *raison d'être* was the dissolution of Canada, was the official opposition, with 54 seats. The western-based Reform Party had 52 seats, and the New Democratic Party nine. The Liberal Party had 177 seats, 100 of them from Ontario. As one noted political scientist remarked, this mix made not only for an "unhealthy balance within the government majority," but also for an imbalance within the federal system as a whole.[5] The election of 1993, which produced this Parliament, revealed regional discontents with particular provincial problems and a national disappointment with the overall performance of the federal government. As well, in the background of many minds loomed the knowledge that another referendum on separatism was due within the year. Peter Donolo, Chrétien's spokesman, pointed out that the prime minister had always considered himself a French Canadian first and foremost, not a Quebecker who was, for the present moment, a Canadian. The appointment of an Acadian as governor general, therefore, in the view of the prime minister, reinforced the idea that the "French fact in Canada is not limited to Quebec."[6] Lucien Bouchard underlined this aspect of the appointment of LeBlanc when he remarked that, during the referendum debates which were to occur within the year, "Mr. Chrétien is going to be able to say...Look...the Prime Minister of Canada is a francophone, the governor general is francophone, the speaker of the House of Commons is francophone, the leader of the opposition is francophone."[7] Manning remained undaunted in his criticism, and defended himself by saying that he was merely articulating widespread public cynicism about the way in which the governor general was selected and the "special perks and privileges attached to the office, such as the exemption of income tax and things of that nature."[8] The *Vancouver Sun* supported Manning, suggesting that, "regardless of his personal qualifications," the appointment of LeBlanc represented "another lamentable step in the debasement of the office."[9]

The day after the nomination, the *Toronto Star* published an analysis of the appointment by their Ottawa correspondent, Edison Stewart, a man who had been born and brought up in Moncton. He opened his article: "His profile is so low that, when word leaked out he was to be Canada's next governor general, the country's national news agency distributed a picture of someone else. No one noticed the error for twelve hours."[10] Stewart turned to Canadian historian Jacques Monet, then president of the University of Sudbury and the acknowledged authority on the Crown in Canada, for his opinion on the wisdom of the appointment. Monet thought that LeBlanc was "a good choice to continue the line that stretches back centuries to Champlain in 1620." Monet commented that the governor general–designate was "probably not as widely known" as some who had been previously appointed, but that he had "all the qualities one would look for. He is a man of great integrity."

Stewart continued his article with a brief account of LeBlanc's career. He had little space, however, to go into much background detail as to why a relatively unknown public figure would receive this appointment. Stewart's article noted that LeBlanc had been born in Memramcook, New Brunswick, in 1927, and had worked as a teacher and journalist and then as a reporter for Radio-Canada. His service as press secretary to two prime ministers, Lester Pearson and Pierre Trudeau, was also mentioned. Stewart summed up his career in Parliament, beginning with his election to the House of Commons in 1972, and referred to the rest of his long service in the Cabinet as minister of fisheries. It is as much a reflection of the lack of interest of "Upper Canada" in the Maritimes in general, and in that industry in particular, that LeBlanc's tenure as Canada's longest-serving fisheries minister was so little known or appreciated. One of his many achievements during these years, was his aid in establishing Canada's two-hundred-mile fishing limit and the shaping of the international Law of the Sea. In the opinion of former fishery union president Richard Cashin, LeBlanc showed himself "a good human being and [had been] an outstanding minister. He brought dignity and respect to people who worked in the industry."

The reaction in the French press, both in Quebec and in the Maritimes, was as mixed as that in the House of Commons: considerable praise and pointed criticism. Senator Louis Robichaud, who from 1960 to 1970 had served as the first elected Acadian premier of New Brunswick, thought that LeBlanc had every qualification necessary for the vice-regal position.[11] In its weekend edition, on Saturday, November 26, *La Presse* summarized the dominant feeling in New Brunswick, particularly but not exclusively, among Acadians. It was, according to the reporter, almost impossible to discover a word of criticism, even among the few Conservatives he could find in the province.[12] One source remarked that Roméo LeBlanc had as much support among anglophones as francophones. The reporter ended by quoting Nelson Landry, editor of the Acadian daily *L'Acadie Nouvelle*, who gave as his opinion that Roméo LeBlanc was "a governor general of the people! That is the best title for [someone] who truly listens to people, who seems as much at ease with the queen as with the humblest fisherman." In terms of opinion in Quebec, the appointment was at first seen as reasonable enough. *La Presse*, already noted, emphasized LeBlanc's Acadian roots.

Le Soleil announced the appointment on November 22, with a brief but accurate resumé of his career, and on November 24, it published a report of LeBlanc's decision to forgo his parliamentary pension while governor general.[13] The newspaper considered that it "was a decision that did him credit and would surprise no one who had followed his career."

A clear division in Quebec public opinion appeared, however, with an editorial by Michel Vastel in *Le Soleil*, published on November 25. It was a corrosive personal attack, not only on LeBlanc's three immediate predecessors and LeBlanc himself, but also on the prime minister. Ed Schreyer, governor general from 1979 to 1984, was categorized as "the defeated premier from Manitoba." Jeanne Sauvé, whose term was from 1984 to 1990, was described as one of Pierre Trudeau's ministerial failures. Ray Hnatyshyn, governor general from 1990 to 1995, was defined as "the Conservative rejected by Saskatchewan's electorate." Vastel considered LeBlanc a mediocre journalist with no great reputation in the Liberal Party, and someone of whom Trudeau had no very high opinion. The root of Vastel's bad humour was made explicit at the end of the editorial. "Historians will perhaps note," Vastel wrote,

> *that since the arrival of Jean Chrétien at the head of the Government of Canada, the speaker of the House of Commons is a Franco-Ontarian, Gib Parent; the president of the Senate a Franco-Manitoban, Gil Molgat; and the governor general an Acadian, Roméo LeBlanc. Is it because those Québécois who were asked by Jean Chrétien, such as Jean Béliveau, refused to serve his administration? Or is it because it's necessary at all cost to wipe out of the memory of the world that Canada was born from political agreement between Québec and the rest of the country?*

Vastel concluded by warning Bouchard that, "in guaranteeing this historic precedent without reservation, [he] approves in advance all kinds of 'alternates' between the Québécois on one hand, and anglophones, Aboriginals, representatives of visible minorities, the handicapped, and francophones from outside Québec on the other."[14]

The time between the announcement of the nomination and the installation is largely spent by the governor general–designate in preparing the speech that he or she will deliver on that occasion. As well as the necessity of saying something about what he hoped could be achieved during the coming years in office, his speech needed to provide, if obliquely, some counter to the criticism raised by the nomination. LeBlanc had already brushed aside the accusation that his appointment was the worst sort of political patronage. On being told of Manning's comment, he remarked, "I didn't know that the world of politics was excluded from consideration for any appointment that might come forward."[15] He had made no comment, however, on the more serious allegations that his appointment was to an office that was an expensive and unnecessary part of Canada's constitution, that it had been the result of a process much in need of reform, or that his appointment had broken an "unwritten convention" of the Canadian federation. These more theoretical attacks on the governor general–designate were combined with an assault from another more personally relevant quarter, that is, from among those in the Acadian population who considered his acceptance of the appointment a betrayal of his heritage.

In recent decades, Canadians have become more and more intrigued by the diversity of customs and traditions the country's people cherish. It is the more surprising, therefore, that the Acadian heritage is, except in the Maritimes, relatively unknown. In most Canadian history textbooks, there is only a brief account of the eighteenth-century Deportation and no reference to the complex heritage upon which the Acadian sense of identity developed. That heritage reaches back to the early seventeenth century, with the 1604 founding by the French of the colony known as Acadia. That year, on an island at the mouth of the St. Croix River, a river which today forms part of the Maine–New Brunswick border, 79 men spent an appalling winter. Samuel de Champlain was among them. In his journals, he recorded the deep snow and the temperatures that froze everything but the cheap Spanish wine. Cider was given out by the pound. He wrote in detail about the dreadful death toll from scurvy that the settlement suffered. Of the 79 men who saw the snow fall on October 6, 1604, only 44 were left alive when the spring melt began in 1605, and 20 of those were sick almost to death. From this disastrous beginning, the Acadian community grew, surviving an extraordinary number of vicissitudes to earn recognition as "the Acadian people—le peuple acadien" from the secretary-general of the United Nations in 1994.[16] At the time of this significant acknowledgement, there were over 300,000 Acadians in New Brunswick, well over one-third of the population of that province. Further, there were more than two million people claiming Acadian descent, some living in the other Maritime provinces, some in Quebec, some elsewhere in Canada, some even further afield, in France and in the United States, all of whom cherished their Acadian heritage.

Close to four centuries had passed between that first expedition and the recognition of Acadian identity by the United Nations. For the first century, the territory that France claimed as Acadia in 1604, lands that today make up New Brunswick, Nova Scotia, and parts of northern Maine and southeastern Quebec, was from 1620 also claimed by England as Nova Scotia. Throughout the seventeenth century, these imperial powers squabbled over this territory being developed by the Acadians. The colony, referred to in the international treaties of the time as "Acadia or Nova Scotia–l'Acadie ou la Nouvelle Écosse," changed hands frequently. By 1713, in the Treaty of Utrecht, it was finally ceded by France to Great Britain, but its boundaries remained a matter of dispute. By this time, the Acadian identity was clearly formed and had become something other than a mere reflection of France or an echo of the French colony along the St. Lawrence River. The Acadian population spoke French but, because of strong economic ties with Massachusetts, had people in their villages who also spoke English. The Catholic religion was of considerable importance in Acadians' lives, but they had little tolerance for priestly control. One commentator called them "the most Protestant of Catholics." With a strong mixed economy and a growing population, as well as a strong belief in their right to live on lands their families had cultivated for close to three generations, the Acadians accepted the arrival of the English in 1713 as something that ought not to disrupt their lives too profoundly.

After 1730, both English and French authorities, whether in London or Paris, Boston or Quebec City, referred to the Acadians as *les français neutres*, "the neutral French." It was generally recognized that the settlers had sworn an oath of allegiance to the British, on the understanding that they would not be required to fight against France. Unfortunately, by the 1740s, the struggle between France and England for the dominance of North America became increasingly bitter and deadly. As the Acadian population increased and cultivated more land, the land itself became more important as a border between New England and New France. Before the declaration of yet one more war in 1756, there was a concerted move by Massachusetts, Nova Scotia, and imperial officials in London (through a naval presence in Halifax) to secure control of the strategic "continental cornice," the land between the northeastern limits of New England and the French position on Île Royale (Cape Breton Island) and Île

Saint-Jean (Prince Edward Island). The colonial authorities in Nova Scotia and Massachusetts were convinced that the Acadians would break their oath of neutrality. In the spring of 1755, matters came to a head and the lieutenant-governor of Nova Scotia, Colonel Charles Lawrence, demanded that the Acadians swear an unequivocal oath of loyalty to the British Crown, without any reservation of neutrality. They refused, and the decision was made to deport the Acadians from lands on which they had lived for three or more generations, to "distribute," in the words of the recorded decision, the Acadians "amongst the Several Colonies on the Continent."

And distributed they were! Some 15,000 to 18,000 people were shipped to the other British colonies in North America, an act that effectively destroyed the first Acadian society. No matter what judgment one makes as to the military necessity of the Deportation, let alone its morality, it had two quite unequivocal results: it sent the majority of the Acadian population of 1755 into exile, and reaction to that event has coloured the Acadian sense of themselves, to a greater or lesser degree, ever since. The sense of Acadian identity after the Deportation of 1755 was different from what it had been before that date. It was built not only on the memories of the few who had remained exiles near their former homes, but also on the experiences of those who eventually returned from the places where they had been sent by force. These Acadians, the link between the pre- and post-Deportation Acadian communities, rebuilt their lives after 1755 within lands that became part of Canada, but not on the lands that their ancestors had cultivated for six generations before their exile. The continued development of Acadian identity during the nineteenth and twentieth centuries wove together a rich heritage of cultural, social, and political customs with new traditions, invented because of the reorganization of life on different lands and the reaction after the exile to the presence of new societies as neighbours. Yet because of the cataclysmic nature of the events of 1755, its memory, like a prevailing wind, shaped the development of Acadian identity over the next two centuries.

The preservation and growth of an Acadian identity after 1764, the year in which their exile was officially ended, was difficult. In Nova Scotia, and later in New Brunswick and Prince Edward Island, the Acadians worked as a collectivity, as a people with a sense of their distinctiveness, as members of communities with specific and deeply held beliefs in their unique identity. But they were now a minority where once they had been a majority, and the struggle to preserve their language and culture was not to be easy. There were always conflicting opinions about the best way to confront their problems, how to improve their circumstances, and how to gain recognition and respect from the more powerful majority.

It is in light of this heritage, then, that the nomination of Roméo LeBlanc as governor general was received with marked enthusiasm by most Maritime Acadians, but angered others. One or two letters were published in the Quebec and Acadian press in December 1994 excoriating LeBlanc for accepting the position, and a few others appeared after his installation. Their general message was the same: how could an Acadian forget it was the British who had deported them, who had ripped people from their homelands, split up families, and driven men, women, and children into exile? To add insult to injury, the British Crown had never apologized, and now an Acadian was to act as the representative of that same Crown in Canada.[17] The writer of one letter, published at the time of the installation, said that he would find it impossible, if the occasion ever arose, to shake the hand of someone, such as the governor general, who could forget the injury done to his own forebears 240 years earlier.

The installation of a governor general is, along with the opening of Parliament, one of the few occasions of official pageantry in Canada. It is also an occasion for the muting of partisan politics, a moment when the idea of a national community is made visible, and beliefs that the country holds in common are emphasized rather than the many issues that divide it. In 1995, the new governor general faced a greater need than had his predecessors to defend the necessity and relevance of the office: Preston Manning, for example, maintained his criticism of the appointment by boycotting the occasion. The general tone of the installation, however, was positive. A number of those who would naturally attend assembled in the Senate Chamber: members of the federal Cabinet; former prime ministers Pierre Trudeau and Kim Campbell; former Progressive Conservative leader Robert Stanfield; and Gilles Duceppe, as representative of Lucien Bouchard. The premier of Prince Edward Island, Catherine Callbeck, and the premier of New Brunswick, Frank McKenna, were present, as well as the former premier of New Brunswick, Senator Louis Robichaud. Justice of the Supreme Court, the Honourable Gérard LaForest administered the oath of office, and the choir Jeunes Chanteurs d'Acadie provided the music. In the audience were many Acadians from all walks of life, who marvelled, as one Acadian journalist wrote, that one of their number would be governor general before there was an Acadian cardinal.[18] The prime minister gave a brief summary of LeBlanc's political career, remarking that he had been in public life since 1972, when he was elected to the House of Commons as the MP for Westmorland–Kent. Chrétien recalled that except for a very brief hiatus, when Joe Clark was prime minister, LeBlanc served from 1974 to 1984 as a minister of the Crown and, for eight of these years, had been the minister responsible for Canada's fisheries, and thus the nation's longest-serving fisheries minister. Summoned to the Senate in 1984, he became its speaker in December 1993. The prime minister pointed out that much of the governor general's time is spent with visiting heads of state, who usually want to talk about politics, and LeBlanc was well prepared for such an activity. Chrétien concluded, speaking directly to LeBlanc, by saying, "I have known you as a man who has not sought glory for himself, but has simply strived to serve the people in Canada."[19]

It is always difficult to speak after having received fulsome praise, even if the praise is deserved. It is even more difficult to do so when assuming a position that is, above all, symbolic, and whose occupant is supposed to avoid making political comments, and at a time when a major part of the country is about to hold a referendum on whether it should separate. To the scarcely veiled astonishment of the national press, LeBlanc delivered a speech that drew considerable approval from most quarters and little outright hostility. He achieved this result by weaving together his perception of Acadian history, the personal experiences of his youth in what became Canada's only bilingual province, and his understanding of particular Canadian national traits into a vision of what he wanted to emphasize during his tenure as governor general. He achieved it also because, at a time when political nerves in Canada were rasped raw by bitter relationships between party élites, when the financial picture was not particularly rosy, and when ethnic rivalries seemed more sharp-edged than usual, he spoke without pretension about what he thought was right with the state of the nation.

In some ways, LeBlanc benefited from the fact that he was relatively unknown, that his political career lay in the past, and that his achievements had not left rancorous debate in their wake. Marc Lalonde, not known for sentimentality or much given to expressing emotion in public, described LeBlanc as someone more at home on the wharves where fishermen worked than in the "salons of Montreal." Other commentators remarked that LeBlanc was not known for being a publicity hound. The *Toronto Star* considered that he "more than rose to the occasion." The

Globe and Mail offered no major criticism, but reported that his
ambition appeared to be to honour "the average Canadian"[20]
and "take on the role with a note of informality."[21] *La Presse*
opened its report by saying that it was "a moment of historical
irony when an Acadian, Roméo LeBlanc, yesterday became the
25th representative in Canada of a Crown that had deported his
ancestors."[22] As for the speech itself, the newspaper merely noted
that it addressed the usual themes of tolerance, compassion, and
the Canadian mosaic. *Le Soleil* and *Le Devoir* were more enthusiastic, and both reported the speech more fully than *La Presse*
and commented more explicitly on its content. *Le Soleil* chose
to emphasize LeBlanc's vigorous assertion that, "if there was one
group of Canadians who could have let their past poison their
future, it's the Acadians," and continued with his description
of the exile. "In the middle of the eighteenth century they were
wrenched from their homes and deported to distant shores."[23]
Le Soleil also included praise for LeBlanc from former Cabinet
colleagues Serge Joyal and Marc Lalonde. *Le Devoir* chose to
emphasize the anecdotes that LeBlanc related about his childhood, living in a village where English Protestants and French
Catholics farmed side by side, each coming to the aid of the other
in times of crisis.[24] What seemed to baffle the newspapers, but
also to stifle criticism, was that the speech seemed a homespun
homily, delivered by an unassuming person who, as the *Toronto
Star* reported, "had moved many in the stuffy Cabinet chamber
to tears."[25]

    It was also helpful that LeBlanc's Acadian heritage was viewed
with something close to approval throughout Canada. While
few Canadians, except Maritimers, had much knowledge about
the Acadian people—except for the story of the Deportation—
LeBlanc's presence attested to the Acadians' survival as a community, which seemed a good "third act" to Canadians in
general. Survival was something that, as LeBlanc emphasized in

his speech, did not happen without a struggle, and a struggle that would have failed were it not for "helping hands from Quebec... [and] in New Brunswick more helping hands that reached out to us as our minority rights were recognized by enlightened people of the majority—people who knew that building a progressive society could not be the exclusive work of the privileged few." Throughout his speech, LeBlanc's choice of illustrations for the points he wished to make persuaded people that he believed what he said. His recollections of village life rang true, with their anecdotes of help between neighbours of differing religious beliefs and languages. When he came to speak about his wish to extend these local attitudes and to encourage Canadians to act as neighbours to one another, he mentioned well-known individual and community stories that had been recently reported in the media, rather than social and political theories. He asked for recognition of "the parents who daily nurture their developmentally challenged children week after week, month after month, year after year. Let us recognize," he continued, "the children who care for parents struck down by an unrelenting illness such as Alzheimer's disease. Single parents, who, in the face of great economic and social difficulties, raise children to be successful adults." Turning to the actions of communities, he said, "Let us honour boat people and the communities who adopted them, the displaced persons, the refugees of this century, who came to the country with nothing but their hands and their hopes and through great effort and hard work have flourished in their adopted land." He concluded this part of his speech by saying, "Let us salute the people of Newfoundland, who live with the worst unemployment rate, and yet have the highest rate of giving to charity." No newspaper picked up this theme. The press preferred instead to focus on his reference to the Acadian history of past injustice and present cordiality. His comment, "Very few of us in this country share the same past, but all of us can share the same future," was seen as a plea for national unity, direct political advice to Quebec separatists, and something close to political interference by the new governor general. However, the press ended their commentaries with general approval of the level of informality that LeBlanc had brought to his installation ceremony.

If the press had time and inclination, there might have been further commentary on the extent to which LeBlanc's career had prepared him for the difficulties he would confront, in particular the need to persuade Canadians that the office was not merely an expensive and superfluous luxury. But there was little interest shown in how someone from a remote Acadian village, the youngest of eight children in a family of subsistence farmers, had traced a career path to appointment as Canada's governor general. Even if the office and its occupant were no more than symbols of the past, both were still worthy of some analysis. After all, the office could be traced back to the beginning of the seventeenth century and Samuel de Champlain. By the mid-1990s, however, Canada was preoccupied with immediate political urgencies. There was a confused sense of *malaise* in the country, as old political alliances fragmented and yet another referendum loomed. Cynicism seemed the order of the day. Journalist Ron Graham captured the mood of the country when he wrote in mid-decade about a media (press, radio, and television) more inclined to report dissent than consensus and a population where the wealthy grew wealthier and the poor found the social safety net wanting.[26] No one had time to give much consideration to the governor general, whose purpose it was to stand outside the fray, to point out to politicians that a prime minister is not a president or monarch, but an elected representative of the people, and to note that a broader community existed outside those systems designed by political ideologues.

The office of the governor general is about ritual and tradition. Without it people become bored with the dull necessity of caring for those institutions without which communities decay. Quite apart from other more esoteric functions, the activities over which a governor general presides are spectacles which are "impressive public relations event[s] for government itself, not for *a* government."[27] One of the most important responsibilities of governors general is to remind Canadians that there is more to Canada that the political processes of the country. In a time of political distemper, the individual who holds the position has more influence over the public mood than at other times. In appointing Roméo LeBlanc to the position, the prime minister had chosen someone who would prove to be a governor general for the time. LeBlanc had seen poverty as a child, had worked as a high-school and college teacher, had travelled widely in Europe in the 1950s, had worked as a journalist for Radio-Canada in the 1960s in both Europe and the United States, and had been the public-relations officer for two prime ministers (Lester Pearson and Pierre Trudeau) and for the Université de Moncton. He entered politics in 1972 and his service as minister of fisheries had earned the respect of fishermen, and the somewhat less enthusiastic support of fishing corporations, during a very fraught period for that industry. As he undertook the challenge of being governor general, he brought to the position both a broad experience of Canada and a great love of the country. Above all, he also brought a strong sense of where he had come from and of the forces that had shaped his career: of a life begun on a subsistence farm on the very edge of the village of Memramcook, New Brunswick. The service he offered as governor general was no more and no less than the service he had given throughout his life to the people among whom and with he lived and worked.

CHAPTER 2

Cormier's Cove

The Memramcook River is one of the small rivers that empties into the northeast arm of the Bay of Fundy. The great tides of that bay, with their spectacular ranges of from ten to fifteen metres most of the year, even higher during the spring, have shaped and moulded the valley of the Memramcook. As a result, it has similar—though much smaller—marshlands, some 25 kilometres in length, than those that grace the Tantramar further east and the more southerly rivers of the Minas Basin. These marshes and the tidal mud flats of the river have meant that farming in the region still resembles Acadian agriculture practised before the Deportation. Low, forested hills rise on both sides of the valley, where the dense, rich grasses grow every colour of green from spring to fall, then change to shades of brown until the snow flies. The centre of Acadian life here is the village of Memramcook itself, and its surrounding settlements and hamlets. The village is about 30 kilometres from the mouth of the river, and more or less the same distance from the city of Moncton. One of the first settlements to be re-established after the Deportation, by 1785 Memramcook had some 160 families within its very broad parish boundaries.[1] In many ways, it became the centre of Acadian development in New Brunswick, yet the valley itself was not exclusively an Acadian enclave. By the opening of the nineteenth century, a variety of anglophone communities had taken root throughout the Memramcook Valley, next-door neighbours to the Acadian communities.

Life throughout the valley from the 1880s to the 1950s centred—and in some ways still does—on forestry, farming, and work for the railway. Then, as now, the railway link between Halifax and Quebec City ran along the eastern shore. The farmhouse where Roméo was born, on December 18, 1927, is on the western side of the valley, not quite directly across from the federal prison at Dorchester. It is part of a small hamlet called l'Anse-aux-Cormier (Cormier's Cove), on the edge of the larger village of Memramcook. The farmhouse and its surrounding land were owned by Roméo's grandfather, and some of the fields had been cultivated in the 1730s. Both his family and his place of birth tied Roméo closely to Acadian life and traditions. The LeBlanc family can trace its ancestry back to Daniel LeBlanc, who arrived in Port Royal (present-day Annapolis Royal, Nova Scotia) before 1650, and quickly became a person of importance in the colony. By the time of the Deportation, his descendants were numerous and spread throughout the Acadian settlements from Annapolis Royal and Grand-Pré to the region of Beauséjour and the Tantramar marshes, as well as along the river valleys of the Memramcook and the Petitcodiac. Roméo was the seventh of the eight children of Philéas and Lucie LeBlanc, who had married in 1911. The youngest child, Raoul, was born in 1930, but died within the year, the victim of dysentery. Roméo's other siblings were: Irène, born in 1913; Antoine, born in 1915; Émilie, born in 1917; Valéda, born in 1920; Alice, born in 1923; and Léonard, born in 1925.

Philéas and Lucie LeBlanc, Roméo's parents

Philéas was the eldest son of Joseph LeBlanc and, as was common among many farm families of the time, lived with his wife and children in his father's house. Again, like many other rural New Brunswickers, Philéas spent a large part of his life working on the farm, and the care of the family land, crops, and livestock was not only his central concern, but also one of the major satisfactions of his life. However, he also worked for forty-three years as a trainman for the Canadian National Railways (CNR), whose line ran from Moncton to Dorchester through the Memramcook Valley, but on the opposite side to the LeBlanc homestead. The need to subsidize the farm income with outside earnings was a stark necessity throughout Roméo's childhood and early adult life. The farm itself was approximately 125 acres, and it supported Roméo's parents and his six brothers and sisters, his grandfather, and, on occasion, his uncle (his father's only brother) and a hired hand. In old age, Roméo's recollections of his early childhood were of a warm family that had enough food, a reasonably comfortable home, but little money for anything except the bare necessities. One of Roméo's strongest memories, however, was his father's generosity to those who needed food and heat. The farm was well able to spare meat and vegetables, if not flour and sugar, and Philéas would send what he could to those less fortunate. During Roméo's childhood, the woodlot provided fuel for the heating and cooking needs of the household, and also an occasional cord of logs for sale. Livestock (cattle as well as chickens), fruit trees, and a large, intensively cultivated garden ensured a food supply. Hunting and fishing, in season, added variety to the menus. The main house was still lived in at the beginning of the twenty-first century, but until the mid-1930s, it had neither electricity nor running water. Running water came to the house in 1938, but not to the barn until 1945. Electricity arrived at the farm in 1934.

The LeBlanc family home, at Cormier's Cove in the Memramcook Valley

The running of the farm was a family enterprise, and there was a fairly clear division of labour between men and women. Some tasks, such as weeding the garden and getting the cows in, were chores for young children of both sexes. Women's work was primarily in the house and its environs, including a great deal of vegetable gardening, the care of the poultry, and many of the tasks associated with the dairy. Planting and harvesting were times when, if there was fine weather, men and women, boys and girls, turned their hands to whatever their strength allowed. In general, men looked after the cattle and pigs, cut the wood, sowed and reaped the cereal crops, hunted and fished, kept the buildings in repair, and often cobbled shoes. Besides being responsible for the garden, women took care of cheese- and butter-making. They also, of course, cooked, cleaned, and preserved food and made and washed clothes. Throughout her married life, like many other wives in rural New Brunswick, both Acadian and anglophone, Roméo's mother carried most of the water for the cooking, the laundry, and the needs of the younger children. The laundry also included cloth diapers, and there were three children under four by 1917. As was then the common practice of housewives in the Memramcook Valley, Roméo's mother baked bread daily, sometimes made with buckwheat flour alone, sometimes with a mixture of locally milled wheat and buckwheat. A wood stove dominated the kitchen, and the meals at midday always included meat or fish, with potatoes or buckwheat pancakes and molasses. One of Roméo's vivid memories was the practice of coordinating the slaughter of a pig or calf with the neighbours, so that the meat of one animal would be shared among several families. This solved the problem of preserving a large amount of meat fresh, particularly in summer. In the fall, meat was salted for the winter and could, depending on the weather, be kept frozen in sawdust. The existence of a large, cool cellar was a vital element in keeping the family properly fed year round. They kept potatoes, carrots, onions, and cabbages there, under earth and sawdust coverings, throughout the long winter months until the arrival of fresh vegetables, lettuce, and onions in late spring. By early July, there were the edible plantains, samphire greens, and salicorne and glasswort, both of which are gathered at the edge of the marshlands. Acadians know the first as *passe-pierre* and the second as *tétines de souris*. The families also harvested and stored apples, while soft fruits, such as wild raspberries and wild and cultivated strawberries, were gathered and preserved for pies.

Roméo remembered his mother as a hard-working woman, whose health was frail. He recalled much more clearly that his sisters were the emotional centre of his childhood. When he was born, his eldest sister, Irène, was fourteen, and had already left the village school to help full-time at home. By the time he was two, his mother was pregnant again with her last child, Raoul, who lived no more than a year. Roméo's care naturally fell into the hands of his sisters, particularly during the final years of his mother's life, when she was mourning the death of her last child. Roméo was eight when she died, early in 1936, and the decade must have been emotionally confusing for the young child. Between the ages of six and eight, Roméo not only lost his mother, but two of his sisters also left the family home. Irène married sometime in 1933. She had been a constant presence in Roméo's life from its beginning. Later in life, he often called her his "second mother." Two years later, Émilie, then eighteen, left for domestic service in the United States, as there was no work available locally. She quickly found a position with a wealthy family near Boston. So Valéda, seventeen, and doing well in school, gave up her studies in 1936 and took over the management of the household and the supervision of the younger children. She always regretted that she had not had the opportunity to finish her education. She eventually married a farmer in 1943, and had ten children. When she first came to oversee the household, Antoine, the eldest son, was working full-time on the family farm and the younger children, including Roméo, were attending school.

Roméo began school in 1932. He attended a one-room school with fifty-seven students and one teacher, which was typical of New Brunswick then. At the opening of the 1930s, New Brunswick had the lowest literacy rate in Canada. Ninety per cent of all students left school before Grade Nine, and the Acadians were, as a whole, less well served by the provincial education system than the anglophones of the province. In the predominantly Acadian counties, only 7 per cent of students finished Grade Six, and under 3 per cent went on to Grade Nine, most of them girls. At the time, the financing of elementary schools in New Brunswick was primarily the responsibility of the local parish, exercised through school boards under the supervision of the Department of Education. While money was sometimes available from the department for buildings and furniture, the upkeep of the schools, including heating in winter and payment of teachers, was a matter for the parishes. Families were asked to contribute according to the number of children they sent to school, and what the parish estimated the family's cash income to be. Roméo had a clear memory of one occasion when his school had a particularly good teacher, who said she could only continue if the school board could augment her salary by buying her a winter coat. One of the members of the board, he recalled, went around the village, asking people for contributions of 25 and 50 cents to make up the five or six dollars necessary for a new coat. Textbooks were also the responsibility of parents, but some provincial funds were available to parishes to help those families who could not afford them.

The fact that elementary schooling throughout the province was barely adequate at this time was as much the result of general economic misery as it was of government policies. Between 1929 and 1933, the value of New Brunswick's major resources fell drastically: "the value of timber production dropped 75%, fish production 47%, agriculture 39% and coal 45%."[2] In 1931, the reported unemployment rate for the Maritimes as a whole was 19 per cent. In 1933, the per-capita income for the region was $185 per annum, just above that of the Prairie provinces at $181, and well below the Canadian average of $262. Most communities paid a dollar a month per individual towards relief, and nothing at all during the summer months. During these years, Roméo was only marginally aware of the economic troubles that surrounded his family. While the family was certainly poor, it had a number of resources that sheltered its members from the worst of the "Dirty Thirties." Unlike the situation in more northern regions of the province, Northumberland, Gloucester, and Restigouche counties, for example, where many lived on the edge of starvation, most people in the Memramcook Valley had enough food, the more fortunate sharing with the desperate. In his eighties, Roméo's brother Léonard spoke of having fresh pork and molasses for breakfast when he was nine or ten, before going out to see to the needs of the farm animals. Roméo did not recall being hungry during the 1930s, but did have memories of walking the two miles to school in homemade shoes, which were not particularly weatherproof. Émilie came back to the farm each summer from Boston and brought him clothing and shoes given to her by the middle-class family for whom she worked. The jackets were always too broad across the shoulders, and the shoes were two-toned, unusual footwear for a kid in Roméo's village. However, he remembered that he put up with teasing from his schoolmates easily enough. After Roméo was eleven, most of his summers were spent as a timekeeper for those employed by the farms to repair the dykes, the essential regulators of the water meadows. Émilie's visits were a time of great joy, tinged with sadness from the outset, because she had only two weeks' holiday. For a glorious week in one particular year, 1939, he was sent off alone to visit Émilie, his father having access to some free passes on the railway because of his job. For Roméo, this visit became a golden memory, although he recalled that travelling to Boston alone had scared him. Thanks to the Saturday-afternoon baseball radio programs, he was already an avid baseball fan, something he remained all his life. He went to the ballpark alone, and cheered for the Boston Red Sox, money for the tickets and hot dogs courtesy of Émilie.

Later in life, both brothers remembered far more about other aspects of their childhood than about what happened to them in elementary school. Yet they both recalled that the family took education seriously, and a punishment at school was reinforced with a strapping at home. What they recalled, from different perspectives, were the changes in family life, the work on the farm, and the complexity of the small local societies. Turnips were grown for cattle feed and weeding and hoeing was the work of the older children. Valéda taught Roméo how to weed badly and heave up seedlings with the weeds, so he would be excused from this chore and allowed to go inside to listen to the Saturday-afternoon baseball programs on the radio. Getting the cows in was a chore for younger children. It was a task Roméo disliked, because it was hampered by the presence of a bull. Young ones were not allowed to rake hay or harness the horses, but Léonard was an exception, because he loved working with animals. Antoine and Léonard were both like their father, in that, though farming was hard work, they found it had its own rewards.

One interesting aspect of the farm work in Cormier's Cove was the contact between the Acadian village and Taylor Village, the anglophone settlement, when it was time for harvesting and building the woodpiles for the winter. Taylor Village was the next settlement along the Memramcook River towards the seashore, no more than two or three kilometres away. It was slightly larger than Cormier's Cove and marginally better off, in large part because there was a bridge across the river between Taylor Village and Upper Dorchester. Built in 1932, it was the fourth bridge to have been constructed at this spot since 1869. Like its predecessors, it would be destroyed by gale-force winds. The storm that brought it down swept through the valley on January 10, 1978. It was never replaced. During Roméo's childhood, however, the bridge meant that Taylor Village had easy access to the anglophone communities on the other side, where the men usually found seasonal work on the CNR tracks. As well, they were employed at haying time by a family who lived across the river. As much entrepreneurs as farmers, this family owned a bailer, which travelled with its crew from farm to farm in the region "pressing the hay." It was then sent to Halifax for shipment elsewhere. Roméo had memories of anglophones being invited into Acadian houses when they came to help, but the reverse not being true.

During his early childhood and his years at elementary school, Roméo clearly recognized the existence of two different societies

Roméo as a child (about ten years of age), c. 1940

among the small communities along the Memramcook River. He had a curiosity about their social practices and remembered that, on Sunday afternoons, when the children were out picking blueberries near the Baptist church, they would stop and listen to the hymns being sung. Then there would be talk about the difference between Mass in the morning and the afternoon singing. Roméo also had vivid recollections of the help given by one village to the other not only at harvesting times but in times of trouble, to repair damage to homes or barns from storms or fires, and the less serious problems of wandering pigs, cows, or horses. There seems to have been no generalized hostility between the two groups at this time, and a considerable realization that the circumstances of daily life were much the same for both communities: the hard work demanded by subsistence farming, with few opportunities for economic advancement.

Roméo was thirteen when he finished Grade Eight, and it

seemed that his formal education would end at that point. None of his brothers and sisters had gone further, partly because there was no public high school nearer than Moncton, some 30 kilometres away, and partly because his father saw little use in book learning. However, the fact that the teachers at his elementary school recognized his intellectual capacity, combined with the existence of the Université St. Joseph in Memramcook, opened his way to further study. This educational institution played a major role, not only in Roméo's life, but also in the lives of many Acadians who came to prominence in Canada. St. Joseph's had its roots in the work of Father F.X. LaFrance, who, in the 1850s, informed his parishioners that he intended to establish a college that would "prepare priests to correct the sins of your tongues, merchants to sell you goods at reasonable rates, doctors to heal you, lawyers to defend you in the courts and even judges who will judge you without ruining you."[3] In other words, his vision was to provide the Acadian communities with their own élites. At a time when the Acadians formed barely 15 per cent (44,907) of the population of New Brunswick (285,594), and less than 12 per cent of the population of the Maritimes, such a vision seemed almost irrational. The assimilation of the Acadians by the anglophone majority appeared to be a foregone conclusion. By 1933, however, the Acadian population in New Brunswick was close to 34 per cent (136,999), and Acadians formed just over 20 per cent of the total population of the Maritimes.

The vision of Father LaFrance took a long time to be fully realized, but it began to take shape in his lifetime, because of his own belief in it and that of another priest, Camille Lefebvre. Lefebvre was born and raised in Quebec, where he entered the Congregation of the Holy Cross Fathers in 1852 and arrived in New Brunswick in 1864. By 1868, he had established St. Joseph's as a small college with a provincial charter and a $400 annual grant from the government. One of the reasons why this educational establishment still existed in 1940 was the passage of the *Common Schools Act* by the New Brunswick legislature in 1871, which actually ended the small government subsidy to the nascent institution. At first sight, this legislation merely worsened the financial straits of St. Joseph's. To receive aid from the government, the act required the institution to erase all displays of religious symbols, submit to government inspection, and follow government rules on pedagogy and curricula. Compliance not only meant the eradication of the religious aspect of the small college, something of concern to the Irish Catholic population of the region as well as to the Acadians, but also ended the priority accorded to French. There was, after all, no protection whatsoever given to the French language and culture in New Brunswick by the *British North America Act* in 1867. The curriculum and pedagogy of the New Brunswick education authorities were, at the time—and for many decades afterwards—firmly centred upon the primacy of English. The apparently unthinking neglect of the French language and Acadian culture by the framers of the 1871 act triggered a support for St. Joseph's that it might otherwise not have received. In spite of considerable difficulties, St. Joseph's slowly developed. In 1898, the college received statutory approval as Université du Collège Saint-Joseph. By 1940, when the question of Roméo's attendance came up, the institution had a faculty composed of 27 priests and 13 laymen, who taught over 300 students, 32 of these enrolled in what was known as a "Grammar School" stream, 191 in the equivalent of high-school courses, and 98 in university-level courses, leading to Bachelor's degrees in Arts or Commerce.

Despite the opinions of his elementary schoolteachers as to his intellectual promise and the existence of a grammar-school year at St. Joseph's, there was another obstacle to be overcome before Roméo could continue his education: his father's agreement to accept the costs involved. Philéas thought that education was for those who spent their lives as priests, a vocation he did not want for a son of his, or for those who worked in an office, something he considered not fit for a man. As the family story goes, the school year had already begun when Roméo and his father drove to St. Joseph's to leave a load of wood in one of the outbuildings. The priest who met them asked why the lad was not in school, and M. LeBlanc replied that there was no money for such frills. The priest then offered to take the load of wood as a down payment on the cost of tuition for the coming year. Obviously, Roméo's elementary schoolteachers had prepared the ground and, as was true in many other cases, the institution stretched its resources to teach a promising student. However, Philéas was not swayed. Luckily, when Roméo's two sisters returned for Thanksgiving weekend, their arguments went on long after Roméo had gone to bed, and persuaded Philéas to let him continue his schooling. Throughout the eight years that Roméo attended St. Joseph's, four years in the equivalent of high school and four years at university, his fees were scraped together with continued help from his sisters. The fact that he had two elder brothers, one of them recently married, living and working on the farm was also probably a factor in his father's acceptance of further education for this son. The land might stretch to support two sons, with some outside work by one of them, but not three.

Roméo boarded in Memramcook village during the four high-school years for $12 a month. He found that his diet contained a great deal more peanut butter for breakfast than he had been used to at home. His first year consisted of a course that St. Joseph's specifically designed for the many students who came from country districts and, as the calendar explained, did not have "the advantages enjoyed by city students of a good preparation" for high-school courses. It consisted of tutoring, according to the need of each student, in English, French, and Arithmetic, with Penmanship and Drawing, History, and Geography.[4] Roméo remarked in an interview he gave in 1977 that he was shocked to find out how poor his command of French actually was when he was thirteen. On his first test in his grammar-school year, he remembered that he made thirty-two mistakes in French spelling and grammar, a disappointing result.[5] The pragmatism that went into establishing this necessary preparatory year was, in many ways, the signature of all the programs taught at the institution, and one of the reasons why St. Joseph's was, in 1940, well on the way to fulfilling the vision of LaFrance. The Congregation of the Holy Cross Fathers, who ran the institution, was a bilingual religious order active in, among other countries, Canada and the United States. Those teaching at St. Joseph's included Québécois, Irish Canadians, and Acadians. Among the latter was Father Clément Cormier, who had studied at St. Joseph's himself. In 1949, he would become its principal and, when it transformed itself into the Université de Moncton in 1963, he would become its first president.

When Roméo completed the equivalent of the provincial high-school program in the spring of 1944, it was clear that he would return that fall to begin his studies for a B.A. It was also clear that, in spite of help from the university, it would be a financial struggle. That Roméo returned to St. Joseph's in the fall of 1944 to begin university studies was once more due as much to his sisters as to the recognition of his talents by his teachers. It was his sisters who argued with their father and their brothers about the need to support Roméo's studies, emphasizing his obvious scholastic success and equally obvious lack of talent for farming.

The entry into "Belles-Lettres," the first year of the B.A. program at St. Joseph's, marked as great an alteration in Roméo's life as the previous move from elementary school into high school. In the first place, it meant that his family, particularly his father and brothers, now believed that his life would be different from theirs, and its path was one that would take him away from farm life to some other world. The difference between the high-school and college divisions at St. Joseph's was considerable, from the type of students enrolled and the curriculum to the attention paid to the student's activities outside the classroom. One of the most significant changes was that students in the college stream were, almost without exception, boarders.

Roméo's day began with Mass at 6:30 a.m., breakfast at 7:30 a.m., and classes at 8:15 a.m., with the time between the end of classes and lights out also being fairly regimented. Furthermore, no other boy who had been in classes with Roméo during the past four years went on to the college stream at St. Joseph's. Those boys had been, to a large extent, from the immediate neighbourhood around Memramcook, or from within the boundaries of Westmorland County. Now his classmates came from across the province and from Quebec and the United States. Moreover, between 1940 and 1944, St Joseph's increased both its student body and its faculty. The student body grew from 321 to 521, and the faculty from 40 to 79—39 priests and 40 lay teachers. This meant that Roméo was exposed to people with much more varied backgrounds than those he had previously known. Both the faculty and students were predominantly francophone, but there was a strong anglophone presence in the university. Among the faculty, roughly 20 per cent of the anglophone faculty members were of Irish heritage.

Among the students, the anglophones were of both English and Irish heritages, and, together, these students made up roughly 15 to 20 per cent of the enrolment. When Roméo enrolled in Belles-Lettres in 1944, there were fifty-one students, of whom eight were anglophone, mainly from Saint John, New Brunswick. The rest of the students came, in almost equal numbers, from the immediate region around Memramcook, including Moncton; from the northwest of the province, particularly Edmundston; from the northern seacoast, around Saint-Louis-de-Kent and

Shediac; and from the province of Quebec. The class also included two Americans. When Roméo's political career began nearly thirty years later, he found that the friends he made during these college years had become an important part of the burgeoning Acadian élite: artists, doctors, teachers, and lawyers.

If the student body brought Roméo a much more varied group of acquaintances, the new courses introduced him to new ideas. There continued to be a great emphasis on French and English studies and, in later years, he credited the weekly essay-writing in both languages for his facility in both languages. The ability to write well was accompanied by the study of the literary classics of both languages: the plays of Molière and Shakespeare, the novels of Dickens and Victor Hugo. As well, there was instruction in religion and Latin, science and mathematics courses, and courses in history, economics and philosophy. The basic vocabulary of Western thought was the core of the curriculum. St. Joseph's provided Roméo with a good, solid university experience. The four years that the degree demanded allowed him access to more than the course materials and the intellectual training that their study required. Academic life was rounded out with attention to contemporary political and cultural questions. There was a collection of general reading material in the small library. Every morning, *Le Devoir*, the newspaper as central to French Canadian political life as the *Globe and Mail* is to anglophone Canadians, was pinned up along the walls of one of the corridors of the college, the pages turned every afternoon. There were weekly debates about the political affairs of Canada, in both English and French. The end of the Second World War and its consequences were frequently discussed. A good exposure to cultural issues, was available, and some students received help to develop their musical abilities, violin as well as piano. Roméo acted in and directed plays; parts were learned in spare moments and rehearsals were in late afternoon. Altogether, his undergraduate years at

Roméo at St. Joseph's College, Memramcook, 1947 (age twenty)

St. Joseph's University gave him a solid general-arts degree, and he graduated *cum laude* in 1948.

As crucial as the educational experience was to his future, in later life two extracurricular activities he took up during his last two years at St. Joseph's would prove as important as his academic training. These were his association with La Jeunesse Étudiante Catholique (JEC) and his editorship of *Liaisons*, the student newspaper at St. Joseph's. His work as editor of the student newspaper would be the stepping stone to his immediate post-graduation employment, while the link with the JEC was a major influence on the development of his political and social ideas. It also brought him friendships with those who became leading Quebec politicians and journalists in the 1970s and 1980s.

In the 1940s and 1950s, the impact of the JEC on young francophone Catholics, both Acadian and Québécois, was extraordinary. Among those who were actively associated with the movement at that time were Réginald Boisvert, Fernand and

Rita Cadieux, Pierre Juneau, Marc Lalonde, Gérard Pelletier, and Jeanne Sauvé. A poet and novelist, Boisvert (1922–1985) became one of the major journalistic voices of the "Quiet Revolution" in Quebec. Fernand Cadieux (1925–1976) became a film producer, whose work was of significance for the development of both the Quebec and Canadian film industry. At the same, he was a journalist whose commentary on social and political life in Quebec was influential. Rita Cadieux became a sociologist, teaching at the Université de Montréal, and an important figure in the Quebec feminist movement. Their home was known for its hospitality, and their house became a meeting place for those who established *Cité Libre*, the journal that became the voice of Quebec reform in the 1950s and 1960s. Pierre Juneau, born in Verdun, Quebec, in 1922, spent much of his early career with the National Film Board. He was the chair of the Canadian Radio–Television Commission from 1968 to 1975 and president of the Canadian Broadcasting Corporation from 1982 to 1989. Marc Lalonde was born at L'Île-Perrot on July 26, 1929. He began a highly successful career as special advisor to Davie Fulton, then minister of justice, in 1959, and went on to hold a number of senior Cabinet portfolios in the governments of Pierre Trudeau. Gérard Pelletier (1919–1997) was editor-in-chief of *La Presse*, the Montreal daily and North America's largest French circulating newspaper, from 1961 to 1964. With Pierre Trudeau, he founded *Cité Libre*. He was elected to Parliament in 1965, and served in various senior Cabinet positions in Trudeau's governments. Jeanne Sauvé (1922–1993) was born in Saskatchewan. She was elected to Parliament in 1972 and became the first woman Speaker of the House of Commons in 1980. From 1984 to 1990, she served as the first woman governor general of Canada. In his memoirs *The Years of Impatience*,[6] Gérard Pelletier recalled that, during the 1940s and early 1950s, all of these people served at the JEC's headquarters in Montreal at 420

Sherbrooke East. It was through the JEC that Roméo, before the age of twenty, met these men and women and formed lifelong friendships with a number of them.

The framework for much of Roméo's intellectual judgment during his youth and early adolescence was Catholicism, transmitted through his family's beliefs and interpreted by the Holy Cross Fathers. The LeBlancs were practising Catholics, neither more nor less devout than the majority of their friends and neighbours. Attendance at Mass on Sundays was usual, the feasts of the church were kept, and parishioners went to confession and communion. Patterns of religious observance regulated the celebrations of childhood through baptism and confirmation, attested to the solemnity of marriage, and provided consolation in the face of the realities of sickness and death. The influence of the parish priests was considerable, but it was in the context of parish councils. Further, clerical influence on family life was tempered by the extent to which the family itself considered the individual priest a person worthy of respect or merely someone to be accorded respect because he was a priest. For Roméo, it was the influence of the Holy Cross Fathers, rather than the observances of his family, that formed the basis of his ideas about religion and politics at this time in his life. As has been suggested, the ambition of the Holy Cross Order was the education of a professional élite. The Jesuits might seek to educate an existing élite, and the Dominicans to form an educated élite, but the Holy Cross Fathers were above all interested in the formation of a new *professional* élite. The teachings, both in the formal courses on religion and by the example of the Holy Cross priests themselves, emphasized the everyday implications of living as a Catholic. It was this orientation that led members of the order to welcome the idea of the JEC when information about the movement arrived in Canada. The students at their colleges in Quebec and New Brunswick were among the first to join the association once it was established in the country.

For many outside the Catholic Church, the JEC has often appeared as an organization that is seamlessly unified. In fact, there have always been almost as many divisions among the Christians of Catholic faith as among those of Protestant faith. One of the greatest of these divisions has been that between those concerned with social justice and those concerned with the authority of the church. With the support of the Holy Cross Fathers and the interest of reform-minded Catholics elsewhere in Canada, two organizations concerned with lay participation became an important force among Canadian Catholics. Their origins were European and were closely linked to the organizations of laypeople that had emerged there in response to the ideas of Pius XI, who was elected Pope in 1922. In his first encyclical, *Ubi Arcano Dei Consilio,* promulgated on December 23, 1922, he outlined the challenges faced by a war-torn Europe, whose people were cynical, dispirited, and confronted with the major social problems of poverty and destitution, unemployment, and political unrest. He specifically rejected the solutions proposed by the Communist movement, as well as those proposed by the Fascists. Pius XI believed that only if there were a renewal of Christian action by the laypeople of the church would the problems of post-war Europe be solved. In the minds of many of the hierarchy, whether European or North American, the idea that the laypeople of the Catholic church had a major part to play in the development of the social role of the church was an affront to their idea of the paramount importance of the episcopate. Despite the doubts of the bishops, however, there was a considerable development of Catholic lay associations over the next decades. Among them were two founded by Belgian priest Joseph Cardijn: the first was La Jeunesse Ouvrière Catholique (JOC) in 1925; the second was the JEC, started as a parallel organization in 1928.

Cardijn acted from a profound belief that Catholicism was more than a set of rules and regulations: it was a faith to live by. He realized that his parishioners, who at the time were poverty-stricken miners on the outskirts of Brussels, needed more than the traditional parish activities centred upon priests and attendance at church. If they were to believe that Catholicism had some relevance to their daily lives and was an attractive alternative to both Fascist and Communist ideologies, action must come from within their own community. So Cardijn began bringing young workers together in small groups, where the talk was about sociology and politics, as well as religion. Discussion about attendance at Mass, confession, and the religious life of a Catholic took second place to ideas about the principles of Christian life and the way in which these should affect society. Cardijn wanted people to believe that there was more to their lives than their present circumstances, to help them decide how and where even small improvements could be made, and to encourage them to have the courage to act. To achieve this aim, whether for the poor and uneducated organized in the JOC, or for the more-privileged gathered together in the JEC, he worked to instill a strong sense in his listeners that an individual could make a difference. The JOC appeared in Montreal in May 1931, and by 1935 was present in the majority of Quebec dioceses.[7] The growth of the JEC was almost equally rapid.

The JEC in Canada started as a result of a study group, held near Montreal at the Collège de Saint-Laurent of the Holy Cross Fathers, in the summer of 1935. By December of that year, there were JEC branches throughout Quebec and New Brunswick. By the summer of 1936, there were seventy-five local organizations. Gérard Pelletier, who was the secretary-general of the JEC from 1939 to 1943, considered that one of its most important results was the connections it developed among young people from all over Quebec and Canada. At a time when telephone calls were expensive, when radio was the basic medium of mass communication, and the impact of the Depression was still strong, the JEC "made it possible," Pelletier wrote, "for us to travel from Halifax to Vancouver and make contact south of the border with young Americans of our generation, from New York to Cleveland, Notre Dame (Indiana) and Chicago...After the war, through the same movement, we came together with our French, Belgian, Swiss and Latin-American comrades."[8] The circulation of its publication, which was first called the *JEC*, but in 1946 was renamed *La Vie Étudiante*, grew from around 15,000 copies in the early 1940s to around 45,000 copies, distributed on the tenth anniversary of its first issue, in 1945.[9] This expansion met with opposition, particularly from the already-established Association Catholique de la Jeunesse Canadienne-Française (ACJC). This group was supervised by the Jesuits and was, at the time, exclusively male, greatly influenced by ideas of French Canadian exclusivity, and rooted in the belief in the necessity of a small educated élite within society.[10] The Holy Cross Fathers, under whose authority the JEC developed, used a much lighter touch and, from the beginning, involved the laity in leadership positions. As early as 1936, the *JEC* publication was in the hands of students, albeit with some clerical oversight.

The way it brought together young people was only a small part of the reason why the JEC became so popular when it arrived in Canada. A much more significant part of its appeal was its challenge to the norms of the Catholic Church in French-speaking Canada. By 1930, a highly conservative, authoritarian episcopate and a clergy much more interested in public observance of the rituals of the faith than in the practice of the cardinal virtues dominated the lives of Catholics in the majority of francophone dioceses in Canada. By 1940, there were clear signs of discontent among the faithful. In that year, a letter to the bishops from Canadian Jesuit Philippe Bélanger remarked on a growing lack of faith and the emergence of "an anti-clerical spirit and an indifference to religion

among the people and élite."[11] Many Catholics were deeply dis-
affected by the lack of social conscience shown by a number of
the hierarchy during the 1930s. Others found that the spiritual
practices that the clergy most commonly enjoined them to follow were less than inspiring. The JEC and its publications came
as a welcome breath of fresh air. There was a strong belief among
the leadership of the JEC that the Catholic Church needed to
be brought to the understanding that the laity were more than
sheep.[12] The influence of prominent Catholic left-wing thinkers
in France, such as Jacques Maritain, was very important. Maritain
had a firm belief in the importance of the laity and the limitations
of episcopal power. He lectured at the University of Toronto in
1940 and saw first-hand the stresses within the Catholic Church
in Quebec. He wrote to a friend, "This time, I've touched obscur-
antism…There is an immense, unspoken anti-clericalism among
the young Catholics."[13] He saw the possibility of a major revolt in
favour of left-wing Catholic ideas among French Canadians, and
thought that it would come within ten years.

While Maritain's religious ideas played a considerable role
in the development of the reform movement among Catholics
in Canada, both anglophone and francophone, between 1940
and 1960 it was the ideas of Emmanuel Mounier that provided
a socialist slant to the JEC.[14] His writings became the reference
point not only for the JEC but also for those who were inspired
by *Cité Libre*. Mounier's ideas blended a strong belief in the personal dignity of every human being with an equally strong call
for social action to ensure that the economic structure of society
provided the conditions necessary for all people to live with dignity.[15] His convictions about the essential worth of every person
meant that he strongly opposed the reactionary and xenophobic
nationalism of European fascism. By the time Roméo became
involved in the JEC, probably in 1946, but certainly by 1947, it
was a dissemination point for the ideas of Emmanuel Mounier

and very definitely an agent for social change in Canadian society—as well as for the renewal of spiritual life within the church.

The most important way in which the JEC spread its ideas was through its newspaper—*JEC*. It was through this medium, from the 1930s to the late 1950s, that francophone Canadians became aware of the galaxy of Catholic writers in France, those who described a Catholicism different from the right-wing traditional church they knew. In 1939, when at twenty Gérard Pelletier became the secretary-general of the JEC, he also took over the supervision of the newspaper. He was quick to pick up the note that had been struck by previous editors: the need to bring to the life of students some idea of a world beyond the boundaries of the books they were prescribed. He was quite clear, as he wrote in an editorial published in the *JEC* in 1941, that the major aim of the publication was "to use humour, ideas and the news to prod the passive, to help those who labour, and to counter poor judgment."[16] To this end, the publication included not only news about what the organization was doing, but also articles about current events across the world and a great deal of information about cultural events in France. Pierre Juneau, writing on the sixtieth anniversary of the international association of the JEC, noted that it was through the publication that francophone Canadians became aware of Georges Bernanos among others.[17]

Roméo became interested in the JEC more from his visits to Montreal than because of the JEC branch at St. Joseph's. The fact that Roméo's father worked for the CNR provided a number of free travelling passes for the family, and Roméo and his classmate Rhéal Gaudet went for short visits to Montreal during the summer. Rhéal was in the same year as Roméo at St. Joseph's, but his course was the more structured Bachelor of Letters, which led him to a career with Radio-Canada. He was from the village of Memramcook itself, and he and Roméo remained close friends throughout their lives. It was during these summertime visits, probably in 1945, but certainly in 1946 and 1947, that Roméo was introduced to the JEC headquarters at 420 Sherbrooke East. By that time, as Pierre Juneau recalled, the JEC was much more a movement than an association. It had abandoned "emblems, hymns, and fees" and there were many young people who "sympathized with the ideas of the JEC, without necessarily becoming members and without feeling themselves regimented."[18] The JEC motto, "See, Judge, Act," ("Voir, Juger et Agir") became catchwords for them, because it gave individuals a right to personal action. It is not clear that Roméo was a member at this time, but he was certainly involved with the movement in his last years at St. Joseph's. His first job after graduation was as one of the editors of *La Vie Étudiante*.

Roméo's interest in student activities, not only at St. Joseph's but nationally, can be traced in the articles he wrote for St. Joseph's student newspaper, *Liaisons*. He became the paper's editor in 1947, and in a thoughtful article, written that autumn, he dealt with the formation of an Association des Étudiants Acadiens (AEA). The seeds had been sown by Acadian students at Laval, sometime during the 1946–1947 academic year, by young men who had taken their undergraduate degrees at a variety of Maritime universities, including St. Joseph's, the Collège Sacré-Coeur in Bathurst, and two Nova Scotia institutions, Sainte-Anne at Pointe-de-l'Église and St. Francis Xavier in Antigonish. In the summer of 1947, their initiative was followed with a meeting at St. Joseph's, which brought together not only students then studying at Laval, but also those from the Université de Montréal and those still being educated elsewhere in the Maritimes. That meeting concluded, in Roméo's words, with a "General Association uniting all Acadian students." He continued, "Unfortunately the time was too short to allow those present to discuss and to agree on the essential question of what precisely our ambitions were and by what means we were going to achieve them."[19] He went on to point out that what had really been achieved was talk, and that forming the AEA was only a first step. To improve present circumstances, immediate action was needed, something more than "shaking with emotion when one comes to the chapter about the Dispersion in Canadian History." Why not, he asked,

> *organize special celebrations for the centennial of [the publication of] Évangéline? Make known a knowledge and love of our history? Help to build a collaboration between the interested young and our newspapers? Encourage expeditions to the important sites of our history? Rebuild links between Acadians and French peoples elsewhere? Support and reveal our talents by organizing concerts for our musicians and regional exhibitions of our painters and sculptors? Publicize both awareness and appreciation of Acadian institutions and associations? In other words, stop wailing and act.*

Roméo articulated his belief that Acadian culture existed and needed to be brought to Canadian attention even more strongly in another editorial written early in 1948, entitled "The Congress Where We Weren't..." Its theme was the absence of students from St. Joseph's at the three important student conferences that were held in Winnipeg, Montreal, and Sackville, New Brunswick, during the spring and summer of 1947. Invitations had been sent to St. Joseph's, but, thanks to administration hesitancy and lack of initiative on the part of the student council, nothing was done. After deploring this blunder, Roméo went on to say why their absence was so regrettable. He pointed out that the students had a duty to act as ambassadors for their university. "Contact with other student groups," he wrote, "is the best possible publicity for the University...since its reputation depends not only on the renown of its professors but on the men that it shapes."[20] Further, he remarked, Winnipeg would have been a particularly good occasion for St. Joseph's, since there had been a demand for bilingual students as translators, a perfect opportunity to show the quality of their university. Why, he asked, didn't the university do anything to create a community spirit among its students? "Since we have ambitions in the area of general culture—and we are not a school for sport—why not intensify our actions in other areas, debates, competitions, conventions."

The final two paragraphs of this editorial deserve to be reproduced at length, since they show his understanding of the social realities of political life, something that would develop and serve him well both as a journalist and as a politician.

> *Even contacts with students with another background and language can bring us useful friendships later on. We will meet them professionally, in business and in political life. If we have created links, what aid and co-operation cannot we expect from them? It would be a circle of men whom we have "acquired" as friends. By such meetings, we will have established connections which we often lack on leaving college...But quite above our own particular interests, haven't we an important duty to fulfil towards both educator and educated? Our present life is not merely a preparation, it is a real life: as real as the first jump made by a parachutist. If the first try is botched, we won't have much chance at a second. This is why we must be interested in the problems that surround us. We must leave our small neighbourhoods to carry elsewhere the light which animates us and replenish it through the spirit of*

others. Each one with his own spark feeds the flame
until, throughout the world, new fire burns.

Just turned twenty, Roméo had become involved in a world of students beyond his own university, a world that fascinated him. He saw a society changing and capable of making even more far-reaching changes. In April 1948, he wrote to Marguerite Michaud, who was in the final stage of her doctoral studies at the Université de Montréal, that it was "undeniable that the student world was in the midst of a radical transformation." He continued,

> *Times have changed since students accepted*
> *everything without asking why and without*
> *discussing their problems. There is a tide of*
> *independence and new initiatives which is sweeping*
> *through the young. Aimed in the right direction, this*
> *attitude could have interesting results.*[21]

He picked up the theme of the importance of a common student experience when he gave the student address to his graduating class. Those who were present remember how nervous he was on this occasion. He needed a pause before he could begin his remarks, but his audience would recall his passionate belief in the broadening experience of university life. He spoke of the mixture of heritages represented by the graduating class, which, he said, had brought together "Acadians from Bathurst, Moncton, Prince Edward Island, friends from Quebec, and Irish co-religionists."[22] He turned the JEC catchwords into "observe, analyse, and advise," and his graduation yearbook predicted that his future would be in journalism.

In September, he left New Brunswick for Montreal, where he earned $14 a week as a member of the editorial board of *La Vie Étudiante*. He took with him a strong sense of an affectionate

Roméo's graduation portrait, 1949 (age twenty-two)

and supportive family, particularly on the part of his sisters, and an equally strong sense of obligation towards them. He also carried with him a love for the Maritimes in general and the Memramcook Valley in particular. He had developed a sense of himself as an Acadian, as a francophone in Canada, who was not from Quebec, but was part of a sprawling community of people who lived throughout New Brunswick and Nova Scotia. He set out for Montreal, a city where, thanks to the JEC, he already had acquaintances, to work at something he wanted to do, with people whose views were, at least on the surface, congenial to him. He seemed set for success.

CHAPTER 3

Transitions and Interruptions, 1948–1955

Roméo boarded the train for Montreal in late summer 1948, "dressed in a $36 Eaton suit and carrying a borrowed suit-case."[1] The next seven years would be a time of unexpected movement, of plans begun and changed because of family needs, as well as unanticipated successes. These were years in which his ideas—not only of Acadian life but also of Quebec society, the place of that province in Canada, and the place of Canada itself—sharpened and deepened. Above all, these were years in which his knowledge of mid-twentieth-century world politics became a matter of both personal experience and academic study.

Montreal in 1948 was an exciting place for such an awakening. It was a time when the city and the country were adjusting to the end of the Second World War. People were coming to terms with their experience of the war and the changes it had wrought. There had been little disagreement over the decision to go to war in 1939. When, on September 10, 1939, Parliament voted to declare war on Germany, there were only three dissenting votes: J.S. Woodsworth and two Quebec MPs. Over the next five and a half years, Canada raised a military force of over one million men and women from a population base of roughly 12 million.[2] The vast majority joined as volunteers. In the early months of the war, the "unemployed flocked to military armouries to enlist. Montreal regiments filled their ranks first."[3]

By 1942, however, the government came to believe that the promise it had given in 1940—that there would be no conscription for overseas service—had to be revoked. The national debate that followed was not as severe as that which had occurred during the First World War, but it was contentious enough. A plebiscite was held to ask the people to release the government from its pledge: the vote across the country was not overwhelmingly positive. Sixty-four per cent voted to allow the government to abandon their promise. Eighty-two per cent of Ontario voters supported the government; in Quebec only 28 per cent did so. Militarily speaking, the decision to send non-volunteers overseas made little or no difference to the Canadian war effort. It produced, however, yet one more divisive issue between anglophones and francophones, since it greatly strengthened the belief among many French Canadians that English Canada was impervious to French Canadian opinions and values. There were also other, more tangible costs: 43,000 men and women were killed and the national debt quadrupled.[4] Many feared that peace would bring a return of the "Dirty Thirties."

Instead, it brought a prosperity that made the Canada of 1948 very different from the Canada of 1939. There were three major areas of change, all of which had an impact on Roméo's life and politics: prosperity itself; the rapidity of urbanization; and the emergence of coherent and articulate voices for political and social change. If the war had quadrupled the national debt, it had also seen the gross national product double and personal savings increase. To considerable public relief, even the demobilization of almost one million veterans by September 1947 did not pose a major employment problem. At that time, the Department of Labour reported that 810,000 already had jobs. Aided by government payment of tuition fees and subsistence grants, another 50,000 enrolled in universities. In three years, university enrolment doubled, veterans going mostly into the humanities, social sciences, and commerce.[5] Poverty and hardship still existed and, as Desmond Morton pointed out, "by the usual definitions of poverty at the time, one-third of Canadians qualified, most of them elderly and rural, too many of them native people and Métis."[6] But, Morton continued, what needed to be remembered is that, in the censuses from 1921 to 1941, two-thirds of Canadians had been so classified. In Cormier's Cove, Roméo's brother Léonard remembered that, by 1948, the price of milk had risen sufficiently for the farm to be more than a subsistence enterprise.

Economic opportunity was, in part, provided by the surge in the housing market, where the growth in construction was extraordinary. "Between 1945 and 1949, no less than 365,900 dwelling units were completed."[7] This reflected the rapid expansion of Canada's population, which in 1948 reached nearly 13 million. The birth rate between 1946 and 1950 reached 27.4 per thousand, a "baby boom." By 1948, there were two and a half million children under nine years of age in the country.[8] Further, this natural increase in the domestic population was supplemented by half a million immigrants between 1941 and 1951, including among them war brides and concentration-camp survivors.[9] It was an expansion that saw Canada's towns develop at the expense of rural villages, whether in the countryside or by the sea. In 1941, urban life absorbed more than 54 per cent of the population. In 1951, that increased to 62 per cent, and within five years, two-thirds of Canadians were town dwellers.[10] The growth of towns and cities, with the expansion of the suburbs, was the most obvious result of the improved circumstances of many Canadians. Roméo was just one of many in the late 1940s who left rural life in the Maritimes to seek his fortune in the cities and towns of Ontario and Quebec. It was in the towns and cities, at this time, where new ideas about politics in general and social policy in particular were beginning to emerge.

Roméo's short summer visits to Montreal in 1946 and 1947 were to a city rediscovering France in books, films, songs, and wartime experiences. He remembered these visits in later life as a time when he began to understand that his experience of life had been narrow because it had been restricted. He bought the recordings of Édith Piaf and the Compagnons de la Chanson, and saw some of the latest French films, such as Clouzot's *Quai des Orfèvres* (the story of French railway workers during the war) and Marcel Carné's *Enfants du Paradis*. His ideas of postwar France and Canada beyond the Maritimes were becoming less vague, less poetic, and more detailed. But it was his time, from September 1948 to June 1949, as one of the editors of *La Vie Étudiante* that marked a turning point in his political development. While he had been considered by his contemporaries as someone more thoughtful and pragmatic than the rest of his class,[11] Roméo was also someone with strong emotions about political life. His sense of Acadian community identity was founded upon his beliefs about its history. He had learned about the Deportation not merely from textbooks but also from living in a river valley where deportations had taken place. He had visited the nearby site of Beauséjour and, as an adolescent, "had walked the ramparts with rage in my soul for my denied heritage."[12] During the months at *La Vie Étudiante*, both the challenges of his work and the people he met provided him with new ideas of what constituted the boundaries between communities and what linked differing societies with each other. His work as editor brought him in touch

Roméo (centre) with friends in Montreal in 1949

with students across Canada. One of his actions as editor was to ask for contributions from his readers, because they represented the differing viewpoints of the various Canadian provinces and, as he wrote, *La Vie Étudiante* was "the national student paper."[13] In later years, Roméo recalled that these months in Montreal opened his eyes to new realities. "I had not anticipated," he told Stephen Kimber in 1975, "finding others who did not share my language or my politics but whose preoccupations, whose objectives were mine. These frustrations, this anger which I had always blamed on my Acadian condition, were only part of the truth. I was faced with the truth of the human condition—a condition that goes beyond language."[14]

It was not only through his editorial work that Roméo found new ways of looking at life, but also through the social contacts that the JEC headquarters provided. Rita Cadieux was the president of the JEC when Roméo arrived, and he was soon invited to tag along to the gatherings that she and her husband hosted. In the 1940s and 1950s, the social net of casual hospitality among young adults in Montreal was a crucially important background to the political alliances that would shape the relations between Canada and Quebec for a generation. Gérard Pelletier recalled that those who went on to establish *Cité Libre* built upon the camaraderie that had united them during the 1940s, when most of them had worked for the JEC.[15] However, it was not only former members of the JEC who met together and argued about political life in Quebec and the social needs of the mid-twentieth-century world. Among those who came together, often in the home of the Cadieuxs, but also in the cafés of Montreal and other hospitable households, were Pierre Trudeau and René Levesque. Roméo in 1948 was on the edge of these gatherings, someone often included, though not, obviously, a major participant. He met Trudeau at this time, whose name and Outremont telephone number show up in Roméo's address book for 1949, although their acquaintance-ship did not develop at the time. Roméo was six or seven years younger than most of those present.

There were, however, two friendships he established at this time, which became of major importance in his life. Beyond the emotional maturity and enrichment that any long-lasting friendship brings, these particular connections helped form many of Roméo's political ideas, especially about Quebec society. Rita and Fernand Cadieux became lifelong friends, whose house was often his home when he visited Montreal for weekends over the next twenty years. Rita's memories of Roméo at this time are of a shy, reserved, charming, and intelligent young man.[16] Fernand was a couple of years older and Rita two years younger than Roméo. The Cadieuxs were part of the academic and artistic life of the city. At the same time, they were active in Quebec politics, at both the provincial and federal levels. Their hospitality was legendary, and their friendship meant that he continued to be aware of the political tides that buffeted Quebec. The other friendship that began at this time was

Roméo with pipe; Fernand Cadieux with cap; Rita Cadieux front
(second from left)

with Gérard Pelletier and his wife, Alexandra LeDuc. When
they met sometime in the fall of 1948, Pelletier was eight years
older than Roméo, and his social and political convictions had
a lasting influence on the younger man. Like Roméo, Pelletier
had been the youngest of a family of eight, and his family's
financial circumstances were much the same.   Like Roméo,
Pelletier had received his undergraduate education from the
Holy Cross Fathers, but he then went on to further studies at
the Université de Montréal. In 1939, however, he left university
to become secretary-general of the JEC, a post he held until
1945. He then spent the next two years as the field secretary
for the World Student Relief Organization in Geneva, a post
which meant, as he wrote, extensive travelling "from Dublin to
Vienna, from Naples, to Brussels to Prague," and through Paris

as often as could be managed.[17] He then returned to Montreal to begin what would be a distinguished career in journalism as a reporter for *Le Devoir.*

By the spring of 1949, Roméo's acquaintance with Gérard Pelletier encouraged him as he looked towards a future in Montreal. Pelletier's success as a reporter was an example to the younger man that a career in journalism was possible for someone who was not of the élite—and, further, that such a career was worth-while in terms of its opportunities for social and political influence. *Le Devoir* at this time was one of the strongest voices against the provincial government of Maurice Duplessis, and Pelletier's reports of its repressive social policies were widely read. This aspect of a journalistic career, the idea that journalists were the balance wheel to other powers within society, whether of wealth, religion, or organized public opinion, was brought home particularly vividly to Roméo in the last months of his stay in Montreal. It was during the Asbestos strike, which began on February 14, 1949, that Pelletier's articles became generally acclaimed throughout Quebec. This was this strike that brought together Pelletier, Jean Marchand, at that time the secretary-general of the Confédération des Travailleurs Catholiques du Canada, and Pierre Trudeau, recently returned from a journey through eastern Europe, the Middle East, India, and China.[18] As John English has written in his biography of Trudeau, "This strike is a fabled moment in Quebec history because it illuminates the class and ethnic differences that fuelled the resentment and dissent in the province."[19] It was also the most severe challenge to the social and economic policies of Duplessis since he had come to power in 1936.

In the eyes of the provincial government, the strike was illegal, and it used every possible means to bring it to an end. For Pelletier, Marchand, and Trudeau, the strike was a justifiable action against appalling and dangerous working conditions,

starvation wages, and foreign ownership.[20] There was violence
on both sides: workers destroyed the property of men brought
in to replace them, and the police responded with brutality. The
local priests were on the side of the strikers. Food and other
supplies were sent from the working-class parishes of Montreal
to Asbestos. Except for the Archbishop of Montreal, Joseph
Charbonneau, the hierarchy were on the side of the American
owners. Because of his support for the strikers, Charbonneau
found himself pressured to resign, and spent the rest of his life in
British Columbia. When the strike ended, it looked, on the surface, as if little had changed; but Pelletier's articles reporting the
bitter poverty of the miners and their families and the actions of
the government, which broke its own laws to bring matters to a
conclusion, made a lasting impression on the public. This strike
marked the beginning of a long period of embittered labour
disputes and was the moment when the "Quiet Revolution" in
Quebec became a probability.

Even though Roméo was very much on the periphery of those
whose activities gave immediate support to the striking workers, and whose efforts marked the beginning of a powerful social
movement in Quebec, his workplace gave him a privileged point
of view to watch what was happening. Gérard Pelletier became
for him someone he greatly admired and whose career he wanted
to emulate. Through the Cadieuxs, Roméo gained confidence in
his own ability to understand the social and political questions of
the time. By late winter 1949, Roméo fully expected to continue
in his position with the JEC, coping with the usual editorial tasks,
writing the occasional editorial, replying to correspondence, and
answering to an editorial board about management problems. At
the same time, he was looking for work that paid more than $14 a
week, plus lodging. Circumstances beyond his control, however,
forced his return to New Brunswick.

In late March or early April that year, his brother Léonard had an accident which handicapped him for the rest of his life.[21] He had parked on the side of the road, and was getting something from the trunk, when a car skidded on black ice and pinned him against his own vehicle, fracturing both legs and causing back injuries. Placed immediately in wooden splints, he was rushed to a hospital in Boston. After a number of operations, he was sent back to Cormier's Cove to convalesce and to face the fact that he would have residual pain for the rest of his life and never again be able to undertake hard manual labour. Quite apart from the personal tragedy of a man who loved farming being chained to office work at the age of twenty-four, Léonard's accident had an immediate and long-term economic impact on the family as a whole. Until then, he had worked the farm with Antoine, his eldest brother, and, in the roughly ten years since 1940, when Antoine married and Roméo left for St. Joseph's as a boarder, the brothers had brought it into a much more prosperous state. Antoine lived in the farmhouse at this time with his wife and growing family, as well as their father. However, though the farm was more prosperous, it still produced little in the way of a cash income. Now there were medical bills and hired labour to be paid, as well as the usual living expenses for Antoine, his four—soon to be five—children, their father, and now Léonard. Whatever Roméo and his married sisters were able to be contribute would be needed and welcome.

Roméo went back home to Cormier's Cove in late August 1949, and quickly realized that a return to Montreal was not possible unless the JEC could provide him with a better salary. Fernand Cadieux wrote to him on September 29, saying that he had sent a telegram to St. Joseph's, confirming that the JEC could not pay him more. The letter was obviously in reply to a long one from Roméo, no longer in existence, in which he had described his situation and told Cadieux of his plans to continue working as a journalist while, at the same time, teaching. In the three-page reply, Cadieux sympathized with Roméo's situation and gave him advice. Cadieux warned him against becoming swallowed up by the life and conventions of an isolated rural community, telling him to find ways to keep his passion, "le feu," alive. Cadieux told Roméo clearly that he must understand that what he had the power to do was important for the health and well-being of Acadia. Cadieux urged him to form a group of like-minded people and share with them his talents, his books, and his resources in general. Finally, he told Roméo to nourish, "*alimenter*," himself by continuing to write to the Cadieuxs and people such as Pelletier, describing the problems he faced in his milieu, to read widely such authors as André Malraux, and to subscribe to periodicals such as *Esprit*.[22] Cadieux's encouragement and counsel must have bolstered Roméo's morale, but in the fall of 1949, his way forward looked unpromising.

There was no question of Roméo going back to work on the farm: that would have meant the addition of another person to feed and clothe, and one whose talent for farming was minimal. The surge in urban development that came to New Brunswick in the 1950s had not yet taken place. He toyed with the idea of going to law school, but the financial situation of the family meant that this was not an option. For the best part of a year, Roméo worked for *L'Évangéline*, the francophone daily published in Moncton. He translated the Canadian and international news reports that arrived in English, wrote obituaries, and carried out a number of reporting assignments. His starting wage was $35 a week, which increased to $45 before he left; but the decision was soon made that he would go back to St. Joseph's in September 1950 to earn a Bachelor of Education. This would permit him to teach in New Brunswick's high schools. It is unclear how the money for his tuition was raised, but somehow the fees were paid, as well as weekly boarding costs in the village of Memramcook. In 2008, at the age of eighty-six, his brother's widow Mélindé recalled how, on Thursdays, Roméo walked the three kilometres between Memramcook and the farm at Cormier's Cove, bringing his washing. On Sunday nights, he left with food to share with others at his lodgings. She recalled that he did all kinds of household chores for her, from sweeping the floors to carrying water and chopping wood. In the spring of 1951, Roméo graduated with a B.Ed., and that September he began teaching in Drummond, a small town in Victoria County in northern New Brunswick, with a starting salary of $2,150 a year.

Today, Drummond is a village rather than a town, with a population of just over 800. It is set in the rolling farmland just south of Grand Falls, and is reputed to have the best soil for growing potatoes in New Brunswick. The land was first settled by Irish immigrants in the 1850s, but by the opening of the twentieth century, Acadians had moved into the area. When Roméo came to teach at Drummond, the population in the immediate area was more than one thousand, 95 per cent French-speaking, and its economy was, then as it is today, centred on the potato crop.[23] In fact, so important is this crop that, at the opening of the twenty-first century, schoolchildren in the region still returned to school in mid-August so that they could be released in mid-September for two weeks to help with the harvest. The purely agricultural nature of the countryside around Drummond, with almost no forestry, was a new experience for Roméo, but the school system had a great deal in common with what he had known when he was younger. The Académie Notre-Dame de Drummond, which had opened its doors the previous year for the first time, had a staff of nine and 282 students, enrolled in Grades One to Eleven.[24] It was, as were all public schools in New Brunswick at the time, still run by a local school board. Financially, almost all the expenses of the physical plant and the teachers' salaries were met from money raised directly from the local population.

In fact, the very existence of the Académie Notre-Dame was

due to the efforts of the local community, led by Father Alfred Lang, who petitioned the provincial authorities in 1947 for a school board for the region, one that would bring together the small villages of Falls Brook, Boat Landing, and Tobique Road with the larger community of Drummond. At the same time, he organized a collection each Sunday in the local churches to help pay for the cost of the new building. If the financing of the education system had barely changed during the past decade, neither had the curriculum seen any major alterations. The provincial government still insisted that all the texts used in the school system be in English, except for the French grammar text, which was the work of two English authors, Fraser and Square. This last was known by Acadian students as "le français carré" and studied for only a few weeks before the provincial matriculation exams. Of course, all provincial exams, except for French grammar, were also set and written in English. Roméo was assigned to teach French and history in Grades Nine and Ten, as well as chemistry. He was a brilliant teacher, especially in the first two subjects. Nelson Lynch was the principal of the academy during these years, and in a conversation in 2007, he spoke to the author of the extent to which former students, still living in the region, talked of the liveliness and interest they had encountered in Roméo's classes. At the same time, it was recalled that chemistry was not his strong suit. On one memorable occasion, when the students were gathered around his desk to watch him demonstrate some particular experiment, Roméo managed to produce an explosion that removed half the skirts of the girls in the class. No one was hurt, but the incident is part of the folklore of the region more than fifty years later.

The two years that Roméo spent in Drummond was a time when major changes were beginning in Acadian life. In 1871, the Acadian population made up 16 per cent of New Brunswick; in 1951 Acadians were 40 per cent of the population, an increase of 340 per cent.[25] It was in the election of 1952 that this demographic showed its strength. The Conservative Hugh John Flemming led his party to a surprising victory over that of Liberal John B. McNair, ending seventeen years of Liberal rule. Four French-speaking Conservatives were elected as part of Flemming's government, and ten of the sixteen Liberal opposition members were Acadian.[26] These results set the stage for the development of the Acadians as a major political force in New Brunswick affairs, and a people who must be considered in the formation of government policy. Many of the same social networks that bound anglophones together in New Brunswick existed among the Acadians, and, over the next years, Acadians showed that they had the same capacity as anglophones for using those networks to bring pressure on politicians. Social connections, formed by attendance at the same church and education at the same colleges, for example, as well as strong family ties, helped the organization of a number of different associations to work for common causes. This coming together was particularly true among the Acadians in the field of education, and, in 1952, education was a province-wide issue, a matter of critical importance to both linguistic communities.

The school population throughout the province had burgeoned with the postwar baby boom: 92,908 students had been enrolled for the 1945–1946 school year; 105,230 were enrolled for 1952–1953.[27] There was a severe shortage of teachers in both English and French schools. Further, particularly in rural areas and above all in the francophone districts, there were far too many teachers with only local licences, many of whom had not finished high school. For the province as a whole, there were 594 such teachers, over 13 per cent of the teaching body.[28] The need to find and hire qualified teachers was marginally more necessary for francophone schools, since the highest illiteracy rate in the province was among the French population, and that was where most of the local licenses were held.[29] L'Association Acadienne d'Éducation (AAE), which had been founded in Bathurst in 1936, was a major and effective lobbying force in this area. Its membership represented the Acadian élite, businessmen, lawyers, doctors, and university personnel, led by Dr. Albert Sormany.[30] While generally interested in all aspects of Acadian cultural life, when it came to education, the association concerned itself primarily with the provincial recognition of the academic value of the Acadian colleges and with their funding. Without the work of the association in this field, there would have been no B.Ed. program at St. Joseph's in 1950 for Roméo to attend. It also considered the problems that the Acadians faced in public schools. What was needed, in the view of these lobbyists, was a complete reform in the way francophone students were regarded by the Normal School in Fredericton, as well a change in the attitude of the Department of Education towards teacher training undertaken at both St. Joseph's University and L'Université du Sacré-Coeur in Bathurst.[31] By 1951, a certain amount of progress had already been made towards reform in these areas: St. Joseph's summer courses were recognized as equivalent to those given by the University of New Brunswick in 1948; those given by L'Université du Sacré-Coeur had to wait until 1958 for similar accreditation.

In the meantime, another Acadian association was at work on these matters, one with which Roméo became closely involved: l'Association des Instituteurs Acadiens (AIA),[32] which brought together francophone teachers from the schools and colleges in 1946. AIA would have had little influence on the Department of Education in Fredericton, without the work of the older organization. The aims of the newer association were the eminently practical ones of looking after the professional interests of Acadian teachers and using every possible means to improve the education of Acadian youth.[33] On his arrival in Drummond, Roméo became not only a member of the association, but also president of the local branch that year. This meant that he was involved locally, regionally, and provincially with teachers who were working to secure a radical change in the policy of the Department of Education for francophone education in New Brunswick. This change was so that francophone students would have the right to study all subjects, except English, in their own language, and, similarly, to write the provincial examinations, except English, in French. The realization of this project necessitated giving much more influence to Acadian teachers not only over curricula, but also in the provincial matriculation examination system. Committees previously staffed by anglophones would now need francophones to select the French texts for the schools and set and mark examinations. A small number of Acadians had been appointed to the provincial committees of the Department of Education during the 1940s, but should the province move towards providing a French education stream within the system as a whole, there needed to be a great many more. Further, there was a need for some rearrangement of provincial finances. While service on Department of Education committees, whether English or French, rarely paid teachers more than expenses, the subsidies previously spent exclusively on English textbooks would to have cover French and English texts. These consequences were, more or less, foreseen by the provincial authorities, who would gradually give ground to the demands made by Acadians during the next two decades, although, as Emery LeBlanc wrote, every concession on the way towards these goals was the result of lengthy overtures and negotiation.[34] What was recognized by very few at this time, however, was that the acceptance of a parallel French-language school system would lead to the provision of French services by other government departments and, finally, to the acceptance by the province of both French and English as the official languages of the courts.[35] However, in the summer of 1952, such developments lay twenty years in the future. When Roméo joined a group of fifty teachers from across the province to spend the month of July helping correct "upwards of 17,000" matriculation papers, the Acadian teachers in the group lobbied the Department of Education officials they met only for the possibility of history being taught and examined in French, a change granted in 1955.

The years 1953 to1955 held something more for Roméo than teaching and politics. They were, after all, the years of his young adulthood, years in which he was doing work he enjoyed that was reasonably paid and brought him into a group of people of much his own age and circumstances. It was still a time before televisions were common, when entertainment was home-based and organized around friendships made at work or through family connections. For Roméo, this net was large and was made up not only of his immediate colleagues, but also of teachers from the villages that were strung along the St. John River between Grand Falls, some five kilometres north of Drummond, and Edmundston, the milltown at the confluence of the Madawaska and St. John rivers, 57 kilometres north of Grand Falls.

The St. John River marks the boundary between the United States and Canada from Grand Falls to well beyond Edmundston. The State of Maine and the Province of New Brunswick have complex social and economic ties, not to mention considerable cross-border family connections. Directly facing Edmundston, across the international bridge, is another mill town, Madawaska, Maine, dependent, as is Edmundston, on the pulp-and-paper industry. Edmundston had a population of 12,000 in 1951, and was the cathedral town for northwestern New Brunswick. That year it boasted two small post-secondary institutions, the Collège Saint-Louis, founded in 1946 by the Eudist fathers for men, and le Collège Maillet, founded in 1949 by the Religieuses Hospitalières de Saint-Joseph for women. It also had a hard-working school board, which was notorious for poaching the best teachers from the surrounding villages for the Edmundston schools, simply by paying them more.[36] All these institutions helped build a cultural life that made the town attractive to young people throughout the region. There were film societies that brought in French films from Montreal, since the local cinemas at this time were showing almost exclusively American films. There were cultural organizations that brought travelling artists and organized community concerts, drawing audiences of over 600 two or three nights in a row, several times during the winter months. There was the occasional theatrical company from Quebec, presenting classical French drama. For Roméo, the town had the added attraction of two or three friends who had graduated with him from Saint-Joseph's, among them Rhéal Gaudet, who was at that point teaching at Saint-Louis.

Nobody had much money, because most of the teachers helped their parents, who had paid towards their education; but there was a great deal of social activity. A few people had cars, and an erratic bus service ran along the river valley that linked the villages. There was a great deal of entertaining at home, often in the form of gatherings of eight or more young people at somebody's family home or, more rarely, at a teacher's apartment. There would be a large country-style meal, more often than not of spaghetti or baked beans and buckwheat pancakes, a few bottles of wine, and dancing with the carpet rolled back. There were good small restaurants, where whisky was served in teapots, because New Brunswick still banned liquor in restaurants. These years were some of the last when rural Acadian life was ruled more by traditional religious observances than by the emerging ideas of secular society. It was not that Roméo and his friends spent their free time under the eye of the clergy or as part of church-run events, but that Catholicism was a reference point in their lives. Teachers were expected to go to Mass every Sunday in the local parish church; if they were absent, they could expect to be questioned on Monday as to the reason. There was a strong expectation that most of the young people would be married by their mid-twenties or soon after. The great wheeling calendar of church observances, the celebratory Masses at Christmas and Easter, the other ritual observances of Advent and Lent, as well as particular saints' days, marked the school year and the life of towns and villages. Louis-Joseph Lachance, the organist at the cathedral in Edmundston, still wrote a new setting for Mass for both Christmas and Easter during these years. The week between Christmas and New Year was still marked by the Réveillon on Christmas Eve. This event, which still occurs in some villages, includes a huge meal at a relative's or friend's house following midnight Mass, when traditional dishes such as tourtière and six-pâtes are served.[37] Along the Acadian coast, of course, oysters were on the menu. The Christmas Day meal of turkey was almost never served before late afternoon, and it was followed by a round of visits to friends, which inevitably led to another very late night. Providing there were no blizzards, or the rare unseasonable thaw, skating and skiing helped the digestion. The celebrations usually continued until New Year's Day. Since the weather in northern New Brunswick is often bitterly cold in late December, these evenings during the 1950s were interrupted around 11 p.m. by people rushing out to start their cars. Those whose engines stalled put their cars in neutral and were pushed by another car until the engine caught. In later years, Roméo recalled this as one of the less stressful and more enjoyable periods of his life. He liked teaching, had begun to make an impact on the bureaucracy of the Department of Education in Fredericton, and had fallen in a love with an Edmundston girl, Gloria David, the daughter of an Edmundston businessman. She was pretty, talented, and a committed Catholic. This more or less tranquil period of his life came to an end in the summer of 1953, when he was informed that he had won a France-Acadie scholarship to study for a year in Paris.[38]

In a letter written to Gloria in December, after he had been in Paris three months, Roméo described the impact of his new life. He was living in Canada House in the Cité Universitaire, the central university residence complex for foreign students at the Sorbonne. That year in Paris autumn was its usual rainy season, with the days growing dark by mid-afternoon. He had caught a cold and felt generally overwhelmed. Before he had left, he remarked that he thought the coming year would be a major turning point for him. Now he wrote that he found himself in the middle of "turmoil," which had been battering at him ever since he arrived. "I was caught in a conformist milieu, stable, doubly confined," he wrote. Now, "I find myself thrown into absolute liberty. There are no longer limits, it is necessary to create them from the outset, there are neither rules nor rights, everyone is charged with his own responsibility; there is no longer a common morality, each one lives as he wishes and no one thinks of challenging this."[39] He continued in this train of thought by comparing his situation to that of Rousseau's character Émile, who was brought up without a structured belief system and then plunged headlong into the everyday world, a world in which he had to make decisions but had no clear idea as to the reasons why he should choose one path rather than another.[40] Roméo elaborated: "We are thrown here into the heart of the free life," he wrote, "nothing fetters our inclinations, au contraire everything tempts us. The ideas of adolescent collegiality, purity, temperance, religious exercises, service to your neighbour—all of this rearranges itself and everyone retains that which they can or wish to keep."[41] In some ways, of course, this situation was no different from the shock that any young person from a small town feels when arriving at a big university in a big city. But this sense of strangeness, of distance from the known community, of being plunged into a different culture, was particularly severe for Roméo and others who came to Paris from French Canada at the opening of the 1950s. In many ways, the similarity of language heightened the feeling of bewilderment, because the immediate cultural references were so different.

Paris in 1953 was the capital of a country still struggling with the aftermath of a war that had cost its people dearly and had shown the nation to be deeply riven. The German advance into French territory in the spring of 1940 led directly to the collapse of the Third Republic and its replacement by what was known simply as "L'État français," the French State. Officials of this government, which had its seat at Vichy, a small provincial health spa in central France, signed an armistice with Germany on June 22 that year. Even while negotiations for this armistice were being concluded, General de Gaulle announced in London that France's war with Germany would continue. In the words of one scholar:

> The German army occupied the northern half of
> the country until late 1942 when it swallowed up
> the rest...Myriad forms of collaboration flourished,
> from obliging the well-armed foreigners to eagerly
> abetting the schemes of the agents of Nazism.
> Resistance to the Germans and Vichy alike sprang
> up, as nuanced in form and aim as collaboration.[42]

At this point there began a civil war in France, which continued to poison French life well after 1945.[43] Politics and social life in 1953 were still moulded by the events of the 1940s, with parties of the Right clustered around de Gaulle, and the Left split by the irreconcilable differences between Communists, who had a grip on 25 per cent of the electorate, and Socialists.

It has been argued by those who defend Vichy France that

the country would have suffered much more had an armistice not been signed. This point of view is difficult to sustain, given the actual price paid by France from 1940 to 1945. Some 92,000 French men and women had already lost their lives before the armistice was signed; another 68,000 were killed during the battles for liberation in 1945. But far more severe were the other losses due to the German presence in France: 160,000 men and women were deported to Germany as "political" prisoners and never returned; 120,000 were sent to Germany as forced labour and died there; and 30,000 were executed for Resistance activities.[44] At the same time, the direct financial cost to France was great: Germany levied somewhere between $8 and $10 billion of payments during the years of the Occupation. Further, the campaigns fought in France in 1945 caused great destruction: over 7,000 bridges destroyed; 38,000 miles of road and 3,000 miles of railway lines damaged; 10,000 commercial and industrial enterprises that needed to be rebuilt; 291,000 homes that were totally destroyed and another 938,000 severely damaged.[45] It is scarcely surprising that, eight years after the end of the war, the country was still coming to terms with what had happened, especially since the liberation had brought in its train "les règlements des comptes." These included at least 10,000 summary executions, as well as another 800 legal executions and at least 39,000 prison sentences.[46]

The pulse of the society, the flow of political ideas in Paris was not only a far cry from the Acadian milieu of New Brunswick, but also radically different from that of Montreal. While there were obviously issues of discrimination within these societies, none were of the magnitude of French anti-Semitism, which had allowed more than 60,000 Jews (men, women, and children) to be deported to the Nazi death camps.[47] While Canadian politics were lively, and relations between the provinces and the federal government strained, there was nothing that compared to the situation produced by the constitution of the Fourth Republic, brought into being in 1946. During its existence, from 1946 to 1958, the tenure of any premier was less than five months, as coalitions between the many Centre parties, the Gaullists on the Right, and the Communists on the Left, came and went. Nor did Canadians produce any intellectual debate to compare with the virulence and brilliance of the clash among intellectuals in France, the passionate disagreements in the press, or books comparable to the writings of Albert Camus, André Malraux, and Jean-Paul Sartre. But it was the crisis of poverty in Paris, the existence of the "bidonvilles"—the shanty towns which had developed on the edges of the city after 1945—coupled with the reaction of the Catholic hierarchy to the worker priests, that were the major intellectual challenge to Roméo's beliefs during his first year in France. Roméo came to France with an experience of rural poverty and of the suffering of the urban working class, but he had never been faced with the knowledge of people dying as the direct result of lack of shelter and food in the slums of a capital. Nor had he faced the challenge of reacting to such a situation as a Catholic. He had heard of the experiences that Pelletier and Marchand had had during the Asbestos strike in 1949, but he had not come face-to-face with people living in destitution, their lives controlled by an authoritarian structure with little compassion. In Paris, however, he was confronted directly with the consequences of abject poverty and state neglect. At this time, Roméo's Catholic beliefs were in flux. He had, very briefly, considered the priesthood at the time of his graduation from St. Joseph's. When he arrived in Paris, he continued to go to Mass and confession. He was also an active member of two Catholic student movements for peace: Chrétiente en Marche and Pax Christi, which led to a connection with the worker priests active in the city.

A "worker priest" was a priest who was "freed from parochial work by his bishop, lived only by full time labor [sic] in a factory, or other place of work, and was indistinguishable in appearance from an ordinary workman."[48] These men were part of a movement that had begun in Marseilles in 1941 by Father Jacques Loew, a Dominican priest who had decided that the only way to help working-class people was to work alongside them. The abandonment of the cassock was almost as revolutionary at that time in France as the idea that priests would labour as factory workers. The number of priests taking this step grew slowly, but when the forced deportation of French men to Germany to work in munition factories gained momentum after 1941, their numbers expanded rapidly. The German authorities turned down a request from the French bishops to allow priests to accompany the deportees. The French then sought volunteers to work "undercover," and twenty-five priests left in secular clothes to work within the German armament factories. After the war ended, the number of worker priests in France grew to over a hundred, and there were several in the poorest districts of Paris. One of the most well-known of these men was the Abbé Pierre, who, while he did not take a job in a factory, combined work among the homeless and the rag-pickers of Paris with service in the Assemblée Nationale. It was at this point, in 1951, that the Vatican became concerned with the worker priests' involvement in direct political action, especially those who had become members of the Communist Party, and the social conditions of the poorest took second place to the fears of international conflict. By the end of 1953, just as Roméo became convinced of the value of worker priests for the poor and of the difference that men such as the Abbé Pierre made in the slums of Paris, the Vatican ordered the movement to be suppressed and the priests to return to their parishes.[49]

There would be other times in Roméo's life when he reevaluated his religious beliefs, but, during his first year in Paris, he thought his way from a questioning of the Catholic beliefs he had been taught to a much more nuanced faith. The worker priests he met brought him to a deeper understanding of charity, suggesting that visiting the incurable and dying in the pauper wards of the hospitals was a more worthwhile action than giving change to a beggar. Roméo followed the debate over the propriety of the lives of the worker priests, and the intransigence of the Vatican in the face of the pleas by a number of French bishops that the priests be allowed to continue their work. In a letter of March 11, 1954, he wrote, "It is difficult to measure the wrenching of conscience of those that are scandalized to see the Church apparently abandon the working class and return to the old conservative tradition which has made it lose almost all its prestige in Europe."[50] His own outrage came out in another letter, dated March 22. He wrote: "I believe in God and His Church, but I accept with difficulty that under pretext of their contact with the communists, one disbands the worker-priests, and two weeks later Cardinal Spellman can, in a public lecture, praise Senator McCarthy...One forbids priests to be workers, but one permits them to be of the middle class, financiers, editors, journalists etc."[51] A description he gave of Catholicism at this time was one he continued to hold throughout his life. "The Church," he wrote in 1955, "was a font of pure water with damn bad plumbing."[52]

In the 1950s, courses of study for overseas graduate students at the Sorbonne could be a somewhat haphazard affair. France-Acadie students were left very much to their own devices. Roméo, who turned twenty-six in December 1953, had a clear idea of what he wanted do and why. Since he saw his future as a teacher in the New Brunswick high-school system, he decided to work with Professor Charles Bruneau, whose field was the teaching of French grammar. In a letter to a friend, Roméo acknowledged that it was a much less poetical choice than enrolling in literature courses, but much more practical, given his teaching assignment. Further, he was hopeful that, if he prepared a research paper in the field, it might lead to some sort of a diploma.[53] His choice of Professor Bruneau was fortunate. By March 1954, the latter was sufficiently impressed by Roméo's abilities to smooth the path for his registration, not for a diploma but for a doctorate on "the teaching of French in a bi-lingual district of Canada: the case of New Brunswick." Furthermore, Professor Bruneau was crucial as a reference for Roméo's application for a scholarship to allow him to remain in Paris for another year. Backed with his strong academic record from St. Joseph's and Canadian letters of recommendation, Roméo received a Royal Society of Canada scholarship for this purpose in 1954.[54]

His application to the Royal Society was helped by the fact that he had taken part in activities related to international affairs. He seized every opportunity for inexpensive travel, going to England and Scotland with a graduate student group in the spring of 1954, and to Germany as part of a study group linked to the *Revue des documents franco-allemande*.[55] He also enrolled in an optional course on the history of international affairs, with a Professor Lanson, whom Roméo described as a sixty-nine-year-old with the energy of someone of twenty-five, who was absolutely extraordinary as an analyst of the present state of the world affairs.[56] This course not only proved invaluable immediately as an aid in understanding the political world in which he then lived, but also helped him later as a teacher at New Brunswick's Normal School. Above all, it was invaluable when he began his career as a journalist in earnest, becoming in the 1960s Radio-Canada's foreign correspondent in London and Washington. The courses that he had taken as an undergraduate had been restricted, to a large extent, to religious history and the history of Britain and Canada before 1940.

The 1950s in Europe were complex enough for those who lived there at the time. The year 1945 had seen the end of large-scale armed conflict between the major powers, but what followed was a very ragged peace. Those who had fought across the globe to defeat Germany and Japan now found themselves at odds among themselves, with the added complications of the atomic bomb and the collapse of the European colonial empires in Asia and Africa. The dominance of eastern Europe by the Soviet Union and the powerful influence of the United States throughout western Europe resulted very soon after 1945 in the state of tension known as the Cold War. International tensions have been a commonplace of relations between states from time immemorial, but as two distinguished military historians have noted, "the development of nuclear weapons and the perfection of new means to deliver them restricted the use of war as a feasible method of pursuing political ends without diminishing the danger of its occurrence."[57] Territorial ambitions were made more acute between the competing powers, because of their bitter ideological differences. The division of Germany into four zones by the Allied armies (American, British, French, and Russian), with Berlin situated in the Russian zone but also divided into sections, led to the Berlin blockade in 1948, an attempt by the Russians to force the other powers to quit the city. The American and British governments supplied their own zones by air, from late June 1948 until May 12, 1949. That year, at the suggestion of Canadian Prime Minister Louis St. Laurent, the North Atlantic Treaty Organization (NATO) was created, whereby the United States, Canada, and Britain accepted military obligations in Europe. By the end of 1952, a NATO army had been organized, with headquarters in Europe. When Roméo began his studies in Paris, Europe was well and truly divided into East and West by the "Iron Curtain," something Churchill had predicted when he invented the phrase in 1946. France had to face the inevitable re-armament of Germany within NATO in 1954.

Professor Lanson's course provided an understanding of the

swirl of these events, but also an analysis of the happenings in Indo-China and North Africa, where France faced the end of its colonial empire. In many ways, while the understanding of the Cold War in Europe was of critical importance for Roméo, as he came to grips with contemporary international affairs during his years at the Sorbonne, his growing understanding of French colonial matters was of more immediate interest to him. In the first place, it added a different dimension to his sense of France as a nation. When he first arrived, France was, above all, the polity and culture at the root of his own. It was also a country from which his own polity and culture had diverged markedly as a result of historical circumstances, circumstances which had also left the Acadians with a strong connection with the British Empire. Now Roméo was to learn something of French imperialism and its importance in post-war France. When he returned to Canada, his experiences in Paris at the time of the struggle for Indo-China and the beginning of the Algerian War framed much of his attitude towards Quebec separatists, as well as his ideas of what it meant to be Acadian.

As British historian Tony Judt pointed out, the continued existence of an overseas empire was significant for the French at the end of the war. "If the French," he wrote, "were not, in their own eyes, quite reduced to a 'helpless, hopeless mass of protoplasm' (Eisenhower's description of them in 1945) this was in large measure due to their continued credibility, as a leading colonial power."[58] If the French officer corps and some members of the French government welcomed the struggle that began in Indo-China in 1949, it quickly became clear, as Judt also pointed out, that "sending young men to fight and die in a 'dirty war' in Indo-China made little sense to most French voters."[59] Six years of increasingly bloody and fruitless fighting ended with the French defeat by Ho Chi Minh's regular and guerrilla forces, based at Dien Bien Phu in the north of

Vietnam. It depleted both the French treasury and its military strength, "costing France more than 35,000 lives, and more than twice the amount of money she had received under the Marshall plan."[60] The final battle for the city of Dien Bien Phu lasted from March to May 1954; its surrender meant the loss of roughly one-tenth of the total French military force in Vietnam, slain or captured.[61] The Vietnamese fielded 50,000 troops, of whom 8,000 died on the battlefield. The French fielded 10,800; more than 2,000 were killed outright, and some 8,000 were captured, of whom only 3,290 were repatriated nine months later.[62] On July 1, 1954, the "Geneva accords" were signed. These divided Vietnam into two separate states, North and South—and France withdrew from the region. On the eve of yet another colonial war in Algeria, France had to accept the loss of control of lands and peoples that had been, in some ways, as central to the French empire as India had been to the British.[63]

Roméo's reaction to the fall of Dien Bien Phu was a mixture of acceptance, a curious regret, and a deeper understanding of what attracted him to France—beyond the link of a similar language and some cultural affinities. Like most of France, except for some politicians of the Right, Roméo saw the fall of Dien Bien Phu as the inevitable conclusion of French power in Indo-China. While he acknowledged that the time had come to end all European colonial exploitation in Asia and Africa, there was regret for the loss of the French imperial ideal, of the belief that the culture of France, its language, literature, its political dream of "Liberté, Égalité, Fraternité" as the foundation of the state, would spread beyond its European boundaries. At the same time, as he returned for a brief visit to New Brunswick in August 1954, Roméo was also clear about what France offered him and why he wanted to continue towards a doctorate at the Sorbonne. The centre of it all was Paris, where Professor Bruneau directed his studies with wit and intelligence, and the Cité Universitaire brought him friends from many countries, in particular a number of Americans, whose future careers would take them into the U.S. foreign service and with whom he would remain in touch throughout much of his life. Paris also brought him a life outside the university, a life of literature, journalism, theatre, music, and films. It allowed him to travel widely enough, and he visited Portugal and Italy during the summer before he left. In a letter dated March 22, 1954, when he had already booked passage by sea to Quebec for the end of August, he wrote:

> *I feel at ease now in Paris, you know: when I returned from Holland it seemed like returning home and I much like the customs man who met us at the border, the girl who sold* Le Monde, *the garçon in the café across the way who made me a fine hot rum because I was cold and my feet were wet. France is all of this to me, it's the old cathedral of course, but even it's more the people I've met, their old custom of shaking everyone's hand, even when leaving just for an hour, it's the smile and the friendly gesture of the guy a little drunk who, in a bar, offers a drink and toasts me because he is happy to learn that I am Canadian and that I speak French, and that I love his country, in spite of all the reasons there are to detest it at times. It's the flower-seller at the métro station who always offers me a carnation because I bought some one day when I felt particularly happy.*
>
> *And France, it's still the Abbé Pierre, who this morning celebrated, surrounded by the most sophisticated intellectuals, a commemorative Mass for Emmanuel Mounier, and who went to the altar*

to put on the priest's robes, in ragged pants and a blue shirt without a tie, but who spoke to us of the hope of the poor and abandoned with fire, filled with the presence of grace. France, it's the café when one sits for hours, sipping a coffee on the terrace, between two lectures, understanding everything and nothing. It's even the woman of easy virtue who invites one to "visit" with a sensitivity and a courage that it is almost painful to refuse her, so much does she seem to act with a good heart, overflowing with human sympathy.

Behind the paint and the hardness of heart, France is still the country of the Joliot-Curies who refused to benefit from the profits of their scientific research and who were quite ready to give anything secret to the Russians, because for them, there were no artificial frontiers between men, in spite of political principles. It's a country of contradiction, it's true, but also a country with a respect for a man and what he represents.[64]

For Roméo, when he considered support for Acadian distinctiveness, it would be to France that he looked, not to Quebec.

When he sailed for Canada, Roméo was hoping that Gloria David would accompany him when he returned. He wrote to her, saying that he knew his year in Paris had changed him and that, if they felt "a strong bond of love between them," they should make sure to undergo a similar development and experience the same influences in the near future.[65] His wishes for this relationship were unfulfilled. Gloria wrote to him soon after he returned, saying that she no longer was in love with him, but "I like you wholeheartedly and irrevocably."[66] Roméo returned alone to Paris in the fall of 1954.

It was the custom of the time among Acadians that the woman returned her suitor's letters when she decided to end the relationship. The half-dozen or so letters that his correspondent sent back throw light on Roméo's development during his first year in Paris, because they are some of the very few personal letters he wrote during in his life that survive among his papers at Library and Archives Canada. He does not seem to have kept a private diary. From this time onwards, it is the replies of friends to his letters, the recollections of his family and long-time friends, and the official record which provide the more personal details of his life. His first year in Paris was a time when Roméo became clearer about what he thought and believed. During his second year, it was more a matter of refining the ideas he had already acquired, rather than discovering new ones; of examining closely how he now thought about his own country, as much as how he felt about France.

The academic year began well enough. His friendships with other students at the Cité Universitaire developed. His studies were reaching a point where comparisons between the systems used to teach French in rural France and those used in New Brunswick provided a fruitful field of inquiry. The most important intellectual challenge occurred, as it did for many in France, with the outbreak of violence in Algeria on All Saints' Day, November 1, 1954.[67] On that day, an organization calling itself the Front de Libération Nationale (FLN) carried out a series of attacks against police stations, warehouses, communication centres, public-utility buildings, and military installations. The FLN was led by young Arab nationalists, who called for an independent Algerian state. The ties between France and Algeria were more complex than those that had linked France to Indo-China, and the immediate reaction of the French government to the violence and the demands was one of intransigence. Not only was Algeria much closer geographically to France than Indo-China, but it was also a settlement colony, where, in a population of ten million, one million were of French and other European heritage. Further, the colony was technically part of the French metropolitan administrative structure. As Tony Judt has pointed out, "The closest analogy elsewhere was Ulster, another overseas enclave in a former colony, institutionally incorporated into the 'mainland' and with a long established settler community for whom the attachment to the imperial heartland mattered far more than it did to the metropolitan majority."[68] The formal reaction of French Prime Minister Pierre Mendès-France to the events of November 1 came in a speech in the National Assembly on November 12, which would open the way for the appalling bloodshed that occurred over the next eight years.[69] He announced, "One does not compromise when it comes to defending the internal peace of the nation, the unity and integrity of the Republic. The Algerian departments are part of the French republic...Between them and metropolitan France there can be no conceivable secession." On July 3, 1962, de Gaulle pronounced Algeria an independent country.

Roméo turned twenty-seven in December 1954. As he watched the Algerian crisis flare more bitterly from week to week, the arguments about French imperialism, in particular, and of all forms of colonialism, in general, were the daily fare of student discussions at the Sorbonne. He spent almost as much time considering the general state of world politics, going to political meetings, and trying to understand the end of European empire, as he did on his thesis. He watched the turning of France towards Europe and towards Germany as an ally: ten years later as Radio-Canada's foreign correspondent in London, he had a rare knowledge of the roots of these political alliances and of the difficulties that the United Kingdom had with both countries. The savagery of the Algerian struggle greatly influenced his reaction to the movement for Quebec sovereignty and the actions of the Front de Liberation du Quebec (FLQ) in the 1960s. But at that time, Professor Bruneau was a continual source of encouragement to him and Roméo began the process of organizing ideas and data for his thesis. He began to frame his comparison between the teaching of Acadians in New Brunswick with that of the differing realities of teaching French in the rural schools of Brittany and Provence, districts of France whose local dialects were far removed from the French spoken in the cities. By Christmas, he was well into the organization of his doctorate, but very soon this work was disrupted by another family disaster, which meant that he was never able to complete his dissertation.

Roméo's eldest brother, Antoine, had married in 1940. He and his wife lived with his father in the family home and managed the farm. With Léonard's accident in 1948, Antoine had become the chief support for his father, as well as for his wife and six children. In 1954, he became unwell and, early in 1955, was in dire straits. By March, Roméo was taking steps to return to New Brunswick, and was in correspondence with the provincial teachers' training college in Fredericton, hoping for employment there. By summer, he was back in Cormier's Cove. Antoine had been diagnosed with a brain tumour. He died early in September. Roméo's income-tax return for 1955 has been preserved, and it shows that he took care of the immediate financial needs of the widow and her children. On a declared income that year of $1,716, Roméo claimed a loan to his brother of $600, the payment of medical expenses of $350 for his brother, and a further $500 for the support of his father, his brother's widow, and the children. Obviously, this meant that he began a new teaching career in debt.[70] At least, however, he had something of a career to develop. He received a letter from J.-Gérard DeGrace, the associate director of the Department of Education, confirming that he had been appointed to the faculty of the Normal School, as the teachers' training college was then generally known.[71]

He was to be paid an annual salary of $3,960, plus a bonus of 4 per cent per month. Once more, Roméo entered, unexpectedly, upon a new stage of his career in the fall of the year.

CHAPTER 4

Teacher to Journalist: Fredericton to Ottawa and Beyond

Roméo's return to Canada—and to the immediate assumption of considerable financial responsibility for his family—was something about which he felt he had no choice. He was the only possible source of money for the hospital bills and for the debts incurred during his brother's illness.[1] The family farm was a subsistence operation and brought in only enough income to cover the bare necessities of clothing and supplies, which had to be purchased. Roméo needed to provide enough ready money to make life bearable for his widowed sister-in-law, her six children, and his father. However, he was fortunate to have a number of options for employment, among them working as the chief assistant to Pierre Juneau at the National Film Board in Ottawa,[2] or as the director of the New Brunswick Teachers' Association, or as a faculty member of the New Brunswick Normal School in Fredericton. He did not seriously consider the job with the Teachers' Association, but in later life Roméo thought that choosing Fredericton and

Atlantic Canada rather than the nation's capital and central Canada was a crucial turning point in his career. Part of the reason for his choice was his attachment to New Brunswick, coupled with a conviction that his France-Acadie scholarship required a return to his own community for a while. During his four years at New Brunswick Teachers' College, 1955–1959, where he taught French and civics, he was a popular and effective teacher. He also played an important part in the ongoing struggle of Acadians for their right to an education of high quality in French in the province. During these years, he also came to understand the need of the English population of rural New Brunswick for a similar improvement in English schools.

When he arrived to take up his new responsibilities, Roméo had to adapt to a series of challenges: coming to terms with the contrast between Paris and Fredericton; between graduate work at the Sorbonne and working in a teacher training college; between the life of student on a generous scholarship and the assumption of major financial responsibility for his brother's widow and her family. In some ways, the multiplicity of events confronting him helped him to accept these major alterations in his life. His salary was reasonable, $3,960,[3] but payment began only at the end of September, and his family's need for financial aid was immediate.[4] The guarantee of employment meant some ease of mind as he began life in Fredericton, a solidly anglophone city with a population of less than 17,000, of which no more than a thousand were French-speaking.[5] It was as foreign a society for Roméo as the cosmopolitan life of Paris had been two years earlier. In the mid-1950s, the French- and English-speaking populations of the province lived, to a large extent, separate lives, divided not only by language, but also by religion. Socially, the two communities were barely acquainted with each other. While most middle-class Acadians were bilingual, the same was not true of English-speaking New Brunswickers. There was considerable

Normal School, Fredericton (Circle St. Anne) graduating class; Roméo centre

wariness on both sides about the way future relationships between the two groups would develop.[6] Even religion did not breach the gap, as there was little co-operation between the Irish Catholics and those who were French-speaking. When he had left Canada in 1953, Roméo's contact with English-speaking Canada had been greater than that of many of his Acadian contemporaries, partly because of his links with Jeunesse Étudiante Catholique when he was in Montreal, and partly because of his involvement with marking matriculation papers in Fredericton when he taught in Drummond. Before he took up his teaching position in Fredericton, however, he had never been exposed for any length of time to life in a milieu as traditionally English Canadian as Fredericton was in 1955, a place where the use of French in general daily life was almost non-existent.

An alteration of his plans for the future, demands of new financial responsibilities, the need to prepare courses at the college level in subject areas that he had not previously taught, all these matters gave him little time to brood about the dreams that had suddenly ended. Although it seemed on the surface barely to have changed, the Canada to which he had returned was, in fact, undergoing a major transformation. St. Laurent was still the Liberal prime minister, having been in power since 1948. Duplessis was still the leader of the Union Nationale and premier of Quebec, having held power even longer, since 1936. The premier of New Brunswick was still Hugh John Flemming, the leader of the Conservative Party in that province, although his government had had a much shorter life, being elected in 1952. Much of Canada was still benefiting from the postwar prosperity, and the recession that had occurred in 1953 was short. The population continued to grow because of the "baby boom": there were one million more Canadians in 1955 than there had been in 1953. Immigration had also played an important role, bringing new peoples from Europe, as well as a fair proportion from the United Kingdom.[7] The development of a safety net for the frail of the country, which had begun to take shape earlier, had been improved by the 1944 *Family Allowance Act* and further strengthened by the 1951 *Old Age Security Act*. There was a growing consciousness at all levels of government (federal, provincial, and municipal), fuelled by strong memories of the "Dirty Thirties," that attention had to be paid to the less fortunate in society.

During the early 1950s, all levels of government initiated changes which were to build a very different Canada from the country Roméo left in 1953. These were developments in what Harold Innis, Canada's most innovative political economist, considered those areas of human invention that determine the quality of life in communities: one being the transfer of knowledge and goods across space, the other being the handing down of knowledge and goods through time.[8] For a federation such as Canada, with ten provinces and two territories stretching across 9,984,670 square kilometres, the need for excellent communication in both categories was and remains crucial. While the railway was still the most important mode of travel, the automobile was gaining ground swiftly. In 1951, 41 per cent of Canadian households owned cars; by 1961, 68.4 per cent would report owning at least one.[9] By that year, as William Kilbourn, a leading historian, pointed out, the automobile had also killed more Canadians than the Second World War. He continued, "Its demands for space and pavement was a voracious consumer of provincial budgets and urban land."[10] It also made the development of suburban life possible, while bringing rural communities much more in touch with life in the cities. In 1948, the federal government agreed to spend $150 million on the construction of a Trans-Canada Highway to link all provinces across the continent with paved roads.[11] Work on this project provided employment opportunities, as well as investment in construction materials and trades, throughout the decade and beyond. The St. Lawrence Seaway, another federally backed undertaking, would allow ocean-going vessels to sail from the Atlantic Ocean to the Great Lakes. It was undertaken with the unenthusiastic co-operation of the United States. This development had far-reaching effects on the transportation links between Atlantic Canada and Ontario, since it relegated road and rail transport between these regions to second place in the policies of the federal government. However, it bolstered the economy of western Canada and strengthened the transport of goods from that region to Montreal, including grain shipments destined for Europe.

For Roméo and many Acadians in New Brunswick, the car not only meant easy connection with distant relatives—his family lived 250 kilometres from Fredericton—but also supported a link to francophone intellectual life. Quebec City is roughly 600 kilometres from Fredericton, and less than that from the predominantly French-speaking population of northern New Brunswick. Then, as now, it is the hub city of French life in Canada, with a world-renowned university, theatres, concert halls, art galleries, bookshops, and a vibrant political life, all working in the French language. Living in Fredericton brought Roméo a knowledge and respect for an anglophone world that had strong links to the United Kingdom and a fairly sceptical view of central Canada. Easy access to Quebec City allowed him a continued connection to many aspects of the life he had known in Europe.

In Canada, in the 1950s, developments in communications were the background and in many ways the necessary support for the simultaneous development of changes in the transmission of knowledge. Rapid transit shrunk space and time. Space and time were bridged by the rapid spread of news on radio and television and by increased access to the accumulated and expanding intellectual resources gathered in schools, libraries, and universities. These developments were largely a result of the Royal Commission on National Development in the Arts, Letters, and Sciences, which had been appointed under the chairmanship of Vincent Massey in 1949.[12] Its mandate was to report on and make recommendations about the general state of Canadian culture, something the commissioners interpreted to mean not only the fine arts and the humanities, but also the universities, communication technologies, and sciences. As well, the guidelines asked them to look at the existing federal agencies involved in these matters and report on what further government aid was needed to ensure that Canadian culture developed and flourished in the future. The commission delivered its report in 1951, and it would play an important role in the intellectual and cultural life of Canada for more than a generation.[13] In spite of some scepticism on the part of the federal government about support for artistic life—Prime Minister St. Laurent told one of his ministers that he was very doubtful about "subsidizing ballet dancers"[14]—and considerable opposition in Quebec, where Duplessis saw its recommendations as an unwarranted interference in provincial affairs, the majority of the *Massey Report*'s most important recommendations were implemented within the decade.

The positive reception of the commission's work came mostly because it built on the foundation of intellectual and social captital that Canada already possessed, rather than suggesting major innovations. Canada already had the National Film Board, the National Gallery, the National Museums— the Canadian Museum of Nature and the National Museum of Science and Technology—and the Public Archives and the Library of Parliament. It had painters, writers, musicians, and scholars, universities and research facilities. What it did not have was any federal agencies for supporting these activities, such as the Canada Council for the Arts and specific research councils, nor did it have any system for the preservation of public records. The Canadian Broadcasting Corporation already existed, but there was an obvious need to obtain additional power to regulate expanding radio communications, as well as the new television networks. The Massey Commission took the elements of the national cultural life that were already in existence and produced a blueprint for coherent growth, pointed out ways in which government support should be given to both intellectual and artistic life, and drafted plans for the continued development of a national radio and communication network. It made the issue of government patronage of cultural endeavours a matter of a national policy, and provided significant aid to the development of Canadian universities as teaching and research institutions. Finally, many artists benefited greatly from subventions of one kind or another given for study, theatrical productions, and publishing, even though some of those who became significant players on the Canadian cultural scene spurned state aid.

By the end of the 1950s, Canada was a more prosperous, sophisticated, and complex a country than it been ten years earlier. The political establishment, however, which looked so solid, was about to be fundamentally altered. In New Brunswick, developments among the population at large, and particularly among the Acadians, resulted in Hugh John Flemming's Conservative government being overturned in 1960 by the Liberal Party, led by Louis Robichaud. The work that began in the late 1940s and early 1950s, which was achieved by Acadian associations such as those to which Roméo had belonged as a high-school teacher, led to a new expression of political will by the Acadian community.[15] Hugh John Flemming's Conservatives were well aware of the demography of New Brunswick, with the Acadians forming 40 per cent of the population. It was the organization of the 200th anniversary commemoration of the Deportation of the Acadians that served as a catalyst for something that was not so much a new as it was a clearer articulation of their collective identity. This articulation was not only to unite their own communities for almost a generation, but also to convince many, if not most, anglophones of New Brunswick that the Acadian desire for the preservation of their heritage within the broader society was an understandable and acceptable goal.[16] One of the most important Acadian sociologists, Jean-Paul Hautecoeur, considered that the organizers presented the past in a way that permitted the future to burst forth.[17]

Roméo was not involved in the planning of the events of 1955, since he did not return to Canada until late spring of that year. However, he knew and admired those who organized the events. Some, such as Father Clément Cormier,[18] had taught him. Others, such as Adélard Savoie, who chaired the organizing committee, later became friends and colleagues. It is not surprising, therefore, that the expression of Acadian identity in the commemorative proceedings was one with which Roméo was comfortable.[19] The celebrations that took place throughout 1955 and encompassed Acadian settlements throughout the province, no matter how small, were a combination of commemorations of past sufferings with a triumphal celebration of present survival and a hopeful vision of future attainments. This interpretation of Acadian experience was very much Roméo's own sense of the narrative of Acadian heritage, tempered by a clear understanding of how many other peoples elsewhere in the world had a similar history. The festivities were supported not only by Acadian institutions such as St. Joseph's University and the Société Nationale L'Assomption (now the Société Nationale de l'Acadie)[20] but also by the government of Quebec and, with formal good wishes and substantial financial help, by both the New Brunswick and the federal governments. The emphasis of the commemoration was less upon the grief of the Deportation than upon those factors which had allowed the Acadians to survive the tragedy. It was less upon old wounds than upon the possibility, in the words of Acadian political scientist Joel Belliveau, that "Acadian society could take its future into its own hands while working with its anglophone neighbours."[21]

As Roméo soon discovered, however, there was another side to the events of 1955. The year might have marked a sea change in the Acadians' sense of themselves and a clear idea of what they wished to achieve, but it did not mean an end to prejudice and discrimination against them in the province. In fact, the very clarity with which Acadian ambitions were stated in the New Brunswick legislature in the spring of 1955 by Lucien Fortin, a Conservative member of the government representing Madawaska, caused anglophone members on both sides of the legislature to voice their opposition to the Acadian desire to resist assimilation. In his speech, Fortin remarked, "What the French want are the means and ways required to keep their cultural and religious heritage," and this meant "official recognition of the mother tongue of both...and proportional participation in public offices."[22] In other words, assimilation was still much desired by the anglophone population, but for the majority of the Acadians it was not acceptable any longer. For many anglophones, the Acadian attitude was considered an unreasonable ambition, a rejection of the best possible values for human society by those clinging with bigotry to a second-rate language and a superstitious set of religious beliefs. In his first weeks in the capital city, Roméo found that his heritage was a hindrance in his search for lodging, a choice apartment being "already taken" the afternoon he went to see it, but available for an anglophone colleague the next day.[23]

The teachers' college gave Roméo a more civilized welcome. Over forty years later, when recalling the time he spent in Fredericton,[24] Roméo emphasized that, on a professional level, he never felt any discrimination, and his relationships with his colleagues were amicable. At much the same time, a number of those who had been on the faculty at the time spoke about their memories of him. At twenty-eight, Roméo was tall, good-looking, well-dressed, with an air of seriousness, but with a very pleasant, open manner and a ready wit. His ability to switch "with ease from impeccable English to controlled French" was seen as a considerable help in bringing together students and faculty from different backgrounds.[25] A number of colleagues described him as "a people person who treated everybody the same," remarking that they considered him "an important thinker who loved to join discussions." The librarian at the time, Eileen Wallace, recalled, "He was thoughtful of others, always making sure everyone was comfortable." The science teacher, Franklin Gilmore, called him "a full-time student of human nature." Gilmore believed this was why Roméo always attended the Saturday-night occasions in the auditorium, where he sat in the balcony, observing "the people sitting around him, never missing a thing, his mind going all the time. People were his forte."[26] Dr. Murray Stewart, who came to the college as its vice-principal in 1956,[27] recalled that he served with Roméo on the French- and English-language curriculum committees and "found him to be friendly, co-operative and supportive, but an educator who kept a low profile."[28]

The September that Roméo arrived in Fredericton there were 23 faculty members and 382 students at the college. Six of the faculty, including Roméo, were francophone, as was about 25 per cent of the student body.[29] At the time, the one-year program licensed its graduates to teach at various levels within the school system. During Roméo's first year of teaching, the Department of Education negotiated an agreement with the universities in the province, whereby "English, French, History and an elective Education subject" would be given credit in certain B.A. programs.[30] This agreement did a great deal to strengthen the reputation of the teachers' college. Roméo's duties were the usual combination of teaching courses, participating in faculty meetings about the academic life of the institution, and undertaking extracurricular work with the students. He taught French language and literature and what then was known as "citizenship and civics," and today is known as social studies. As well, throughout his years at the college, he chaired the committee, composed of four faculty members and seventeen students, that produced the bilingual yearbook, *Tutoris.*

Roméo was, of course, well aware of the difficulties that faced francophone students wishing to know and use their mother tongue in the province. Although the situation looked much as it had two years earlier, in common with the shifting ground underlying federal and provincial politics, the linguistic politics of New Brunswick were also changing. The provincial education system was still desperately underfunded, too few of its teachers were adequately trained, and most schools, particularly in rural areas, were understaffed. The school system remained largely a matter of local school boards, constricted by the economic circumstances of the communities they served. A Royal

Commission on School Financing in New Brunswick, which had reported in 1954, emphasized the extraordinary lack of balance in the economic resources available to schools in the countryside as opposed to those in urban areas.[31] This disparity was particularly, though not solely, between Acadian rural schools and those in the cities. Since French was not recognized as an official language in New Brunswick, the staff and students in the Acadian areas worked with the additional handicap of having to use English in all their classes, except for the courses in the French language itself. In his last year at Drummond, Roméo had been one of those working for the right of French-speaking students to write the provincial matriculation examinations in History in French. A letter to Angèle Godin, the secretary of the Association des Instituteurs Acadiens, from the Director of School Services for the Department of Education asserted that all matriculation examinations, except that for French II, must be written in English.[32] The lack of official status for the French language within the province was also reflected in the training provided for Acadians at the teachers' college. In 1955, there was no provision for an equivalent licence for those whose first language was French and who would be teaching in the francophone areas.

Roméo's appointment was, however, a sign of change, much of it due to the man who had recruited him, R.H. Chapman. He had been appointed Director of Education for the province in 1953, and held this position under both Conservative and Liberal governments until 1966. Chapman was an inspired appointment. He was clear about the need to improve the quality of education throughout the province for both linguistic groups. He was a New Brunswicker, born and bred, from Port Elgin, and had himself graduated from the teachers' college in 1919. Before he took up this appointment, he had been not only the principal of three high schools, but also the superintendent for Westmorland and Albert counties.[33] He proved particularly skilled in navigating his way through the minefield of linguistic concerns and religious interests that bedevilled education issues in the province. One of Chapman's first actions in 1953 was to ensure that "practice teaching for French-speaking students [at the teachers' college was] in schools where the language of instruction was French."[34]

Roméo went to see Chapman at the end of his first week in Fredericton to point out that he had been hired to teach French language and literature, as well as history and politics, *in French.* However, Roméo explained, the library at the college contained almost no books in that language. Chapman gave him a sympathetic hearing and, with the full support of Dr. Wallace, who had been appointed as principal of the college that same year, sent Roméo to Quebec City with $3,000 in his pocket, with orders to bring back the books necessary for the proper education of his classes.[35] Many years later, Roméo remarked that the majority of the anglophones he met during his years in Fredericton had been sympathetic to the difficulties of the Acadians.[36] Part of this reaction was due to Roméo's own ability to argue in a reasonable way for Anglo-French co-operation, and so to avoid useless conflicts. His childhood in the Memramcook Valley had made him well aware that poverty was not something endured only by Acadians. He knew from personal experience that students coming from the rural areas of the province were unsophisticated but proud, were ignorant but not stupid, and, above all, had a strong desire to learn. He was able to emphasize the common experiences of such students and break down the French-Catholic/English-Protestant barriers that separated the groups. During his four-year chairmanship of the large committee for the yearbook of the college, which was dominated by the seventeen students drawn from both English- and French-language groups, he succeeded in establishing a successful working atmosphere, something remembered years later by others who had been members of the committee. At the same time, he acted as faculty adviser to the Cercle Sainte-Anne, the association regrouping francophone students at the college, and the Ciné-Club Lumière. These activities were to stay in his memory, and would also help to keep his memory alive.

It was as a classroom teacher, however, that he made a lasting impression on the students. In 1997, volunteers told his son, Dominic, when he ran for Parliament in his father's old constituency, that they were going to work for his campaign or vote for him because "your father taught me, you know." Part of Roméo's success came from his knowledge of the difficulties that the students faced and his realization of the extent to which he had to prepare them for what he wanted to teach them. William Biden, who was in charge of curriculum during these years, remarked that Roméo "saw the disadvantages of the Acadians in the education system of the 1950s and he wanted to do something about it; thus, the French students had great respect for his teaching."[37] In his classes he introduced additional materials and made them relevant to the students' past experiences and future needs. In particular, the students appreciated the broad-ranging classes in civics and political issues. During these years, Roméo was a frequent freelance correspondent for Radio-Canada, recording commentary on local politics at CFNS, as well as on national and international events that he considered needed a Maritime viewpoint.[38] It was inevitable that his classes benefited from this activity. His students recalled the breadth of his knowledge of world affairs and his growing familiarity with Canadian politics.

Of course, there was much more to Roméo's life at this time than just teaching and freelance journalism. He was a frequent visitor to his family home at Cormier's Cove, and he was often in Edmundston, where the friends that he had made when he taught in Drummond welcomed him enthusiastically. He went to Montreal two or three times a year, keeping in touch particularly with Rita and Fernand Cadieux. He carried on a

voluminous correspondence with family, friends, and acquaintances, who wrote to him from across the world; he kept many
of their letters. Unfortunately, in most cases, his letters to them
have not survived. Friends writing from within New Brunswick
told of the concerns of the teaching profession, of marriages, of
the births of children, and of their reactions to the wider problems within Canada. These letters provide a fascinating account
of the experiences of young Acadian adults in the late 1950s.[39]
These were the years when many in this age group were questioning the strictures of the Catholic Church and the influence
of priests on the conduct of teachers—both inside and outside
the classroom. The local diocesan authorities required that lay
teachers teach the Catechism and be seen to be leading a life
that included strict attendance at religious celebrations, over and
above Sunday Mass. This was now being challenged by Roméo's
contemporaries. Another frequent topic of concern among his
correspondents was the ongoing battle for the recognition of the
right to use French as the language of instruction. There were,
of course, comments on books read, films seen, and social life
enjoyed. Letters from friends in Europe followed a similar pattern, but what is interesting about them is the extent to which
those whom Roméo met in Paris kept in touch with one another
over the next ten years.

It was through such correspondence that Roméo heard of
an opening at Radio-Canada in Ottawa. In June 1959, Roméo
left Fredericton for the nation's capital. Despite his success as a
member of the faculty during the four years he was at the teachers' college, he had always kept his link to journalism, through
his freelance work for Radio-Canada. His friends who worked
elsewhere for the network also kept him informed of possible
openings in their areas. One of the most important of these
friends was Rhéal Gaudet, Roméo's contemporary at St. Joseph's.
Rhéal's family was somewhat better off economically than

Roméo's, and he was able to combine a career in teaching journalism immediately after graduation. Rhéal also had the good
fortune, with some scholarship money and no family crisis to
finance, to take courses in French history and civilization in Paris
for two years, his last year in the city being Roméo's first. In 1955,
Rhéal worked full-time at CKCH, Hull, as chief announcer and
program director.[40] In December 1957, he was offered work with
Radio-Canada in Montreal: a two-hour, five-day-a-week radio
program with René Lévesque and Jacques Languirand. Rhéal
suggested that Roméo apply for his old position. While this did
not prove successful, it was through Rhéal that Roméo learned of
an opening for a journalist for Radio-Canada in Ottawa, in 1959.
His application for this post was accepted, in large part because
of his years of freelance broadcasting, but also because of helpful
references from Fernand Cadieux and Pierre Juneau. It was also,
as he said in an interview, the result of the general reluctance
of Quebec journalists to move to Ottawa. As he remarked in
1959, Ottawa was, in some ways, almost as much an anglophone
enclave as Fredericton.[41]

Throughout his life, Roméo took time to make up his mind,
considering every possible factor. Deciding to leave teaching for
journalism was no different, and he talked at length to his colleagues and his friends. There was no doubt that, since 1957,
Roméo had found Fredericton more and more confining. But
would he be any good at full-time journalism? Should he, perhaps, go to the National Film Board? Or stay where he was? Some
of his doubts were effectively squashed when a colleague asked
him bluntly, "How will you ever know if you can bat in the big
leagues if you don't play?" Recalling this period of his life in later
years, Roméo remembered it as being one full of doubts and conflicting desires. Apart from his longing for a career in journalism,
a significant factor was his wish to be in a much more cosmopolitan environment, somewhere that had a greater francophone

Roméo during his days as a reporter in Ottawa, 1959

presence. It was not that he found his English colleagues in any way unsympathetic. He remarked in an interview in 1975, "One thing I discovered—which reinforced what I'd been feeling in Montreal and Paris—was that...I had as many allies with the English staff as with the French." However, Fredericton in the 1950s was a city of strong Loyalist heritage; it was beautiful, but, in every sense of the word, provincial. It was overwhelmingly anglophone, casual anti-Acadian prejudice was everywhere, occasionally bursting forth in bitter hostility. The social life of the New Brunswick capital was without any significant Acadian presence.

There was also a personal reason for Roméo's move. One of his most important correspondents during these years (1955–1959) was a young woman from Chicago, whom he had met when she was serving in the American Embassy in Paris. Evidence in letters from mutual friends between these years indicate that Roméo went to the United States a number of times and proposed to her by letter in 1959.[42] The letter in question, which, according to the custom of the time, was returned to Roméo on the rejection of his offer, is a poignant document. In it, Roméo recalls the first time he saw her in Paris, the difficulties that separation over the past years had caused them both, he having returned to New Brunswick and she to Chicago, and the extent to which a recent meeting in Montreal had overwhelmed him. He found himself, he wrote, unable to tell her what he felt when they parted at the airport, and so had written instead. This heartfelt letter reveals the extent to which earlier experiences had left him with almost no emotional self-confidence. It was not so much the earlier failure of his romantic relationship with Gloria David, but the fact that the motherly nurturing he had received as a child, loving as it had been, came from women—Irène, Emilie, and his mother—who seemed suddenly to vanish from his daily life. Once again, in 1959, Roméo received an emotional blow, as his proposal of marriage was turned down by a woman with whom he was clearly very much in love.

The move from teaching to journalism, from Fredericton to Ottawa, was one of the few occasions when Roméo made a change in his life because he wished to do so, not because family circumstances and financial pressures required it. This move proved to be another major turning point in both his professional and personal life. Professionally, during the next seven years, he became a highly successful journalist. Personally, his posting to London for Radio-Canada gave him the opportunity to court Joslyn "Lyn" Carter, the woman who would become his wife. The change from Paris to Fredericton had been a shift from the cosmopolitan to the provincial. The journey from Fredericton to Ottawa was the reverse. It was a shift from a provincial capital, where political life had yet to undergo any major upheaval, to the capital of Canada, at a time when the country was undergoing a transformation in national political life. When Roméo arrived in Ottawa in the fall of 1959, the Conservatives, led by John Diefenbaker, were still finding their feet, as the governing party with an overwhelming majority. Quebec was coming to terms with the death of Duplessis, who had been premier from 1936 to 1939, and again from 1944 to 1959. The politics of the late 1950s structured the way in which Canadian governments, at all levels, developed for much of the next decade. International relations, federal-provincial relations, social and economic policies, questions of citizenship and regional priorities, about which there seemed to be a comfortable national consensus in 1955, were matters for passionate public debate after 1958.

Roméo learned his craft as a political journalist between 1959 and 1962, coming to an understanding of the shifting priorities of Canada's major political parties and the personalities of their leaders, as well as the twisted web of relationships between Quebec City and Ottawa post-Duplessis. It was a particularly turbulent time in Canadian politics, and provided him with an extraordinary opportunity to observe at close range the establishment of new patterns in the political life of the country. His fluency in French and English meant that he was very often asked to be present when other journalists interviewed the political newsmakers of the day. In fact, during his first year in Ottawa, he spent much of his time organizing the broadcasts of both the prime minister and the leader of the opposition. As a result, he became known by members of both the Conservative and Liberal parties, which gave him an experience of working with a wide variety of politicians. He often acted not so much as a translator but as an interpreter of the subtlety of the ideas of those being interviewed.[43] Within a few months, however, he became one of those reporting on the workings of the federal Parliament for Radio-Canada.

Roméo was in New Brunswick when Diefenbaker was first elected prime minister, and it was this election that brought about the political turmoil that Roméo now watched. The defeat of the federal Liberal Party in 1957, a party that had governed Canada for twenty-two years—from 1935 to 1957—by a prairie lawyer from Saskatchewan, who had been a member of the House Commons since 1940, startled the whole country. The Conservatives won 112 seats, the Liberals 105, the Co-operative Commonwealth Federation (CCF) 25, Social Credit 19, and there were four independents. Diefenbaker and the Conservatives succeeded largely because of the energy and enthusiasm of the leader, helped by the complacency of the Liberal Party. The Liberals were convinced that the personal popularity of Prime Minister Louis St. Laurent would easily overcome any disaffection the voters felt for the party itself. After all, he was fluently bilingual and had had a distinguished career in international and corporate law before entering politics in 1942. When he succeeded Mackenzie King as prime minister in 1948, the Liberals continued to flourish, seeming to govern Canada without difficulty through the negotiations that led to Newfoundland joining Confederation and the work of establishing equalization payments to the provinces, as well as through the consequences of the Suez crisis and its impact on the Commonwealth and the issues of Canada's involvement in the Korean War. In 1956, there was no obvious sign that St. Laurent could not easily defeat a unilingual western criminal lawyer. One of the most important Cabinet ministers at the time, C.D. Howe, allegedly said that the Liberals would win even if they had "to run [St. Laurent] stuffed."[44]

Instead, the oratory of the western defence lawyer and practised politician captured many, if not all, first-time voters, and the Conservatives won a majority of seats.[45] Shortly after the election the Liberals retired Louis St. Laurent, now seventy-five. They did not turn to Paul Martin, Sr., who had served the party since his election to the House of Commons in 1935, had entered Cabinet in 1945, and was appointed as minister of national health and welfare in 1946, but instead chose Lester Pearson, who was two years younger than Diefenbaker. Pearson had taught history at the University of Toronto, then served as a distinguished diplomat, who played major roles in the founding of both United Nations and the North Atlantic Treaty Organization. He was elected to the House of Commons in 1948 and, in 1957, was awarded the Nobel Peace Prize for helping to bring the Suez crisis to a conclusion. During its first months in office, the Diefenbaker government failed to impress the Opposition, despite the energy it displayed at this time. To a large extent, this failure was because the Opposition supported the government's legislation. It would have been difficult for the Liberals to oppose an increase in the Old Age Pension payments from $46 to $55, or similar increases to the disabled and to veterans. Nor would it have been popular to stand in the way of a reduction in income tax and the extension of benefits to the shipbuilding industry. Criticism of work undertaken to help prairie farmers sell their wheat was not an option either. By January 1958, the Liberals were convinced that the electorate would understand that the government program was really Liberal policy, and that the Liberals should be the ones to carry it out. On January 22, Pearson requested in the House of Commons that the Conservatives resign and allow the Liberals to form a government without an election.

Even before Diefenbaker started to speak, Pearson knew he had made a colossal mistake. He later recalled that, as he sat down, he knew "his first attack on the government had been a failure, a fiasco."[46] He was right. His move gave Diefenbaker the opportunity to present Canadians with the clearest possible picture of Liberal arrogance, an attempt "to bring the Liberal Party—defeated, discredited, and failing in the opinion polls—back to power without an election."[47] The prime minister responded with a blistering two-hour speech, in which he started with the charge that the Liberals' request to return to power was no more than the arrogant reaction of a "party saturated with fear of what the electorate will do to it."[48] He then ripped apart the Liberals' criticism of the Conservative economic policies. To make his points, he used a report leaked from the records of the previous government to a friend of his. Ten days later, on February 1, Diefenbaker asked for and obtained the assent of Governor General Vincent Massey for a general election.

It became clear during the 1957 election campaign not only that Diefenbaker was an outstanding orator, but also that his vision for Canada was considerably different from the traditional, comfortable image that was projected by the Liberals: of an understood co-operation between Anglo-French élites. As William Kilbourn pointed out, "he was the first unhyphenated Canadian to be prime minister...and had brought into politics the sort of people who had not been there before."[49] Among the newcomers were not only more MPs from the western provinces, but also, at the Cabinet level, Michael Starr, the first Ukrainian, appointed as minister of labour, and Ellen Fairclough, the first woman, appointed as minister of state and then as minister of citizenship and immigration. In the1958 campaign, enthusiasm for Diefenbaker's dreams of "One Canada" and the development of the North reached fever pitch. In *This Game of Politics*, Pierre Sévigny wrote of the phenomenal interest in the campaign throughout Canada. The Conservatives' popularity in the West was to be expected, but Diefenbaker's enthusiastic reception in Quebec was unprecedented, especially given the lukewarm reception he had experienced in the province the previous year. Sévigny considered that "the Diefenbaker speeches were masterpieces of emotional appeal." After listening to many of them, he wrote that the prime minister spoke "of a vision of Canadians who would, with the Conservatives, develop a new faith in the future, new sources of inspiration based on what this country would be like under competent rule." Sévigny believed that, when people left the meetings, "They were never too sure of what [Diefenbaker] had said, nor [were they] certain it made absolute sense. But they were happy."[50] The result on March 31 was a landslide, which buried, as John Duffy wrote, "the remains of the political system of the King–St. Laurent era, replacing that system's incremental co-option of regions, classes, and language groups with a new politics of national purpose."[51] Diefenbaker and the Conservatives swept the country, winning 208 seats, with a majority of votes and seats in every province except Newfoundland. The Liberals managed to hold on to 48 seats, the CCF, 8.

In September 1959, Roméo moved into a small apartment in Ottawa, which he shared with Jim Taylor, another young New Brunswicker who was working for the CBC. They became lifelong friends. By this time, Canadian political life had settled down a little, though there were, of course, the perennial problems: federal-provincial relations, the health of the economy, and international relations. Roméo quickly learned how to cope with the demands made on a professional journalist for the national francophone radio network. His broadcasts from New Brunswick for Radio-Canada during the previous four years always had federal politics as their context, but they had been essentially about Maritime—and, especially, New Brunswick—concerns. Roméo was now part of a team covering federal politics and public affairs for francophone listeners from coast to coast: not only Acadians in Atlantic Canada, but also the huge French-speaking population of Quebec, as well as Franco-Ontarians, Franco-Manitobans, and the scattered French-speaking population of the rest of western Canada, not to mention those in the Northwest Territories. Radio was still extremely important in the political life of the country, but television was gaining ground rapidly, and within eighteen months, Roméo was involved in the occasional broadcast in this medium.

At first, his work was primarily as a producer and scriptwriter, for both French and English news. During his first months in Ottawa, his bilingual abilities, coupled with his good manners and general friendliness, meant that his senior colleagues helped him to recognize the politicians and their aides. He also spent time renewing his acquaintance with Montreal and his friends there, in particular Rita and Fernand Cadieux. It could not have been a better time for Roméo to learn the ways and means of federal politics. The years 1957 and 1958 saw a major reorganization among the people holding power in Parliament; 1959 to 1962 saw the results of that reorganization being played out. During these three years, Romèo gained considerable insight into Canadian political life that not only was an immediate aid to his burgeoning career as a journalist, but also would prove invaluable when he became an MP in the 1970s. He was a witness to the arrival of the West as a major force in federal politics, and the parallel decline of Quebec influence. He watched Diefenbaker struggle to implement his vision of "One Canada," with, as historian Michael Bliss wrote, "human rights for all and collective privileges for none."[52] This vision was a strong contrast to the emerging policy of many Liberals from the province of Quebec, who wanted to recognize a special status for that province. Roméo also learned the ways an Opposition could influence government policy, even when that government had an overwhelming majority. The fight over Diefenbaker's *Canadian Bill of Rights*, passed in 1960, was an object lesson about the different visions of how the Canadian federation should be managed. As an act, it had no teeth, because it had no power to bind either future Parliaments or the provinces. Ironically, much of the intention behind it came into being with the passage of Trudeau's *Charter of Rights and Freedoms* over two decades later. In 1960, however, its discussion showed, more than anything else, how diverse and divergent the regions of Canada had become.

By the end of 1960, Roméo had moved from working mostly as a producer to being a broadcaster in his own right. That year he was made a member of the Press Gallery.[53] Clark Davey, whose distinguished career as a journalist went from reporting for the *Chatham News* to twenty-seven years with the *Globe and Mail*, recalled what the parliamentary Press Gallery was like at that time:

> *It was without doubt the most crowded, noisy and disorderly space on the Hill...The vast majority of reporters had no other working offices...CBC [and] Radio-Canada operated out of studios cramped into the seventh floor, attic-like space in the Château Laurier just across the Rideau Canal locks from Parliament Hill.*[54]

He also remembered the remarkably friendly atmosphere among the reporters:

> *A member of the Gallery was a member of a unique journalism-cum-political club. And unlike today's stultifying security, gallery members had incredible access. They had their own door at the end of the hall into the gallery itself, little used today except on special occasions, above and behind the Speaker's chair in the Commons. Their membership cards gave them entry to the private lobby/lounges for MPs behind the curtains in the House. Cabinet members were only a phone call away and, in fact, reporters who arrived on the Hill very early were able to find Prime Minister John Diefenbaker at his desk in the East Block and check story ideas with him. It was a heady time to be a parliamentary correspondent.*

Roméo now covered not only federal politics, but some aspects of Canada's external affairs. His assignment to cover both the Democratic and Republican conventions in the United States that same year came partly because of his facility in English as well as French.[55] This talent also meant he was often sent to New York to report on the United Nations. Such assignments were also a recognition of the ability he had acquired earlier, as a freelance broadcaster, to report concisely, accurately, and interestingly about public affairs. By mid-summer 1961, he was as much a commentator and interviewer, very often about Quebec matters, as a reporter. At this time, the complicated patterns of federal-provincial relations, in particular those involving Quebec, were of great concern for the federal government. There were only three Quebec MPs in Diefenbaker's Cabinet, none of whom were in charge of major government departments, and he had no close adviser on his staff in the area of Quebec affairs. Jean Lesage became premier of the province on June 22, 1960, with a very different view of political affairs from that held by Duplessis. Lesage was to remain in power for the next six years, overseeing what has come to be called the "Quiet Revolution." His first Cabinet included René Lévesque. There was an attempt that fall to work out a new plan for sharing tax fields, but it ended in deadlock, to a large extent because of opposition from Quebec. Over the next months, Quebec politics, at both the provincial and federal levels, became of increasing interest, not only for politicians but also for the general Canadian public.

For Roméo, this state of affairs meant that he was assigned, with some regularity, to report on political issues in Quebec. One such assignment was an interview, in July 1961,[56] with Réal Caouette, then Quebec leader of the Social Credit Party. Caouette's economic views were based on the need for "provincial autonomy," and he spoke with fervour about the necessity to control large corporations and financial institutions. His power base, and that of the Créditistes in Quebec, was an appeal to those who felt marginalized by an intellectual and urban élite. In the 1962 federal election, Social Credit won twenty-six seats in Quebec along with four in western Canada, and held the balance of power in the House of Commons. Caouette was always a federalist, but interviewing him gave Roméo the chance to talk with a Quebec politician whose sense of the province was close to those of the emerging separatists, not because of sympathy with the ideas of the latter but because of frustration with the lack of respect shown by the federal government for the countryside. Fernand Cadieux and Gérard Pelletier had shown Roméo the urban and intellectual life of Quebec, the needs of factory workers and miners. Caouette was a window on rural Quebec.

In the same way, an interview with Thérèse Casgrain on September 1, 1961[57] introduced Roméo to yet another aspect life in Quebec: the attitudes and concerns of women. Thérèse Forget was born into a wealthy family and married Pierre Casgrain, a successful lawyer and politician, and together they raised four children. In 1921, she became a founding member of the Provincial Franchise Committee for women's right to vote in Quebec, and it was in large measure due to her leadership that this was granted on April 25, 1940.[58] Women's rights were only a small part of her social activism, which included human rights in general. The occasion for Roméo's interview with her was the transformation of the Co-operative Commonwealth Federation into the New Democratic Party (NDP), and their discussion centred on the place of Quebec in the new party and the place of women in political life. In many ways, the latter was the more important subject for Roméo, since the 1960s saw the emergence of women's rights as a matter that needed to be addressed, and the women's movement in Quebec was a major force in Canada in this effort. Roméo's sympathy for the struggle for equal rights for women was of long standing, and sprang, in part, from the great support he received throughout his life from his sisters.

Of all the assignments that rounded out Roméo's knowledge of the varied strands in Quebec life, however, those related to the Chaput affair were some of the most significant.[59] This matter hit the headlines towards the end of November. It gave Roméo the opportunity to observe, at close range, the emergence of an important part of the separatist movement in Quebec, and provided an insight into the bitterness of many francophone federal civil servants.[60] Marcel Chaput was a chemist who worked for the Department of National Defence. In 1960, he published a series of articles in *Le Devoir*, protesting the lack of French usage in the department. That same year he became one of the founding members of the Rassemblement pour l'Indépendance Nationale (RIN). He was elected its president in October 1961, and in November he was suspended without pay for violating employment laws that forbade civil servants from holding a political office. In December, he resigned, although at that time the RIN was not a political party but an association that had been formed to provide educational information about the cause of Quebec independence. At that time, the possibility of a serious challenge to Confederation developing in Quebec seemed less than imminent, but within seven years de Gaulle's "Vive le Québec Libre" would be greeted in Montreal with wild applause.

By the end of 1961, Roméo had clearly established himself as a professional journalist with both the CBC and Radio-Canada. A large part of his work concerned the affairs of the federal government, matters such as the speeches made to the United Nations by the minister for external affairs, Howard Green, on the fallout from the use of nuclear energy in neighbouring countries, in October 1961, and the return of Prime Minister Diefenbaker from his visit to Japan, in November 1961.[61] Roméo was part of the Christmas broadcast, "Nöel à travers le monde," for which he reported on affairs from Rome.⁶² His most important work during the first six months of 1962 was covering the election, something he enjoyed. It was also something that would prove immensely valuable to him when he took up the position of press secretary to Prime Minister Pearson in 1967.

It was this election that showed the seismic shift in Canadian political life, which had begun with Diefenbaker's victory and been carried forward by the ending of the Duplessis régime in Quebec. The Conservatives' tumble from the overwhelming majority victory of 1958 to the status of a minority government in four years was due to a variety of factors. It was less a loss for Diefenbaker personally than it was a defeat by forces beyond his control. In part, it did come about because Diefenbaker's charismatic oratory could not compensate for his method of governing and his inability to accept and act on criticism. However, it also occurred because the Liberal Party managed to find a vision for Canada's future that was founded on a coherent international policy and an understandable program of social legislation. The loss also owed something to the emergence of the NDP, with former Saskatchewan premier Tommy Douglas as its leader, and to pressure by the American government. But it was also due to a large extent to the fundamental shift in politics in Quebec, where Jean Lesage and his Cabinet successfully began major changes to modernize Quebec, not only ending the repression of the Duplessis regime in political life but also changing the role of the Catholic Church in education and social welfare.

Roméo took part as one of the panellists for Radio-Canada's program on the results of the 1962 election,⁶³ results as varied as the forces that had produced them: the Conservatives won 116 seats (a loss of 92); the Liberals won 99 (a gain of 50); Réal Caouette's Créditistes won 26 in Quebec; and the NDP won 19, of which 12 were in western Canada. Similarly, opinions on the panel about what had produced these numbers were equally

diverse. Diefenbaker was given credit for a number of achievements, but was seen as the author of the Conservatives' defeat.
He was praised for his concern for individual rights, but criticized for his blindness to the need for social institutions which
would interpret those rights. It was agreed that he had an awareness of international events and their importance, but he had
been unable to see the change in world politics that had occurred
since 1956. He had opened trade with China, which annoyed the
Americans but tripled the income of western farmers. Further,
if the Liberals had gained seats in British Columbia, elected a
majority of Ontario MPs, and taken almost half of the Quebec
ridings, the Conservatives held many of the rural ridings, as well
as the prairies. In many ways this election was as significant as
that in 1958. The latter had changed the political landscape of
Canada, but the 1962 election laid bare both the new political
positions of the parties and the new rhetoric of political debate
within the country.

Roméo's experience of this election was particularly timely
because he left Ottawa sometime in late July to begin five years
as a foreign correspondent for Radio-Canada, first in London
and later in Washington.[64] His knowledge of the way in which
the various parties and their leaders reacted to the mood of
this particular electorate provided him with the grounding to
understand the elections of 1963 and 1965. The 1962 election
also deepened his interest in federal politics, and he left Ottawa
reluctantly. Pearson wrote him a brief letter at the end of July
to thank him for dropping a record off at his office. In it the
leader of the Opposition said: "I can well understand that your
preference would have been to remain here, for what might be
termed this 'unusual' session but I hope it may not be too long
before we will have you back home."[65] One can understand the
reasons for his employers' actions: the opening in London, with
responsibility for European matters, must have seemed a natural

slot for Roméo, bilingual and with considerable knowledge of European politics, now a seasoned reporter with experience of international affairs, particularly on questions concerning the United Nations.[66] For him, it was one more move, albeit within the profession he had sought, just at the time he felt really comfortable where he was. It was not something he could turn down, however, and it would bring him both professional honours and personal happiness.

CHAPTER 5

Foreign Correspondent: London and Washington

Roméo was now in his mid-thirties and had often enough adapted to new challenges in new surroundings. His official posting was as the London correspondent for Radio-Canada and, over the next two years, his assignments would take him to much of Europe, the Middle East, and, occasionally, back across the Atlantic. His considerable reluctance to leave Ottawa was partly because he felt at home in the capital and partly because he felt confident in his work as a parliamentary correspondent. He now went from a city of under one million to one close to ten million, from a North American pattern of living to a foreign culture, and from the familiar society of numerous acquaintances and many friends to one where he knew almost nobody. In Ottawa, the apartment he shared with Jim Taylor on Laurier Avenue, was a comfortable walk to work, fifteen minutes away. In London, he lived in a flat at 25 St. George's House, 72 St. George's Square, London SW1, in the reasonable-but-by-no-means-fashionable Islington area of London, and his work, in Portland Place, W.1, was a good half-hour walk away. The changes in his domestic life were matched by radically different technical and organizational working conditions. In Ottawa, most of his work had been live broadcast from the studio. In London, tapes for television had to be made and sent by motorbike to Heathrow Airport to be put on the morning flight for Montreal. This got them to the studio for the evening newscasts. Roméo later remembered that the technical staff was helpful, but there was a fair amount of stress involved, because the time difference imposed a short deadline between covering an event and reporting on it. His first months in London he spent learning on the job, and he recalled that it was a time that had much in common with his first months at teachers' college.[1]

The rapidity of Roméo's rise among the journalists employed by Radio-Canada had been remarkable. He had arrived in Ottawa in 1959 with no formal journalism training, which was not unusual at the time, because there were few courses for francophone journalists in Canada before the 1970s. What was unusual was his move within two years from helping in the studio as a producer to his position as full-time parliamentary correspondent. Ever since 1950, he had worked part-time as a freelance journalist, but this transition to a London posting after barely three years as a professional journalist was a vindication of his decision to leave teaching. Now he faced yet another series of challenges. In Ottawa, his workload was centred on Canadian public affairs, in particular Parliament, with assignments elsewhere in Canada and, occasionally, at the United Nations. During those years, he acquired a reasonable knowledge of the major players in Ottawa and the various policies they favoured. One of the most important differences between Ottawa and London was the type of general knowledge he required. He quickly had to gather a new and accurate catalogue of references for contemporary European issues in particular and international affairs in general.

He needed to become as familiar with the names of European heads of government and their ministers as he had made himself with the names of federal and provincial ministers in Canada. He had to amass a background of information about the questions preoccupying European politicians in the way he had assembled such information about the concerns of members of Canada's legislative assemblies. Above all, he needed an understanding of the complex politics of the developing European Economic Community (EEC), also known as the Common Market, and the impact this entity had on the United States.

Another Canadian, Ed Higginson, who worked in London at this time as a cameraman for the CBC, soon became a close friend of Roméo's.[2] They often worked together over the next three years. Writing to the author about his memories of this time, Ed recalled a party just after Roméo arrived, "a get-together with some of the other correspondents."[3] Roméo was invited and, "although he was a little hesitant, he showed up...He was not a drinker like most of us," Ed continued, "and he settled in a chair, able to observe and have passing conversations with others. He seemed reserved but very friendly, and seemed to enjoy being together with other CBC correspondents and crew... He probably had a glass or two of wine and left quietly while everyone else continued to live it up."

The 1960s were a period when there was a comradeship among the people working for the CBC and Radio-Canada and a great deal of help for newcomers to the field between both networks. The general high quality of the work of Canada's foreign correspondents was due as much to the extent to which they helped one another as to their own particular abilities. Roméo soon established friendly relations with those he met at work. At a time when hard drinking was common, it never mattered that Roméo was a moderate wine drinker, very rarely drinking spirits. He almost never commented adversely on those who drank

Ed Higgenson, CBC cameraman, Roméo, and Morley Safer in Berlin, 1963

more, just saying, one time, that "he was the one who remained sober and drove the others home."[4]

At the beginning, most of his reporting involved assignments suggested by producers and program administrators.[5] His immediate broadcasts concerned news events on both sides of the Atlantic, such as the referendum on amending the constitution of the Fifth Republic in France in the second week of October 1962, and the Cuban missile crisis some ten days later. Europe and North America were still very different polities in the early 1960s, but the Cold War made close relations between the continents crucial. In particular, the impact of France on international affairs was a matter of concern not only for Europe in particular, including the British Isles, but also for the United States and Russia. Roméo's first broadcast as a foreign correspondent was on October 13, 1962,[6] and dealt with the background of the referendum in France that amended the constitution of the Fifth Republic.[7] His time at the Sorbonne proved a solid foundation for his work. The Fourth Republic had been established in 1947, but its political life was torn apart by bitter debates over the way to solve the social and economic problems that beset the country. As we have seen, Roméo had been in Paris in 1954 when the military disaster of Dien Bien Phu occurred, forcing the French from what soon became known as Vietnam, Laos, and Cambodia. He was also a witness to the emergence of the Front de Libération Nationale in November 1954, the organization that became a major player in the coming struggle for Algerian independence. In 1958, General Charles de Gaulle became the last prime minister of the Fourth Republic as the only way to avoid rule by a military dictatorship. Four years later, the general reworked the constitution to be closer to his ideas of what France needed. Roméo's short report on the new constitution was sufficient to give people an understanding of the importance of the result of the vote, which took place on October 28. For the first time since 1789, republican institutions received a majority.[8] Roméo's next broadcast about French affairs linked de Gaulle's new powers with his foreign policy, a policy that was decidedly pro-German and disdainful of Anglo–American opinion.

Before this broadcast took place, however, Roméo was assigned to comment on the United Nations' reaction to one of the most bitter and dangerous episodes of the Cold War: the Cuban missile crisis. Going from commentary on the domestic politics of France to describing an international duel of superpowers demanded considerable mental agility, but during the 1960s such rapid shifts from one major event to another were typical for Canadian foreign correspondents. The Cuban missile crisis occurred between October 15 and October 28, 1962, but its roots went back to 1959, when Fidel Castro had taken control of the country. Within a year, he openly aligned himself with the Soviet Union and, on January 3, 1961, the United States severed diplomatic relations with Cuba. On July 27, 1962, Castro announced that the Soviet Union had invested heavily in his country, and would defend it against any aggression from the United States. By mid-October, there was photographic evidence of missile sites and intermediate-range missiles in Cuba. On October 24, American President John F. Kennedy placed his country on its highest military readiness since the end of the Second World War, and demanded that the Soviets withdraw their missiles and that the sites be destroyed. October 27, 1962, was one of the most tense days of the crisis, filled with meetings among top government personnel in both the United States and the Soviet Union. Tension was further heightened that day when an American U-2 aircraft was shot down over Cuba and the pilot killed. At the same time, the American navy dropped a number of "signalling depth charges" on a Russian submarine off the coast of Cuba, unaware that it was armed with nuclear-tipped torpedoes, and had orders to use them should the submarine be damaged. By the afternoon of October 28, however, a deal was reached between the United States and the Soviet Union, which defused the issue and saw the missiles removed from Cuba.[9] The memoirs of those who were in power at the time, both in the United States and the Soviet Union, record their feelings that nuclear war had been very close.[10] The day before, in West Berlin, Roméo recorded a report dealing with the uproar at the United Nations over the issue.[11] One of the reasons for this recording venue was the shortage of Canadian staff. Cameraman Ed Higginson and soundman Morley Safer, who was in Poland shooting a half-hour magazine show, were sent to West Berlin, where Roméo joined them. Because of flight departure times and the connection through Frankfurt, both the footage from Poland and Roméo's tape were shipped to Toronto, where Roméo's piece was to be fed to Montreal. As Ed remembered, "the feed from Toronto to Montreal was screwed up," and Montreal was "convinced, because of their distrust of the English Network staff [that] this was done purposely in Toronto."[12] When Roméo heard about it, he made sure that, from that point on, his work always went directly to Montreal. Ed observed, "There were never any loud or raucous debates from Roméo...His motto seemed to be to co-operate and get along rather than cause any fuss, but he could stand up firmly if he felt he was being unfairly treated."

Roméo's last major broadcast in 1962 was as part of the Radio-Canada team for the television program "L'Année dans le monde," which surveyed the domestic and international events of the past year. During the program he commented on the Common Market and the negotiations of this organ-ization with Great Britain. The Common Market had come into being in 1957, when Belgium, France, Italy, Luxembourg, the Netherlands, and West Germany signed the Treaties of Rome. It had its roots in the agreements reached previously between France and West Germany over the coal and steel industries, and these two nations were the dominant partners. Britain was not party to the Treaties of Rome, but in 1962, British Prime Minister Harold Macmillan sought entry to what had become known as the European Economic Community.[13] As Roméo reported, the negotiations were not going well.[14] It soon became clear that the stumbling block was de Gaulle, aided and encour-aged by the upper echelons of the French civil service. De Gaulle believed that, if the British were forced to choose between Europe and the United States, they would choose their American allies. On January 4, he clearly outlined his opposition to the British, saying, "England is in effect insular, she is maritime, she is linked through her exchanges, her markets, her supply lines to the most diverse and the most distant countries, she pursues essentially industrial and commercial activities, and only slight agricultural ones. She has in all her doings very marked and very original habits."[15] On January 14, 1963, France vetoed Britain's application to join the EEC.

If de Gaulle led France to use the veto to stop the five other countries in the EEC from accepting Britain's application, it was part of a major movement to turn his country away from the possibility of close ties not only with Britain but also with the United States. The next action he took was of equal significance: it was the Élysée Treaty, also known as the "Friendship Treaty," proclaimed in Paris on January 22, 1963. It was intended, as its preamble announced, to bring about "the reconciliation of the German people and the French people." Roméo was in Paris at the time, and he remembered, almost forty years later, the deep impression the event made on him.[16] He recalled night-long bitter debate in the French Parliament, a debate so acrimonious that the building was ringed with tanks, their guns pointing outward into a turbulent crowd. Among those against the treaty were many who had lost family members to forced labour in Germany and many who had fought in the Resistance. For some people, the treaty seemed of little significance, more an expression of pious hopes than concrete proposals. Roméo saw it at the time in a way that many later came to view it.[17] For him, this treaty was much more than a symbol of a French wish to resist Anglo–American policies. It was a measure designed not only to end the bitterness between France and Germany that had remained after 1945, but also as something that would lead towards the development of much deeper co-operation between the two countries. There had been a number of agreements between the two former enemies since 1955; now both countries would encourage the growth of

further links between their economic, social, and political policies. As far as Roméo was concerned, the obvious anti-British
and anti-American bias of the treaty was far less important than
the strength it gave for the future development of the Common
Market, to which Britain would gain entrance in 1973. At the
time of its signing, he saw it as a magnificent achievement by
two old men to bring an end to the dwelling on past wrongs. De
Gaulle was seventy-three in 1963; Konrad Adenauer, the chancellor of West Germany, was eighty-seven.

Throughout 1963, Roméo worked mainly out of London,
covering the repercussions of de Gaulle's policies within the
Common Market and the reaction in Europe to events in North
America. He was, however, in Canada for the federal election that
took place on April 8. This election, not quite ten months after
the last, centred on the issues of nuclear power and Canadian–
American relations. On election night, Roméo commented on
the results from the Maritimes.[18] The election produced yet
another minority government, this time in favour of the Liberal
Party. Lester Pearson won 129 seats, the Tories won 95, and the
NDP, 17. In Quebec, Social Credit won 20 seats, and in the West,
its related party won four. By the end of the month, Roméo was
back in London, once more reporting on de Gaulle and his opinion of European needs and trans-Atlantic issues.[19] For Roméo,
however, his interviews with Quebec Premier Jean Lesage in
London and Brussels during the second week of May were much
more interesting than his broadcasts about European politicians.
Lesage had been premier since 1960, and what became known as
the "Quiet Revolution" was well under way. A provincial hospital
insurance plan had been put in place; a Department of Cultural
Affairs and another one for federal-provincial relations had been
established, both for the first time in Canada. Reforms to a broad
range of social policies were in the works. The main purpose of the
Quebec premier's visit to London was the opening of "Maison du

Québec." In the interview with Roméo, Lesage pointed out that it was really a "re-opening,"since the first "Maison du Québec" had been established in 1911 and closed in 1936 only because of the financial crisis of the Depression years.[20] He went on to say that it was important for Quebec to have a visible presence in London, the capital of the Commonwealth, and emphasized that it was of great importance for Quebec to profit from European technical advances in order to counter unemployment in the province. Lesage stressed that, however central the idea of "Maîtres chez nous" was for the policies of his government, the need for financial capital in Quebec made it necessary to attract funds from outside the province. In the second interview, two days later in Brussels, he repeated Quebec's need for European industrial knowledge and capital investment.[21]

Throughout the spring and summer of 1963, Roméo's broadcasts were mostly about events in Britain, where the political scene was undergoing a major transformation. By this stage, Roméo's reputation among the producers and editorial staff within Radio-Canada was excellent. To a large extent, he suggested many of his assignments. One of these occasions was the fate of the Conservative government of Harold Macmillan, which had been elected in January 1957 and was now facing growing opposition from the Labour Party. Harold Wilson had emerged as Labour's leader at the beginning of 1963, and he proved to be an outstanding leader of the Opposition. Although Macmillan tried to adapt to the demands for change with a major Cabinet shuffle in mid-summer, his administration was side-swiped by the "Profumo Affair," which developed around a liaison between then–secretary of state for war John Profumo and a call girl who was also a close friend of the Russian attaché in London. The whole affair brought the government into general disrepute, above all because Profumo lied about the matter in the House of Commons. In his broadcasts on this issue, Roméo stressed the ideological differences between the Conservative and Labour parties, rather than focusing on the social gossip.[22] Labour's program included more money for education and health, while the Conservatives relied on their past record to counter the growing discontent in the country. By the fall, the political debate in Britain was sufficiently heated that Roméo considered it distracted the country from other events. Labour, he said, was so caught up in presenting itself as a real alternative to the Conservatives that little attention was paid to the retirement of Germany's Konrad Adenauer in October of that year, and his replacement by Chancellor Ludwig Erhard.[23]

For Roméo the summer of 1963 was memorable for the death of Pope John XXIII on June 3. He had met the Pope briefly, and recalled the feeling among the crowds in St. Peter's Square when the Pope appeared. For Roméo, John XXIII was a man who "radiated goodwill towards men, not merely a criticism of their sins, a feeling of love even for journalists."[24] It was also during this summer that Roméo organized his domestic life in London and established a routine of taking his laundry to the local laundromat, accompanied by one or more friends. As the coins clinked into slots and the machines whirled, Ed Higginson recalled wide-ranging discussions. "Roméo," Ed remembered, "was interested in the well-being of others, looking at government programs that covered health care, pensions for seniors and young Canadians...As he listened and put his clothes in the dryer, he would patiently explain his views on the subject/subjects under discussion." Ed continued:

> *Roméo had a very dry sense of humour and used [it]often to make a point...We would talk about our younger days, our upbringing...he told me that his family was hard working, but did the best they could for the large family...It was obviously quite emotional for him when he discussed the fact that*

*he was the only one of the children that could have
an advanced education and gave his sister[s] praise
for help in his early years.*[25]

With the fall came the event that marked the year around
the world: the assassination of President John F. Kennedy
on November 22, 1963. Its impact was profound. Eighteen
years later, three sober Canadian historians wrote with emotion about the event: "On that late fall day, the death of John
F. Kennedy in Dallas stunned Canadians. Like Americans they
stopped to watch what they could not believe." For these historians, the assassination meant that "the light seemed much
farther away and blackness so near."[26] With perceptive judgment, they pointed out, "It was not our public history but our
private selves that changed most." The public impact was, of
course, international. In common with other national networks,
CBC and Radio-Canada broadcast special programs about the
tragedy. Roméo reported on the immediate reaction of the
British government and of the coverage by British media of the
events surrounding Kennedy's funeral.[27] In common with many
others, Roméo remembered wondering whether Vice President
Lyndon Johnson, who immediately became president, would
continue the domestic and foreign policies of his predecessor.
On a personal level, Kennedy's death also had a major influence on Roméo. The tragedy brought to a head his wish to be a
commentator on the political future of his own country. He had
been impressed, for instance, with the determination of Prime
Minister Pearson—even though he headed a minority government—to attend to the problems posed by the rising discontent
of many in Quebec. Pearson's response was to establish the Royal
Commission on Bilingualism and Biculturalism on July 19, 1963.
Roméo's continued fascination with Canadian politics, only
strengthened during his absence from Canada and the drama

of events in Dallas, gave him the final spur to write to Gérard Pelletier on November 30, asking for his help in obtaining a posting back to North America.

Roméo opened his letter by saying that he felt that his work in London was more a literary endeavour than a matter of political analysis, leading to commentary that was not only blandly unbiased but also uninvolved, to the point of being platitudinous. He wanted, he wrote, to be present at the important events that were taking place in North America. "You are," he continued, "aware of my views on Canada's problems—I believe it worthwhile to work against the break-up of this country, and I believe that the French-Canadian journalist must broaden his outlook so that a number of 'national' problems are really considered the business of the nation as a whole."[28] While Roméo was ready to admit that his time in London was, from a number of points of view, a useful experience, he deplored his absence from North America at a time when "there is a nationalist crisis at home, a racial crisis in the United States, a political change in Washington and the possibility of elections in Canada."[29] The powers-that-be took no immediate notice of this appeal.

Roméo's assignments in 1964 were much more to his taste, because many concerned international affairs that, while centred in Europe, directly involved Canadian interests. The first of these involved the island of Cyprus, which was granted its independence from Britain in 1959. By 1963, open fighting had broken out between the Greek and Turkish communities, and Greece and Turkey were poised to intervene. Roméo reported on the international conference that was convened in London in January 1964.[30] The British government attempted to settle the matter without United Nations or NATO involvement, but this proved impossible, and the United Nations took up the issue in February. Roméo reported on the gravity of the situation in a broadcast at the beginning of March, which included interviews

Roméo in London, foreign correspondent for Radio-Canada, 1965

with a number of United Nations delegates.[31] Later that month, Canada was asked to consider sending troops as peacekeepers. Backed by the prime minister, Paul Martin, Sr., then Canada's secretary of state for external affairs, agreed to this request. The role Canada played at the time of the Suez crisis of 1956–1957, a role that had earned Lester Pearson a Nobel Prize, gave Canada international credibility as a negotiator. On the night of March 13, a small party of Canadian officers were flown to Cyprus. They were quickly joined by the 1st Battalion of the Royal 22nd Regiment.[32] Later commentators agreed that Canadian actions prevented the international tension from erupting into a widespread conflict.

The politics within NATO became increasingly tense as the year went on. Roméo broadcast a lengthy report on the annual meeting of the foreign ministers of the fifteen member states, which took place in the Hague in May. Some member states, in particular Holland and the United States, wanted to expand the membership. France and Great Britain stood against any merging of their military commands. Paul Martin, Sr., emphasized Canada's belief in the value of the organization in its present form.[33] A week later, Roméo was briefly in Ottawa as a member of a broadcasting team assembled to comment on the idea of a new flag for Canada.[34] The views expressed in this program by the journalists who were involved covered most of the arguments brought forward by the politicians, before the idea and a proposed design were introduced in the House of Commons on June 15.[35] The strong opposition of the Canadian Legion was mentioned. The support of most of the opposition parties was discussed, the general belief being that a new flag would provide a symbol of national unity without reference to past imperial ties. The press emphasized the paradoxical nature of the enterprise at a time when Canada was experiencing a particularly bitter division between its anglophone and francophone citizenry. What was not foreseen by the panel was that the adoption of the flag would take six months of increasingly bitter debate before the House of Commons finally approved a new design on December 15, and the Senate accepted it on December 17.

When Roméo returned to London, his attitude to this foreign posting underwent a considerable change. As a result of his organization of friends to go to the laundromat, he met his future wife: Joslyn Carter.[36] She was a young Canadian, born in Montreal in 1942, the only child of a couple who lived in the predominantly anglophone district of Westmount. Her mother was the daughter of James Johnston, who lived in Thetford Mines until asbestos was discovered—literally in his back garden. The sale of his property made him a moderately wealthy man and allowed him, with his wife and three children, to move to Montreal. On his death, his money was divided among his two surviving children: Lyn's mother and her uncle. One son had been killed in Second World War. Lyn's father was John Lemesurier, who had been a corvette captain in the war. After 1945, he studied law and joined the firm of P.S. Ross and Sons. By the time Lyn was in her teens, he had become an alcoholic. Lyn was sent for her high-school education to boarding school at King's Hall in Compton, Quebec, from which she graduated at the age of sixteen. She then spent two years at Trinity College, Dublin, where she studied French and Spanish. When she met Roméo, she was working at a number of temporary jobs and shared an apartment in London with a friend, Diana Fowler, who had also attended King's Hall. Diana worked at the time on the administrative side at Langham Place, the headquarters for both the CBC and Radio-Canada.

On one particular Saturday afternoon, Diana invited Joslyn, quickly known as Lyn, to bring her washing along to the laundromat party. Many years later, Lyn recalled her first impression of Roméo. He was clearly the organizer of the occasion. The other Canadian there was Morley Safer, who had just joined the American CBS network as their London correspondent. At thirty-seven, Roméo was some four years older than Morley, and quite definitely the most domesticated of the four. The washing being done, everybody went back to Roméo's apartment, where Lyn watched him sort the laundry, produce food and wine, and steer the conversation, while Diana and Morley teased. For Lyn, just twenty-two, whose father was, in her words "a brilliant accountant and an unreliable alcoholic," Roméo was something new: an attractive, successful, responsible man. During the last three months of 1964, Roméo realized that he wanted to develop their relationship, and he was fortunate that one of his major assignments was the coverage of the general election in Great Britain in October of that year.

Looking back on his time in London, Roméo recalled that covering that election was an education in the differences in

Roméo, Diana Fowler, and Morley Safer at Diana's marriage
to her first husband

the political life between that country and his own.[37] Having
observed both provincial and federal elections in Canada at close
quarters, Roméo now travelled the countryside of the United
Kingdom. He was quick to seize on the obvious differences that
population and geography made: Canada stretched over nearly
four million square miles, with a population of less than 25 million; the United Kingdom had some 55 million people squashed
into 95,000 square miles. While there were many local issues,
such as the problems of unemployment in the north of England,
Roméo felt there was a much greater awareness of and concentration on the national policies of the parties. He attributed this
focus to the apparent unity of Britain in 1964, as opposed to the
mosaic of Canada's federal and provincial structure. The problem of Northern Ireland was only just emerging as a major crisis
for the United Kingdom, and the separatist tendencies within
Wales and Scotland had not yet become politically important to

either major party. The way the Conservative and Labour parties managed to cover up their internal disputes, although both were deeply divided internally by struggles over leadership just before the election was called, seemed to Roméo to be due, in large measure, to the dominance of the cities.

The election was held on October 16. Roméo provided a half-hour program on the major issues facing Great Britain. The broadcast contained an on-camera opening, several lengthy interviews with relevant footage complementing the interviews, a well-placed musical background and sound effects, as well as his narration track. Ed Higginson remembered Roméo editing the footage himself and being very pleased with the reaction to the tape in Montreal. The program analyzed the political and social questions that were a matter of major debate during the campaign. A crucial element in the program was the reporting on the way the campaign was fought in Glasgow and in other centres where unemployment was rising and questions about the welfare state were particularly sharp.[38] At the same time, Roméo was able to convey the fact that the election as a whole came at the conclusion of thirteen years of Conservative rule. The possibility, and maybe necessity, of change was the underlying theme of the political rhetoric of the Labour Party, whose leader, Harold Wilson, promised to implement reforms in a number of areas. Together these would achieve a "meritocracy," a world where politics would be more a matter of merit and achievement rather than of patronage and personal connections.[39] Above all, Wilson promised more funds for research for the development of technology and science, as well as for more general education and social welfare. He won a narrow victory, about which Roméo reported on election day.[40] The last major broadcast Roméo made in 1964 concerned the dissension that had arisen within the EEC over de Gaulle's opposition to West Germany's demands for change in the agricultural policies of the organization.[41] This dispute would not effectively end until de Gaulle departed as president of France in 1969. The year 1964 wound up with Roméo's participation in a journalistic round table on the events of the past year, which took place on January 3, 1965.[42]

During the more than two years that he had been stationed in London, Roméo's capacity for clear and succinct reporting gained him the respect of both management and colleagues. As well as the broadcasts specifically mentioned in this chapter, he also reported on other events that stirred public interest.[43] Among these were Soviet leader Nikita Khrushchev's visits to Egypt in May and later to the Scandinavian countries in July, as well as the unilateral declaration of independence by Rhodesia from Great Britain in November 1965.[44] He also occasionally reported in English for the CBC. As a result, his reputation grew among the management of both networks. His wish to return home was common knowledge in Ottawa.

In March 1964, he was asked if he would be interested in a federal civil-service position, that of Director of Information Services in the Department of Citizenship and Immigration, an offer he rejected.[45] Just before Christmas 1964, Roméo made a brief visit to Canada, primarily to see his family. However, during the few days he was there he also talked with people in Prime Minister Pearson's office, as well as others close to the then-head of the CBC, J. Alphonse Ouimet. Dick O'Hagan, a New Brunswicker in the Prime Minister's Office, discussed the possibility of Roméo coming to Ottawa, and the conversations between them led to a meeting between Roméo and Pearson in London in early January 1965, at which the possibility of Roméo joining the prime minister's staff was broached. At the same time, Roméo had conversations with Ouimet about his future with Radio-Canada. As a result of these discussions, Roméo wrote to Ouimet in April 1965, pointing out that the prime minister needed an answer to his offer.[46] Roméo mentioned that he did not particularly want to quit the CBC or his London posting, but he felt his work was not particularly challenging and was ephemeral in nature. He concluded by saying that he wrote because Ouimet suggested that he should. In the end, Roméo turned down Pearson's offer and, in August 1965, he was appointed the senior correspondent for Radio-Canada in Washington.

The last months of Roméo's time in London were hectic. Many of his assignments were a continuation of reports on matters about which he had already broadcast, such as Franco-German relations, French domestic affairs, and British foreign policy.[47] A new experience came in February with an invitation to speak to the Royal Institute of International Affairs about Canadian policies in general.[48] Roméo's memories of that occasion were of the total incomprehension of his audience of the realities of francophone life in Canada and of the tangled nature of the relationships between Quebec and the federal government. Towards the end of the event, on being asked why anglophones in Quebec should adapt to changing circumstances, he remarked that their choice would be to adapt or leave. Shortly afterwards, he had an interview with a BBC journalist on the preliminary report of the Royal Commission on Bilingualism and Biculturalism, by now commonly known in Canada as the Laurendeau–Dunton Commission, after the two men who chaired it, André Laurendeau and Davidson Dunton.[49] For John English, the accomplished biographer of both Lester Pearson and Pierre Elliott Trudeau, it was "perhaps the most significant royal commission in Canadian history."[50] The commission was controversial from the start. Many of all political stripes felt either that it would do nothing or, as Maurice Sauvé, a Cabinet minister from Quebec, believed, it would make matters worse. It was said that those in the West considered it unnecessary pandering to Quebec interests, and many in Quebec believed it was no more than a face-saving measure by the federal government to counter the unjustified complaints of anglophone prejudice. Indeed, Laurendeau and Dunton had released their preliminary report largely because the hearings that took place from the inception of the Royal Commission were often belligerently hostile to their work. They became convinced that "Canada without being fully conscious of the fact, [was] passing through the greatest crisis in its history."[51]

Roméo was fortunate that his BBC interviewer was Erskine Barton Childers, one the network's most distinguished journalists. He was the eldest son of Erskine Hamilton Childers, Ireland's fourth president, and grandson of the Irish nationalist Robert Erskine Childers, who was executed during the Irish Civil War. This pedigree meant that the interviewer allowed Roméo to present his ideas about the importance of the commission's report without having to explain in detail the tangled emotional history behind the present political realities. If there were many differences, there were also similarities between the Anglo-Irish troubles and the Quebec problem in Canada. Roméo's connections with those who formed the driving force behind the changes taking place in Quebec, the architects of a major part of the "Quiet Revolution," men such as Fernand Cadieux and Gérard Pelletier, allowed him to comment about the underlying problems faced by the commission. His travels during the 1963 federal election had taken him from one end of the country to the other, and he was also able to speak with sympathy about western Canadian views.

Asked by Childers to explain the unexpectedly strong public reaction to the commission, Roméo remarked that it was probably the first time that the opinions of the general public, rather than those of the élite—university teachers, civil servants, and politicians, who were careful of their words—had been solicited and heard.[52] Childers wondered how such a crucial issue could have remained undiscussed in the first place, and Roméo pointed that one of the roots of the difficulty was a Canadian reality. "You must remember," Roméo said, "that British Columbia is as far from Quebec as Quebec is from London. Then English-speaking Ontario is very conscious of the problem because of the federal capital; but the western areas of Canada frequently considered that the French Canadian problem was just another minority problem." He went on to talk about the specific difficulties in the federal civil service, which did not provide francophones with service in their language—nor sought so to do. Before the interview concluded, the question of Quebec's sense of mastery over its own economy was touched on, as well as French Canadians' feelings about the degree of their acceptance throughout the rest of Canada. Roméo made the point that he believed English Canada would be much more startled by the report than Quebec, where such questions had been discussed for more than a decade. Childers concluded the interview by saying, "Well now, after this extremely gloomy preliminary report, is the Royal Commission going to be able to offer specific hopes, solutions?" Roméo replied, "I'm sure that is what the federal government and all responsible people in Canada are hoping for. I suspect that they will at least remove some of the irritants in the present situation."

By the end of April 1965, Roméo knew that he would soon be on his way to Washington, although this new posting was not made public until an announcement in *La semaine à Radio-Canada* at the end of July.[53] Before he left London, however, there were two more interesting assignments. The first involved an interview about his experiences, or rather a report of events witnessed. This was an account of Algiers at the time of the coup on June 19,[54] led by Houari Boumediène against Ahmed Ben Bella, who had become the first president of Algeria in 1963. Roméo was in Algiers at the time, and his observation of a military coup at close quarters was an experience of political change without the ballot box that marked a new stage in his political education. The second assignment was his last major European broadcast. It concerned the situation in Greece, which provided Roméo with another lesson in the variations of political chaos. Trouble had been brewing in that country all summer, as Prime Minister George Papandreou fought divisions within his own party. By early August, a group of young army officers began to agitate for major changes in the constitution, something apparently supported by Papandreou. Fuelled by rumour and gossip, matters boiled over into what became known as "The Aspida Affair."[55] Ed Higginson remembered that he and Roméo travelled to Greece and were in "the legislative chamber in the Greek Parliament when the place erupted into chaos...Romeo and I shot some film of the mêlée, looked at each other and then we departed before one of the flying chairs headed our way."[56] The tape was broadcast on August 8.[57]

Roméo welcomed the transition from London to Washington, not only because he was pleased to be back in North America, closer to Canadian political life, but also because it meant that he was nearer Lyn Carter. However, his constant travel and her mother's health made life complicated for them. Ever since January, they had become increasingly important to each other. Mrs. Carter had arrived in London in 1964, but suffered from cancer and decided to return to Montreal early in 1965, since it was clear that her condition was terminal. Lyn's father was absent from their lives throughout this period, and Lyn had accompanied her mother back to Canada in March, to stay with her until she died at age forty-four in October 1965. In this period, they came to understand the very different lives each had led before they met. She was fascinated by his interests, and he was enchanted by her willingness to learn. On their first date, Roméo had questioned Lyn about what political causes were important to her, and she answered "cruelty to animals."[58] He then asked her whether she cared about the problems of Jews and Blacks.

She replied, "But I don't know any."[59]

In Washington, Roméo was at least on the same continent, as Lyn coped with the sorrow of her mother's illness. He was able to telephone frequently and visit Montreal fairly often.[60] Moreover, while he was occupied with moving across the Atlantic and dealing with the bureaucracy surrounding accreditation as a foreign correspondent at the White House and the Pentagon, Roméo was assigned to cover the Canadian federal election that took place on November 8, which meant broadcasting sessions in Montreal throughout the month of October.

Before the 1960s came to a conclusion, Canadians would have voted in four federal elections: 1962, which produced a minority Conservative government; 1963, which produced a minority Liberal government; 1965, which produced yet another minority Liberal government; and 1968, which produced a Liberal majority government led by Pierre Elliott Trudeau. Although it did not result in a majority victory for the Liberal Party or alter the makeup of Parliament to any great degree from its predecessor, the election of 1965 introduced a major alteration in the political life of the country, because Pearson persuaded Jean Marchand, Gérard Pelletier, and Pierre Trudeau to run as candidates. Their success at the polls brought a strong reinforcement for Pearson and his work for the survival of Canadian federalism. As John English wrote, "For Liberals it was a coup, for Quebec politics, a shock."[61] These men were different in character, personality, and careers, and in their understanding of the best political path for Canada to follow. They were all active participants in the "Quiet Revolution," and were all convinced federalists. Jean Marchand brought with him a knowledge of the Quebec labour scene and a sense of the industrial economy of Quebec. He served immediately as Pearson's Quebec lieutenant. Since Roméo had first met him in 1947, Gérard Pelletier had become one of Quebec's most influential journalists, as editor-in-chief of La Presse,

North America's largest-circulating French-language daily, from 1961 to 1964. He knew the important movers and shakers in Quebec's intellectual life on both sides of the sovereigntist-federalist debate. At the time, Pierre Trudeau seemed to be the least significant acquisition for the Liberal Party, but his clarity of thought about constitutional matters in general and the politics of Quebec in particular soon made him one of Pearson's most valued advisers. The acquisition of these talented individuals, the "Three Wise Men" as they were immediately dubbed, gave the prime minister new life in his battle for the preservation of Canadian unity and changed for the better the French Canadian presence in federal affairs.

Roméo's assignments during the 1965 election were those of commentator and political analyst. His first broadcast was on September 27 from Montreal,[62] as a member of a round table with a number of leading Quebec journalists. It marked the recognition by Radio-Canada of his promotion to senior correspondent. The moderator, Pierre Nadeau, had worked for Radio-Canada since 1962, and was well-known for his ability to keep the members of a panel focused in a civil discussion. He had just been informed that he was to be sent to Paris as the senior correspondent. One of the other panellists was Jean-Marc Poliquin, who had a varied and distinguished career, most recently as literary editor at *Le Droit*. He had been a political commentator for Radio-Canada since 1964. He was known for his ability to place contemporary arguments in their historical context. This broadcast was very much a general discussion of the party platforms and what the two major parties hoped to achieve, along with some analysis. Among other plans, the Liberals promised to implement a national medicare program within two years and a Canada Pension Plan, while the Conservatives promised to improve the existing Old Age Pension payments and reduce personal and corporate income taxes. Roméo took part in two other similar broadcasts on October 3 and 24, and was part of the team that covered the election itself in November.[63] This work allowed Roméo to regain the expertise about federal politics he had had three years earlier, as well as familiarize himself with the new trends and rhetoric in federal-Quebec relations.

He returned to establish himself fully in Washington in December, a move influenced a little by Lyn's decision to return for a short while to London. He adapted more easily to Washington life because of the friendly welcome he received from the two senior correspondents who worked for the CBC there, James Minifie and Knowlton Nash. Minifie was one of Canada's most distinguished foreign correspondents, having covered the Spanish Civil War in the 1930s and reported from London during the Battle of Britain. He was first posted to Washington in 1945, and returned frequently to the capital. Roméo considered that he learned more about journalism from him than from any other individual. Knowlton Nash, born on November 18, 1927, in Toronto, was almost the same age as Roméo. He had begun his career in journalism in the late 1940s, and had been a regular contributor to the CBC from Washington since 1958. Together, he and Roméo founded the CBC/Radio-Canada Correspondents Association. Roméo became its first president in late 1965. According to Knowlton, it was entirely due to Roméo's determination and tact that the association was a joint Anglo-French endeavour.[64]

Radio-Canada announced Roméo's posting to Washington by pointing out that listeners to *Téléjournal* already knew him as a journalist with a clear and pleasant voice, whose reports were both elegant and accurate.[65] The publication also noted that Radio-Canada would now have two correspondents in Washington, the other being Guy Lamarche, a younger man who was known for his work as an interviewer. This double posting allowed Radio-Canada to continue to assign Roméo work on matters outside the United States. In fact, his first assignment in 1966 was to chair the lengthy press conference given by CBC President Alphonse Ouimet on January 11.[66] This assignment was a signal that Roméo's reputation was high among influential Liberals. It also highlighted his command of both languages and the respect in which he was held by his fellow journalists. At this meeting, Ouimet was faced with giving his response not only to an advisory committee report about the relationship between private and public broadcasters, and that between the CBC and Radio-Canada, but also on the issue of union-management relations within the corporation. In essence, the head of the corporation was defending his record on all these matters. Arguments about them had become more intense in the past decade, during Ouimet's tenure. The national network was repeatedly condemned by private broadcasters as élitist, inefficient, and biased, while the national networks judged commercial television as shoddy purveyors of American culture, dominated by the pursuit of ratings and revenues. By 1963, the president of the Canadian Association of Broadcasters, a Newfoundlander named Don Jamieson, said, speaking of the CBC, "There are few better places than a state-controlled broadcasting system with which mediocre talent can rationalize its failures so conveniently while calling on the state for help." Douglas Fisher, the CCF broadcasting critic, remarked that Jamieson "could be as brutally frank as any old robber baron and as piously high-minded as an Archbishop."[67]

The prime minister came to recognize the need to find some solution to what was becoming a major irritant on the political scene. In 1965, he had appointed not another royal commission, but an advisory committee. It was headed by Robert Fowler, the same man who chaired the Royal Commission on Broadcasting, which had issued its report in 1958. Alphonse Ouimet disliked that report, and was not particularly pleased by the one which

Fowler now presented to him. On the other hand, there were few in the national broadcasting system, and very few among journalists in Quebec, who were at all happy with Ouimet. His chairing of the lengthy press conference showed Roméo's ability to control the expression of conflicting points of view, keeping them from becoming a rancorous public debate. It helped that he had recently organized a joint Anglo-French union for the foreign correspondents at the corporation and that he had a good personal relationship—more civil respect than warm friendship—with Ouimet. It also helped that those most angered by the report were the owners of the private broadcasting networks, rather than working journalists. Recommendations that fewer American programs be imported and Canadian talent be paid more were received positively by Roméo's colleagues. Ouimet might have been unhappy with the criticisms of the CBC—that it broadcast too much American programming, that it was far too centralized, that it should capture more advertising revenue, and that it failed miserably as a cultural bridge between English and French Canadians—but the private networks were enraged by the scathing criticism of their programming. Fowler referred to it as "systematic mediocrity."[68] Although Ouimet escaped public humiliation at the press conference, he resigned within the year. It took two years for the government to follow up on the advice tendered and pass the *Broadcasting Act*, which confirmed the CBC's position as a national broadcaster and created the Canadian Radio-Television Commission.

Roméo returned to Washington in mid-January 1966. Remembering this period of his life, he recalled his growing admiration of the United States at a time when that country was facing prolonged and bitter debates about foreign and domestic policies, especially the war in Vietnam and the turmoil of the civil-rights movement.[69] While he broadcast far more often about the war during coming months, Roméo found the ongoing struggle for the entrenchment of civil rights the more riveting subject. There were more dramatic years than 1966 for civil rights. In 1964, the *Civil Rights Act* outlawed many forms of racial segregation and saw the murder of civil-rights workers in Mississippi, while 1965 was in many ways the most dramatic. That was the year of the "Bloody Sunday" march in Selma, Alabama, when 600 civil-rights marchers were attacked by state and local police using tear gas and billy clubs, and the Watts Riots in Los Angeles, which lasted five days and caused $40 million in damage. But in 1966, violence in Chicago showed that Illinois was capable of as much intolerance as Georgia. On June 14, Roméo was in Washington and reported on the civil-rights march that took place in the capital that day.[70] This form of public action, together with debate in the Senate on the general question of civil rights,[71] were examples, in Roméo's mind, of a great and complicated democracy working through one of its most serious and divisive crises. He remembered many of the speeches in the Senate as being the most moving examples of the best of political rhetoric.

The question of the war in Vietnam was, in Roméo's mind, more a matter of international power politics, of conflicting ideological arguments, and of hypocrisy on the part of the combatant power, than a moment of major historical importance for the world. He was influenced in his ideas on the conflict by the American anthropologist Gerald Hickey, with whom he had become friends when both studied at the Sorbonne in the 1950s. They corresponded occasionally throughout the intervening years, during which time Hickey worked in the Vietnam highlands, first as part of his fieldwork for his doctorate and later as part of research projects for the Rand Corporation. By 1966, Hickey was thoroughly disenchanted with American policy in Vietnam, writing in his autobiography, "By and large American leaders were suffering from vincible ignorance about Vietnam nationalism because it was something they did not care about."[72] Another influence was his continuing friendship with Morley Safer, who reported from Saigon for CBS from 1965 to 1967.[73]

Roméo was accredited to the White House and the Pentagon while he was in Washington. His broadcasts about Vietnam during January and early February were sufficiently impartial in the eyes of the American authorities that he retained these privileges.[74] It was, after all, a time when domestic American criticism of administration policies was becoming more widespread. The year 1966 was when American military involvement in Vietnam mushroomed: in December 1965, the total number of military personnel there was 184,000; in December 1966, it was 425,300.[75] Throughout the year, domestic opposition to the war increased, and it became for President Johnson the dominant issue of the last three years of his presidency. Johnson renewed air attacks in late January 1966 and by early July Roméo was reporting on American raids on supply lines in North Vietnam.[76] By midsummer, Johnson was actively searching for a way to end the war and its continuously rising cost. As a result, when the leaders of Australia, South Korea, New Zealand, the Philippines, and Thailand suggested he attend a conference in Manila on the matter, Johnson announced his acceptance on October 1.[77] Roméo was to go as well.

Between the opening months of the year and early September, Roméo's personal life became much happier. He and Lyn continued to write to one another with increasing frequency during January and February 1966, after Lyn returned to London following her mother's death. In March, Roméo went to London on assignment to cover the British general election, which took place on the March 19.[78] By the time Roméo returned to Washington, arrangements for Lyn's return to Montreal were in place, and by September plans were being made for their marriage. During these same months, the possibility of a major change in Roméo's

professional life was once more being discussed. The offer that
came this time was very different from those that had previously
come his way. Those had been simply explorations of possibilities, but they meant that Roméo's name was one that was
considered when the prime minister was in need of a new press
secretary. Now there was a firm proposition to consider. In early
1966, Richard O'Hagan, who had been the prime minister's press
secretary since 1963, let it be known he wanted to resign. Over
the summer and into the early autumn, a concerted effort was
made to persuade Roméo to go to Ottawa as O'Hagan's successor. During these weeks, Roméo was preparing for his first trip
to Asia, socializing with Lyn on her visits to Washington, and
discussing when and where they would marry, as well as contem-
plating a major shift in career. He also broadcast regularly about
Vietnam and other American issues. Leaving with the presiden-
tial entourage in the second week of October meant a new set of
problems and gave Roméo time to think, not so much about his
coming marriage plans, which were well in hand by then, but
about the opportunity to return to Canada.

Before he left Washington for Manila, Roméo reported on the
21st session of the General Assembly of the United Nations, which
opened on September 22, 1966.[79] He followed this assignment
with a number of broadcasts on why Johnson was undertaking
a seventeen-day visit to the various countries involved in the
war.[80] For Johnson the war in Vietnam had become an agoniz-
ing dilemma. Robert Dallek, one of his many biographers, wrote
that "even as he decided to escalate the war, Johnson had deeper
and more clairvoyant views about Vietnam than contemporaries
could possibly have imagined. He believed his own rhetoric about
the need to fight in Vietnam; at the same time, however, he could
see the makings of the quagmire ahead."[81] He hoped by this trip
to encourage the troops in Vietnam and to rally his supporters
in the South Pacific. Roméo's first broadcast was from Manila,

where preparations were being made for the conference.[82] It took place on October 23 and 24 and resulted in expressions of platitudes and wistful hopes, but no concrete plans for the resolution of the region's problems.[83] Roméo brought together his impressions of the journey in a broadcast from Washington on November 7, commenting on the warm reception that greeted Johnson at the Cam Ranh Bay Air Force base in Vietnam, the welcome of the governments of Australia and New Zealand, and the angry protests at the airports in Wellington and Brisbane.[84]

Throughout the tour, Roméo acted as a reporter, not as an editor, and he made no predictions about what impact President Johnson's tour would have on the United States and the world. When he talked about it in later years, Roméo was more concerned about the Vietnam War in general than about his own brief experiences there. His recollections of the second half of 1966 were mostly about his personal life.

CHAPTER 6

An Unexpected Path
to Political Life

Roméo and Lyn were married in a Catholic ceremony in a parish church in Washington's Georgetown neighbourhood on December 17, 1966. It was a small wedding party, with several of Roméo's friends, including James Taylor, with whom he had shared an apartment in Ottawa; Ed Higginson and his wife; James Minifie and Knowlton Nash and their wives; and one or two other Washington acquaintances. When the LeBlancs returned from their honeymoon in Martinique, it was for only six months before they left for Ottawa and the Prime Minister's Office. In later years, they remembered these months, full of happy adaptation to marriage, with fondness. There was also the anticipation of another type of journalism experience for Roméo, one that involved less travelling. This opportunity came through the auspices of Marc Lalonde.

Lalonde had known Roméo since they both worked for the Jeunesse Étudiante Catholique. Both men were influenced by the teachings of Mounier and believed that political life was a proper

Roméo and Lyn at their wedding on December 17, 1966 in Washington, DC

avenue to effecting social change. At the same time, both were influenced by the ideas of Gérard Pelletier and Fernand Cadieux about Quebec politics. Lalonde had gone on to graduate as a lawyer from the Université de Montréal in 1954 and then graduated from Oxford University, where he took a degree in Philosophy, Politics, and Economics. His academic career concluded with a Diplôme d'Études Supérieures en Droit from Ottawa University in 1960. That year, Lalonde returned to Montreal to practise law. Already one of those who considered that Quebec's future was as part of Canada, he was quickly welcomed back by the Cadieuxs, the Pelletiers, and Trudeau, who were actively discussing the matter. By the time of the 1965 election, he had become fully engaged with "les trois Colombes" (Marchand, Pelletier, and Trudeau), who had decided to run for the federal Liberals. It was in his capacity as an important Quebec Liberal that he went to talk to Roméo, but he also went as someone who had not lost touch with a fellow JEC member, someone who had followed

Roméo's career with Radio-Canada and was himself about to become a member of the prime minister's staff.

Lalonde's visit laid the groundwork for Roméo's accept-ance of the offer. His arguments started with an analysis of the present state of Canadian political life, particularly in Quebec, and continued with the pitch that Pearson needed someone with Roméo's talents. Roméo had been a parliamentary cor-respondent between 1961 and the fall of 1962, and had been brought back from London to cover the 1963 and 1965 elec-tions. Even when abroad, he had not lost touch with events occurring both federally and provincially in New Brunswick. What Lalonde provided was information about how Pearson planned to move forward from the disappointing result of the 1965 election. It was not that the Liberal Party and its ideas had been rejected out of hand. There was the encouraging election of Trudeau, Marchand, and Pelletier in Quebec, and fifty-six seats out of a total of a possible seventy-five in the province. Support in Ontario, British Columbia, and New Brunswick held for the Liberals, while the Prairies mostly remained loyal to Diefenbaker and in Nova Scotia ten Conservatives out of a total of twelve seats were elected. But the Canadian electorate was uncertain about the Liberal government's past record and plans for the future. Roméo needed to know, in some depth, how Pearson was going to react to the challenges. It was clear that Pearson was not going to abandon his determination to foster a federation that worked, where people in all provinces knew that Canada was a country with a complex heritage and, above all, where both the French and English languages were cherished at the federal level. This vision meant a just accommodation of the wishes of Quebec, within the constitutional framework of the country. Therefore, it was necessary that the government's emerging bilingualism and biculturalism policies be fully understood—not only in Quebec, but also in the rest of Canada. Here, Roméo's talents and experience were a major attraction for leading Liberals. He was completely bilingual, and came from a province whose premier, Louis Robichaud, was moving its divided population of Acadian, United Empire Loyalist, and Irish to an acceptance of the legitimacy of each other's civic rights.

When Pearson telephoned him to offer the position, Roméo said yes. It was not so much that the prime minister took the trouble to call him that made up Roméo's mind; it was the conviction that there was something that needed to be done that people he deeply respected felt he could do, something that he also thought should be done.

By this time, Roméo had come to a profound belief in the value of his Acadian heritage and an equally deep conviction that Canada was a country which allowed his people to survive and develop. What Roméo took from Acadian history was "la Survivance," not "Le Grand Dérangement."[1] The inescapable knowledge of what happened in 1755 and its consequences was as much a context for his own political identity as knowledge of the treatment meted out to the Irish by the English was to many of those in modern Ireland. But the knowledge of past wrongs and present injustices was not the determining factor of his political views. His early life in the Memramcook Valley gave him an appreciation of what successful Acadian farm life could be on fertile land. His undergraduate years at St. Joseph's brought him a wealth of knowledge of the differing experiences that built the Acadian communities throughout the Maritimes, of the breadth and depth of Acadian culture. His friendship with Fernand Cadieux and Gérard Pelletier in Montreal when he was twenty-two, both men having seen immediate post-1945 Europe, drove home that Acadian suffering had parallel examples in the past, and worse, in the sufferings of many other people in the present. His experience in France, at a time when that country was withdrawing from its imperial ventures, acquainted him with imperialism as an historical and common feature of human communities. His years teaching in Fredericton, when changes brought about by Hugh John Flemming's government laid the foundation for the extraordinary work undertaken by Louis Robichaud in the 1960s, brought an understanding of how to work with people of different religions and languages. He came to the realization that neither past injustice nor present prejudice should be the overwhelming determinants for contemporary political judgments. Here, he echoed the view of an Acadian woman in Cheticamp who, discussing the Deportation with the author in the early 1960s, remarked that the English who carried it out were not her present neighbours. For her, as for Roméo, what was the important was the need to correct present problems, not review the roles of victim and victor and argue again matters of historical guilt. History was important as a guide, but it was not the final voice for the resolution of the problems of the present.

Talking about his decision to leave Washington in an interview after he retired as governor general, Roméo emphasized that, at the time, the job was to be only a contract for a year.[2] He and Lyn enjoyed their life in Washington, a city he found beautiful, exciting, friendly, and interesting. He took a leave of absence from the CBC and sublet their apartment on the understanding that he went as an interim replacement for O'Hagan, with a responsibility to recommend his own successor. Even though Roméo thought that it was a temporary assignment, he made it perfectly clear that his position was the prime minister's press secretary, *not* the "prime minister's *French*-language press secretary."[3] He often recalled demanding this clarity in conversations in later years. It was partly professional pride, but it was also a shrewd judgment about what he needed if he was to be taken seriously by all his colleagues. He also made it clear that his duties required unrestricted access to the prime minister, since his work was as a "press secretary," not as a "public-relations" expert. His experience as a White House accredited journalist gave him the opportunity to see how President Johnson worked with his press secretary, Bill Moyers, and to consider what he needed in order to carry out a similar task in Canada. Roméo pointed out to Lalonde that "a press secretary may not tell everything he knows, but he must know everything. That means daily access to the prime minister."[4] Pearson agreed to these conditions and, in late spring 1967, it was officially announced that he would join the PMO on September 1.

The most important broadcast he made in his first months on the job was an interview he gave to his colleague Henri Crusene on January 1, 1968 explaining why he had accepted the position. During the fifteen-minute interview, Roméo spoke first about his belief that "if your prime minister asks you to do something you have to have a very good answer for refusing to do it."[5] He went on to say that he believed deeply—"je crois profondément"—in Canada's survival as a country, not because he thought it perfect: being an Acadian and knowing Canadian history made that hardly likely. But, he continued, at a time when Canada was on the brink of a major evolution, he felt that, as a Canadian, he had a right to feel as much at home in Vancouver and the Yukon as in Quebec and New Brunswick. He wanted to be involved in Canada's development, because he was convinced that it would and should survive. Crusene asked him if this move meant that he had political ambitions. Roméo pointed out that he still had his lease on his Washington apartment, that he had a short-term contract, and that it was not the position but the man that attracted him—"je ne suis pas attiré au poste mais à l'homme." He added, however, that one never knew what the future might hold.

Crusene pursued the matter, asking if Roméo really believed he would be able to return to his work as a journalist. Roméo answered that he hoped so, although there would obviously be a need for a period of "decompression," such as a deep-sea diver required when returning to the surface. Crusene pressed: did he really believe he would retain any shred of credibility as an impartial political commentator after serving as press secretary to a Liberal prime minister? Roméo's response was that he believed journalists had a right to political opinions, in the same way as other Canadians, and remarked that, in Canada and especially in Quebec, there were journalists with known nationalist, federalist, and separatist opinions all working at their trade. After all, he continued, journalism is a profession with it own norms and discipline. He expected journalists to write or speak of what they had actually heard and seen. It would not do, he suggested, to castrate journalists politically because of their profession. Roméo pointed out that there were journalists who managed to return from politics to journalism. After all, many readers were not naive. It is clear that Crusene felt Roméo would find the task impossible, while Roméo considered it entirely feasible.

Roméo continued to work as Radio-Canada's chief correspondent in Washington until mid-July 1967, although the majority of broadcasts from the American capital were done by his colleague Guy Lamarche. Roméo remained president of the Canadian Foreign Correspondents Association until the end of June. His last official act on behalf of this group was an acerbic letter written to the accounting department of the CBC, with copies to every possible interested party, regarding the manner of expense accounting the corporation required of its foreign correspondents.[6] The letter argued the need for some latitude in appending receipts for foreign expenses, especially for the currencies of Latin American and Asian countries. The appeal had little effect on the corporation's policies. His own major broadcasts from Washington during these months dealt with American foreign policy, Vietnam in particular, and the general topic of American-Russian relations.[7]

Roméo and Lyn did not settle permanently in Ottawa until the late summer, although there were a number of lengthy preparatory visits as Roméo was introduced to the work of the Prime Minister's Office. The PMO, as it is most often called, is sometimes confused with the Privy Council, which is the secretariat of the federal cabinet, the purpose of which is to provide non-partisan advice and support to the prime minister and government departments in general.[8] The PMO is made up of the prime minister and his/her top political advisers and administrative staff, all of whom are the personal choice of the prime minister. It is a reflection of the needs, substance, and style of the sitting prime minister, and thus a changeable entity. The numbers employed vary greatly, as do the ways in which its personnel are used. When Roméo arrived, there were ten members in the PMO, of whom Marc Lalonde was Pearson's senior adviser.

The first week Roméo began regular work in the PMO was very nearly his last. He came with very different work experience than his predecessor, Richard O'Hagan. O'Hagan was a newspaper man and worked in the advertising world before becoming special assistant to Pearson, then leader of the Opposition, in January 1961. In April 1962, O'Hagan continued to work with Pearson as his press secretary.[9] He worked on the belief that his job was to present the government and its policies in the best possible light. With broad experience in radio and television and work as parliamentary correspondent, Roméo came to the position with the idea that his main job was to explain what the government was doing, rather than be its public-relations expert. It was this understanding of his work that had led Roméo to insist that he be part of the weekly meetings between the prime minister and his senior advisers. According to an interview he gave in 1977, when he discovered that one such meeting was already in progress with the prime minister, Lalonde, and Gordon Robertson, the clerk of the Privy Council, Roméo went straight into the meeting and informed the prime minister that "he had merely taken a leave of absence from the CBC...he had only sublet his apartment in Washington...he had not unpacked. He could, he told Pearson, be on the next plane back to the U.S. capital."[10] Pearson made sure Roméo was included in all future meetings. It was an arrangement that would continue when Trudeau replaced Pearson as prime minister in April 1968 and retained Roméo as his press secretary.

While both jobs demanded a similar knowledge and set of skills, and can be considered equally the work of a professional journalist, there is a considerable difference between the practice of journalism as reporter and editor and the practice of journalism as press secretary. The first involves gathering, sifting, and giving comments on information about the contemporary scene; the second involves the communication of government information about the affairs of state to the media. The most formal definition of Roméo's duties came only in April 1968, when Trudeau took office. The memorandum in question explained, "The Press Secretary is the Prime Minister's principal advisor with regard to all matters related to the transmission by the government of information of all kinds to the communication media...he is also concerned with the press and information policy of the government as a whole...advises the Prime Minister regarding Press conferences, broadcast[s] and interviews...advises on public-relations aspects of...public statements."[11] How these guidelines worked in reality depended on the personal relationship of the people involved and the exigencies of the moment. Roméo was particularly fortunate to make the transition from Radio-Canada to the PMO with Lester Pearson, someone with a long experience of Canadian government and politics who was happy to introduce Roméo to the complex world of federal affairs.

The change in Roméo's professional focus also meant a considerable adjustment for Lyn who, during the months since her

Roméo and Prime Minister Lester Pearson, 1968

mother's death, had come to know Knowlton Nash and his wife, as well as James Minifie and his wife. Both couples were helpful and much-appreciated friends. During the months before the LeBlancs left Washington, Lyn had also begun to know and like the city and feel secure in the life she led there. Ottawa was a town that Roméo knew well, even though the people he knew there were more acquaintances than close friends. The move meant a new beginning for Lyn, the establishment of a home for herself and Roméo. They rented a house for a year in Rockcliffe, on Buena Vista Road, and spent part of the summer settling in and part in New Brunswick in the Memramcook Valley. While she had travelled to Nova Scotia and New Brunswick with her mother when she was in her teens, Acadian society was unknown territory for Lyn. The family welcomed the newlyweds with warmth; they stayed with Léonard, who had recovered to a certain degree from the 1950 injury to his legs and spine. He had obtained employment at Radio-Canada in Moncton and had moved out of the family home to his own small house. Roméo's obvious happiness did a great deal to ensure their welcome, and Lyn's ability to speak and understand French reasonably well was a help. Roméo had always remained close to his siblings and their families, even if the dire need for his financial and emotional help had by now lessened. He visited them whenever possible, brought presents, and often managed to help them financially without embarrassing them.[12] The news that Lyn was pregnant also pleased Roméo's extended kin.

During the ten months he worked for Prime Minister Pearson, Roméo came to grips with what his position meant on a day-to-day basis. In many ways, it was akin to the chief editor's work at a newspaper. The editor sets the tone for each issue, chairs the meetings, oversees assignments, but leaves the detailed work to be carried out by equally competent people heading specific departments. From the outset, Roméo saw his primary responsibility as ensuring that Pearson had as succinct a view as possible of general public opinion, as expressed in the newspapers, public-opinion polls being much less common then. These months also brought Roméo a greater understanding of the present state of Canada, as viewed by the Liberal Party, and insight into the beliefs of English Canada, above all of Ontario. There was an essential sympathy between Pearson and Roméo, who later remembered times when they were able to talk at length. Although from very different backgrounds, both men had a feeling for Canada as a country that informed their thinking about its politics. Both men cherished a sense of the particular histories of the communities in which they had been born and raised. Both saw Canada as a framework which made possible the growth and development of traditions they held dear. Both had experiences of other countries in their youth, and both were convinced that the present time was one of both danger and opportunity for Canada. As Pearson wrote in his memoirs, "My own conviction was that national unity was the major question facing Canada";[13] he "saw no way of holding our country together unless English Canada adopts a new attitude towards the intention of our French-speaking compatriots to maintain their identity, their culture and their language as a special fact of life within Canada."[14] For Roméo, this view was the ideal that Louis Robichaud was on the verge of achieving in New Brunswick. Even if larger, the problem at the federal level seemed not that much more complicated. Over forty years later, Roméo recalled these conversations as being some of the most important and enjoyable learning experiences life brought him.

Quite apart from helping Roméo discover what it was that Pearson wanted him to do as his press secretary, perhaps more importantly such talks showed the extent to which an English Canadian, brought up in a devout Protestant family in Ontario, could understand the complex nature of Quebec politics. Pearson's viewpoint was sophisticated and based on friendship with elected politicians from both parties working at the provincial level. It was informed by a lifetime of experience in international politics, which made him fully aware of the influence that French ambivalence towards separatist aspirations might have on Canada-Quebec relations. For Pearson, by 1967, a major factor in the relationship between the federal government and Quebec was the attitude of de Gaulle and a number of French intellectuals and civil servants towards the separatists. Roméo particularly remembered one conversation, which took place on a long car journey, about the background for Pearson's immediate reaction to de Gaulle's "Vive le Québec Libre" remark in Montreal during his abbreviated visit to Canada at the time of Expo 67. Roméo was still in Washington when the visit had taken place. In this and other conversations, Pearson gave Roméo an account of the relationship between the federal government and Quebec since 1963, when Pearson became prime minister with a minority government, albeit one that won forty-seven out of seventy-five seats in Quebec.[15] It was an invaluable briefing for the new press secretary and served him well when he continued in the position with Prime Minister Trudeau.

Roméo's career as a foreign correspondent had benefited from the graduate courses in international relations he had taken in the 1950s at the Sorbonne. Now he had what amounted to a graduate tutorial in contemporary Canadian politics from Pearson. As most successful journalists did, Roméo constantly read background material for the context of the stories he was covering. He had also followed, even when out of the country, the twists and turns of federal politics. But what Pearson provided was a narrative of a prime minister's thinking about one of the crucial developments of the contemporary scene: the impact of France on Ottawa-Quebec relations, something which became a major issue for the Canadian government during the next two years. As Roméo moved into the PMO, with the responsibility of advising the prime minister on the questions journalists would ask and what information they considered they had the right to know, this detailed knowledge of the evolution of immediate past policies that Pearson related was invaluable.

Jean Lesage had been premier of Quebec for nearly three years when Pearson took office, crucial years, which saw the development of the "Quiet Revolution." These were the years when Lesage and his colleagues, among them René Lévesque, began a legislative program that would bring major reforms in the way the provincial government worked. They were also years when a significant portion of people in the province began to work towards a special status for Quebec, within confederation if possible, but, if not, then as part of a separation of Quebec from Canada. As Pearson later wrote, "The violence associated with the extremist *Front de Libération du Québec*[16] began just before and continued intermittently during my régime, becoming somewhat more serious toward the end." He continued, "This escalation reflected...the growth of the violent separatist movement which in turn mirrored the extreme aspect of the Quiet, at times not so quiet, Revolution...All this was very disturbing and undoubtedly affected our attitude to Quebec."[17] Throughout his years as prime minister, Pearson held firmly to the belief that Quebec's demands for powers to protect and develop the culture and heritage of its people could be accommodated within the Canadian confederation. The sympathy for the separatists from certain influential people in France irritated him considerably. When this sympathy grew into obvious support for Quebec's right of independent action in international matters, Pearson's irritation turned to annoyance.

Since 1961, de Gaulle's minister of cultural affairs, André Malraux, had paid increasing attention to links with Quebec. Jean Lesage, in turn, welcomed the new consideration shown to visiting Quebec dignitaries in Paris. By the end of 1964, a preparatory agreement for an educational "entente" between Quebec and France was reached, and on February 27, 1965, it was signed by these parties. At the same time, Canada and France exchanged diplomatic "notes" in which Canada became the diplomatic cover as the sovereign state, along with France, to the agreement. The Quebec government, and particularly those wishing for a weakening of federal power, considered this accord, in the words of Paul Gérin-Lajoie, who signed it on behalf of the Quebec government, "the political instrument of a distinct cultural group."[18] What particularly galled Pearson, and something he conveyed fully to Roméo, was de Gaulle's growing disdain for Canada.[19] It was one of the first times that Roméo heard someone from Ontario speak from the heart about the roots of his emotional commitment to his country. Certainly, it would have been the first time Roméo listened to a man, twenty years his senior, who had fought in the First World War, and had had a distinguished career as a diplomat, talking about what Canadian history meant to him and what impact the present attitude of France toward Canada had on him.

Twice in less than fifty years, Canadians had been allies of France. Now the Canadian ambassador to that country, Jules Léger, suffered a pattern of barely veiled insults. The attitude of France seemed to be, in the words of John Halstead, chief of mission in Paris, "to receive Quebec ministers because they are French Canadians but to fail to receive French Canadians because they were Federal Ministers [which] was equivalent to saying that only the Quebec Government and not the federal Government represented French Canadians."[20] Pearson's attitude towards de Gaulle became a matter of intellectual disagreement in March 1966, when de Gaulle asked for the removal of Canadian troops stationed in France as part of the NATO force.[21] Not only Pearson but also diplomatic opinion generally, in Canada as well as in the United Kingdom and the United States, was uneasy when France withdrew its support for a NATO military presence there. But, as Roméo discovered, what finally had turned the irritation and annoyance of an outstanding international Nobel Laureate diplomat into outright anger was de Gaulle's request that Canada remove its troops, coupled the general's subsequent stand towards the fiftieth-anniversary ceremonies at the Vimy Ridge memorial on April 9, 1967. The French disdain for Vimy could have been foreseen, because de Gaulle had already studiously ignored the British commemoration of Dunkirk, which took place in 1965. However, the fiftieth anniversary of the Battle of Vimy Ridge was, for Canada, an occasion of much more significance than the Dunkirk ceremonies. Vimy was a battle in which the Canadian Corps had borne the brunt of the fighting. Thirty-five thousand Canadian troops were committed to capturing the German defences of the mines and factories that lay in the plains beyond the ridge. It took three days of heavy fighting to achieve this goal, and more than 10,602 men were wounded, of whom 3,598 died.[22] Lieutenant-Colonel Alexander Ross, DSO, who was there at the time, in command of Canada's 28th (Northwest) Battalion, later wrote: "It was Canada from Atlantic to Pacific on parade...I thought then that in those few minutes I witnessed the birth of a nation." For Pearson, as for many other Canadians of his generation, Vimy Ridge was one of the most important moments in the history of the country. Roméo sympathized fully when Pearson told him of his remark to the civil servant who spoke to him during the Vimy memorial ceremonies about his regret that Canadian troops were leaving France. Pearson suggested he ask de Gaulle if, when this occurred, the hundred thousand Canadian dead in French cemeteries should also be taken to Germany.[23]

General de Gaulle arrived in Canada on his official visit as head of state to Expo 67 in July of the centenary year. Roméo was kept informed of the way the PMO handled the press during the unhappy event. It was hardly surprising that the visit went badly. There was some talk of not issuing an invitation to de Gaulle, but that would have produced a major break in relations between the two countries and outraged Quebec. In June, the widow of former Governor General Georges Vanier had eaten lunch with de Gaulle and reported to the Canadian Embassy that she was "stunned" to be told by him that "only a free and independent Quebec will be able to save North American civilization."[24] When a French warship, the *Colbert*, arrived at Quebec City on the morning of July 23, it did not fly the Canadian flag, the normal courtesy to the host country. The general then refused to ride in the carriage with Governor General Roland Michener.[25] From then on, the visit went from bad to worse for the government, and culminated with de Gaulle's infamous speech on July 24, from the balcony of Montreal's Town Hall. He led up to his final phrase with the revelation of a deeply held personal memory, and announced that he would reveal a secret that his audience would not repeat. "This evening," he said, "here and all along my journey, I have found myself in the same type of atmosphere as that of Liberation." Then he concluded, "Vive Montréal! Vive le Québec! Vive le Québec libre!"[26]

It was a performance that released a tidal wave of emotions: for the separatists it was the articulation of a promise, an anointing of the journey to the Promised Land; for the thousands of Canadians who fought to liberate France from German occupation, the idea that the situation in Quebec was in any way comparable to that of occupied France was beyond credence.[27] For Pearson and his Cabinet, it was an unwarranted intrusion in the affairs of another country, a view shared by French newspapers on both the Left (the Communist *L'Humanité*) and the Right (*Le Figaro*). The next day, the prime minister sent a strongly worded rebuke to the French Embassy, which read, in part: "Canadians do not need to be liberated. Indeed, many

thousands of Canadians gave their lives in two world wars in the
liberation of France...Canada will remain united and will reject
any effort to destroy her unity."[28] Roméo believed that Pearson
was far more deeply hurt by de Gaulle's shunning of the Vimy
Ridge memorial than over the Expo 67 incident. De Gaulle left
Canada the next day, although not before attending a luncheon
with Jean Drapeau, the mayor of Montreal, who informed him
that French Canadians had survived with little help from France
for over two hundred years and would continue to do so in
the future within a strengthened Canada. Pearson watched the
speech on television and telephoned the mayor immediately to
thank him for words which "would do much to heal the wounds
inflicted on our country in the last few days."[29]

The contrasting events of the summer of 1967—the glow of
pride and national enjoyment that marked the opening of Expo
67 in Montreal and the reality of the clashing political ambitions
of a large number of Canadians—would be part of the country's life during the coming decades. As historian Desmond
Morton wrote, "The euphoria dissolved...On November 18,
1967, Lévesque launched his Mouvement souveraineté-associ-
ation. In Canada's hundredth year, the forces of disintegration
had found a compelling leader and a program."[30] The question
of Canadian unity cast a shadow not only over the politics of
the coming decades, but also over the achievements of past federal governments—even, temporarily, Pearson's record. In his
case, however, the announcement of his resignation as leader of
the Liberal Party on December 14, 1967 (his seventieth birthday
had been in April that year), followed as it was by an election
within six months, dispelled some of the criticisms. December
14 was also the day Roméo's son Dominic was born in Ottawa's
Civic Hospital. Roméo was torn as to where he should be. Lyn
told him he should go to the office; Pearson told him he should
go back to his wife and child. He returned to hold his first-born.

The *Ottawa Citizen* headline for the day was: "Lost a Leader, Gained a Son."

In many ways, defending the record of Pearson's five years as leader of a minority government was not difficult. As Blair Neatby, a political historian of repute, wrote, Pearson had "fundamentally altered Canadian identity by introducing the flag, Medicare, a national pension plan and comprehensive welfare measures, and by focusing attention on Quebec's challenge to national unity."[31] In the view of Monique Bégin, the legislation that Pearson managed to pass, even with a minority government, laid the foundation for Canadian society for the remainder of the twentieth century: "a major expansion of post-secondary education federal funding, manpower training initiatives, the community and regional development program (the Fund for Rural Economic Development (FRED) and the Agricultural and Rural Development Agency (ARDA)), the Company of Young Canadians, the Royal Commission on the Status of Women and a divorce act."[32] This catalogue does not mention the many regulatory initiatives in the areas of transportation, broadcasting, and labour codes. The difficulty was less the record of the government than the atmosphere of chaos that surrounded its achievements: disputes within the Liberal Party and among Cabinet ministers, the poor handling of government errors, such as the Rivard case, which concerned a narcotics-peddling thug,[33] or, more seriously, the deterioration of Canada's relationship with the United States. It was this reputation for inefficiency and poor administrative practices that the next leader of the party, to be chosen at the convention held from April 4 to 6, 1968, had to counter before the coming election.

Roméo's appointment as press secretary signalled more than just careful attention to the way in which the PMO shaped communications with Quebec. It also presaged a sea change in the way the PMO handled the media in general. This change was

Roméo with his son, Dominic, age one month, January 1968

partly due to the realization throughout the English-speaking world that television was more than just radio with pictures, that it was capable of influencing public opinion in a very different way than either print or audio communication did. This impact was brought home to the PMO through an incident very much like others over the previous five years when the Liberals shot themselves in the foot: the mangled presentation of the budget, which, on the procedural motion for third reading, was defeated by two votes on February 19, 1968.[34] For journalist Anthony Westell, the way this defeat was dealt with was the moment when the Liberals discovered television. The defeat of Bill C-193 immediately led to a demand by the Opposition that the government resign, something that, as Westell underlined, was "echoed almost unanimously by the press." Pearson, Westell continued, "accepted that tactical advice of his press secretary, Romeo LeBlanc," to use the television networks "to put his arguments for a reprieve to the nation...The nation listened, and then sent its instructions in a flood of mail to the opposition: End the crisis so that the government [can] get on with the budget intended to shore up the dollar and hold its party leadership convention."[35] Whether it was public pressure on the politicians or negotiations between two men (the newly elected leader of the Conservatives, Robert Stanfield, and Prime Minister Pearson) that actually ended the matter is debatable. It is certain that the opinion of Eugene Forsey carried considerable weight. According to Gérard Pelletier, who talked to him on the telephone during this period, Forsey was "hauled out of bed for a rush consultation...[and] put his fantastic memory to work and quoted I don't know how many similar occasions, British and Canadian precedents, with dates and places, and concluded in the same breath: 'If the government thinks it must resign for a little blunder like this, it must be out of its mind.'"[36] It soon became clear that having someone with a long track record as a radio and television reporter made the strategists in the PMO much more aware of the way television could inform the public.

When Trudeau decided to run for the leadership of the Liberal Party, he asked Marc Lalonde and Roméo to remain in the PMO should he win.[37] Lalonde was one of those who had supported Trudeau's decision to run federally in 1965 and had no hesitation in agreeing. Roméo's assent took minimally longer, and it was the excitement of Trudeau's plans for constitutional renewal, rather than his vision of the character of Canadian society, that finally persuaded him. Trudeau's ideal of a "Just Society," something that sprang from his strong belief in the law as a major determinant of the political health of the state, was not as compelling for Roméo as Pearson's commitment to the provision of a "safety net" for the frail in society. The Liberal convention chose

Trudeau over Robert Winters by 1,203 votes to 954. The sheer excitement of the election that followed, called on April 23 for June 25, decided Roméo, wholeheartedly but not uncritically, to work for the new prime minister. In many ways, as John Duffy pointed out, it was the Diefenbaker election of 1958, but this time a made-for-TV version with Trudeau "greeted like a rock star with screaming girls...straining to touch his sport coat."[38] Roméo vividly remembered one occasion in Toronto when he and Trudeau found themselves on the shaky roof of a garden shed, where they had jumped to escape the press of the crowd. Trudeau wrote in his memoirs, "Everybody came in droves to rallies where I was speaking...In Montreal, where the nationalist intelligentsia was already trying to make me into 'the traitor of Quebec'...the huge area of Place Ville Marie was swarming with people."[39] As Gordon Robertson pointed out, it was not just a hugely popular campaign and a reasonable political program that swept Trudeau to power, it was also his personal courage on the eve of the election when demonstrators threw rocks and bottles at him and other dignitaries as they stood watching the St. Jean Baptiste Day parade in Montreal.[40] Most of the other notables fled, but Trudeau did not. He later wrote, "As a democrat, I will never accept that a small group of agitators can make someone invited by the majority take to his heels by throwing a few stones at him."[41] When the votes were counted, the Liberals won 155 seats; the Tories, 72; the NDP, 22; and Social Credit, 14.[42]

Immediately after the election, Trudeau's priorities were appointing his Cabinet and deciding the agenda for his government. This transition allowed Roméo and his family time for a few weeks of holiday in New Brunswick. They rented a ramshackle cottage that had been built on the coast between Shediac and Cocagne, on a small spit of land in the parish of Grande-Digue. Originally built as a summer house for some nuns from Montreal, it was surrounded on three sides by the sea. It consisted of one large room, with a kitchen on the north side and a chapel attached to the south side. There were no additional rooms on the west side, but on the east side there was a bathroom and a series of little bedrooms. The fact that it was outside any village, just part of a straggle of houses built at intervals along the coast road, relatively isolated, with a small woodlot and an unencumbered view of the sea, made it a beautiful property. The next year they purchased it and, over the coming years, would slowly transform it, at first into a summer home, then into a year-round dwelling. Since the building rested on the skimpiest of foundations, its transformation meant digging out a basement, as well as rewiring, replumbing, and, above all, adding effective insulation. It quickly became a beloved refuge from Ottawa life for the LeBlanc family.

A return to life in Ottawa at the end of summer meant a return to regular work with the new prime minister, a very different man from his predecessor, one whom Roméo knew only slightly. They first met in 1949 as part of the group befriended by the Cadieuxs and Pelletiers, but after that they had little more than a passing acquaintance. Roméo was the younger by eight years, which made for a more significant difference then than it did in 1968, when Roméo was forty-one and Trudeau was forty-nine. The disparity in background and life experience also needed to be bridged. During the last months of 1968 and the beginning of 1969, there were times when Roméo's advice to the prime minister on how to handle journalists demanding information about his private life was not well received. Trudeau chafed at the interest of the press, and took unkindly to suggestions that he should be more discreet. On the more important level of the business of government, however, there was little or no conflict between the two men. In common with most press secretaries to prime ministers, Roméo considered his first responsibility was always to the prime minister. The personality differences between Pearson and

Trudeau were largely responsible, in the opinion of journalists, for Roméo being less open after 1968. The affable, suave, and experienced diplomat Pearson allowed his press secretary a freedom of comment that his successor did not. As well, Pearson's own contacts with the media were less abrasive than those of Trudeau.

Trudeau decided, even before taking office, on two matters which needed immediate action: one administrative, the other legislative. In his memoirs, he wrote that one of the first things to be done was to "review the way government itself was run."[43] The reorganization that took place between the summer of 1968 and the spring of 1969 did not involve Roméo in the doing, but it did demand that he learn where the new paths of communication within the government ran. Looking back on what changed, Gordon Robertson believed that the alterations were significant, in terms of the "fundamental discipline [necessary] for the coherence of the government," but he thought that ministers' freedom for the policies of their own departments was diminished.[44] The changes undoubtedly helped the passage of that most significant piece of legislation the following year, the *Official Languages Act*, assented to on June 9, 1969. Pearson began plans to deliver such legislation in 1966.[45] Trudeau wrote, "Within weeks of the federal election, I formed a work group that was to draw up, following the general outlines provided by me, a text that would eventually become the Official Languages Act and produce a veritable revolution within the public service in Ottawa."[46] In the words of Robertson, who as Clerk of the Privy Council had much to do with the actual wording of the legislation, "the objective of the policy was to make it possible for more Canadians to use and be served in their own language."[47] It passed with far less overt opposition in Parliament than the establishment of the Canadian flag had aroused, but there was certainly much subsequent bitter and long-lasting debate on the matter throughout Canada, especially in Quebec. There were a number of reasons for the relatively calm reaction in the House of Commons. The Liberals had a majority, and the measure was supported by the leader of the Opposition, Robert Stanfield. Another reason was the organization of its presentation to the public. Roméo and his staff not only coordinated the prime minister's contacts with all branches of the media on the subject, but also helped oversee the public statements to the general public about the legislation by individual Cabinet ministers. Many of those who worked hard for its passage—Jean Marchand, Paul Martin, Sr., Gérard Pelletier, Gordon Robertson, and Mitchell Sharp, to name but a few—all wrote in their autobiographies that Trudeau deserved credit for using every means at his disposal to see that the bill became law. In their view, without his determined leadership, the legislation would not have come to pass.

Being prime minister means there are always a host of issues that need action, the importance of which are as great as those the leader has set as his priority. It took some time for Trudeau to understand that, for the prime minister, Canada's foreign relations were one such set of issues. It took considerable argument from Gordon Robertson and other senior officials to persuade him to attend the Commonwealth Conference in London in January 1969. Trudeau needed almost as much persuasion to acknowledge the unquestionable importance of Canadian–American relations and to agree to a three-day visit to Washington, from February 28 to March 2, 1969, accompanied by Roméo. Trudeau's main interest in foreign affairs at this time was the attitude of France to Canada, with a close second being the politics of the Third World. Roméo received a warm welcome from former colleagues in the capital, but Trudeau was less enthusiastically received. Since this visit was the first by a major foreign leader to President Richard Nixon, Trudeau was nevertheless treated with appropriate ceremony.

Canada's lack of wholehearted commitment to American action in Vietnam, which had been unequivocally expressed by Pearson, was resented by the Americans. Trudeau himself was seen as an unreliable ally.

Most of 1969 and the spring of 1970 was taken up, for both Trudeau and Roméo, with the daily routine of governing Canada. Roméo's papers include twelve spiral notebooks that contain a partial record of his daily routine between September 1967 and May 1970. Roméo was not the tidiest record-keeper and these notebooks are mostly scribbles to himself about what he needed to do in the upcoming days. They are supplemented by a haphazard collection of memos, to and from the prime minister and from other members of the PMO, many of them from Lalonde. Their substance is the stuff of daily chores, interviews to be arranged for the prime minister, meetings Roméo had to attend with other ministers, relations with various members of the press and media outlets, comments on topics raised in interviews, and letters from the general public that the prime minister wished to answer. The most important part of the week was the meeting, usually on Monday mornings, with the prime minister, Marc Lalonde, and either the clerk of the Privy Council or, more usually at this period, the deputy clerk, Marshall Crowe. Recalling the meetings of this group that he attended between 1969 and the end of 1970, Crowe said that there was an established pattern to the conversations: Trudeau summed up the matters he considered needed attention; Marc Lalonde gave his opinion and ideas as Trudeau's senior political adviser; Marshall brought forward the ideas of the Privy Council—and his own. At this point, Trudeau would turn to Roméo and ask, usually in French, "And what do you think we should do?" Marshall said that Trudeau, who wanted advice on what should actually be done that day and that week, always paid considerable attention to what Roméo recommended.[48] Looking back at this period of

At the White House in 1969 with Trudeau (left) and Nixon (centre);
Roméo bottom right

his life, Roméo remembered, above all, how hard people worked
and the insight it gave him into the machinery of government.

There were short breaks from work and, in the summer of
1969, Roméo and Lyn went again to the sea, to the cottage that
was now their own, in Caissie Cape, the official name for the
area of the Grande-Digue parish where it was actually located.
This summer was very important for Roméo, not only because it
meant time with Lyn and Dominic, but also because it provided
opportunities to strengthen his links with his siblings and their
families who remained in the Memramcook Valley. Further, it
came at a time when Roméo was thinking about the direction he
wanted his professional life to go. He had come to Ottawa two
years earlier, clearly intending the move to be only a pause in his
work as journalist. However, by the end of 1968, it had become
obvious to him that returning full-time to that work would be
difficult. Marriage and fatherhood, in particular, made Roméo
realize the benefits of a life with less travelling. He found family

life a great pleasure. The idea of taking up teaching once more, with an appointment at the Université de Moncton, was something he began to consider. As for credentials, he had taught courses at the Teachers' College in Fredericton, and they were accepted for credit by the University of New Brunswick. He had also completed the residency requirements for a doctorate from the Sorbonne.

These summer weeks also gave him the opportunity to meet friends and discuss what Acadian politics and society had become by the end of the 1960s. It was not only Acadian society that had developed during the years he had worked outside the province; it was the province as a whole, anglophone and francophone, which had undergone something akin to the "Quiet Revolution" in Quebec. This development was due in large measure to Louis Robichaud, who became premier of the province in 1960 and initiated extraordinary political and social changes that benefited New Brunswickers in general. These changes drew the Acadians into the public life of the province. Roméo had left New Brunswick the year before Robichaud came to power, but he kept himself well-informed about the reforms Robichaud implemented. What Roméo learned during his summer vacations were the details of the struggle there had been to achieve the changes, a struggle not only between some anglophones and Acadians, but also within the ethnic enclaves. New Brunswick's problems were exacerbated by the fact that it was, and is even today, Canada's most rural province, with 73,437 square kilometres of territory stretching from the Baie-des-Chaleurs to the Bay of Fundy. In 1960, its sparsely distributed population was under 600,000. Further, Acadians who were centred in Madawaska and the north of the province, those of the "péninsule Acadienne"— Caraquet and Leméac—and those around Moncton no more agreed with one another about politics than did the English-speaking inhabitants of Woodstock, Fredericton, and Saint John. Moreover, the fighting within and between the Liberal and Conservative parties crossed ethnic and religious lines.

Robichaud began as he meant to continue. In his first months in government, he established the Byrne Commission, whose work transformed the county council form of government and made the provincial government the central authority, responsible for education, hospital services, and the administration of justice. As Arthur Doyle has pointed out, Robichaud left "a modern network of public schools and hospitals across the province, in depressed as well as prosperous counties, and a reformed, and more equitable, system of taxation for financing those services."[49] Robichaud's reforms meant scarce tax resources were more equitably distributed, and New Brunswick was given structures to cope with twentieth-century challenges. The establishment of the Université de Moncton in 1963[50] and the passage of the *Official Languages Act* of New Brunswick,[51] generated the strongest opposition to the premier. The first came about as a direct result of the Royal Commission on the Status of Higher Education in New Brunswick, which was established on May 6, 1961, with John Deutsch as Chair. The commission's report was published the following year. It recommended, without mincing words, the need to establish a post-secondary French-language institution, which would bring together the scattered resources of the three small existing colleges—Sacré-Coeur in Bathurst, Saint-Louis in Edmundston, and St. Joseph's in Memramcook— an institution that was able to compete on equal footing with the University of New Brunswick and Mount Allison University. The creation of the Université de Moncton brought forth not so much a chorus as an opera of criticism. There was fierce opposition from some faculty and staff of the francophone colleges, as well as from the faculty and administration of the University of New Brunswick, who considered that UNB had been, and would continue to be, perfectly capable of providing the necessary access to post-secondary education for Acadians.[52] Nor, as Roméo learned, had much of this debate diminished over the past six years. As to reaction over the official-languages legislation, whether at the federal or provincial level, opposition continued to be strong and the debate remained heated throughout the summer of 1969 across the province. Returning to New Brunswick brought Roméo face to face with a province digesting great social changes.

Meanwhile, Ottawa in the fall of 1969 was a return to the familiar, but equally drastic changes were in process—though the work was at the direction of others. As a journalist, Roméo had achieved considerable independence. As a member of the PMO, he had little control over which matters were granted priority. He offered advice, which was often but not always heeded. He interpreted, but did not originate, policies. At the beginning of 1970, he was openly considering the people he might recommend to replace him. Oddly enough, it was accompanying Trudeau on a tour of the Pacific in the spring of 1970 that made Roméo begin to consider in earnest his next possible employment. The lure of foreign travel was always a siren call, but he disliked the separation from his family, and the trip itself was exhausting. Gordon Robertson included an account of this extensive visit in his memoirs.[53] The itinerary included New Zealand, Australia, Singapore, Malaysia, Hong Kong, and Japan. It began badly with the New Zealand prime minister comparing Canada and his own country, asserting, "We have our Maoris and you, Prime Minister, have your French Canadians."[54] In Australia, Trudeau frightened his hosts by snorkel-diving at the Great Barrier Reef just after one of their politicians had died from a shark attack. Remembering the trip later, Ed Higginson, who was there as cameraman for the CBC, recalled the way Trudeau would "escape" from his officials and worry his entourage about where he was and with whom. Robertson summed up the tour by commenting that the idea of a "Team Canada" had not yet emerged. At the end of the 1960s, Canada's interest in the countries visited was not particularly intense.

The LeBlanc family once more summered in New Brunswick, and Roméo talked with Adélard Savoie, the president of Université de Moncton, about the possibility of a teaching appointment there in the fall of 1971, but the atmosphere in Ottawa in September 1970, when the LeBlancs returned, relegated such thoughts to the background. The relationship between Quebec and Ottawa had not improved since the spring. The provincial election, which had taken place on April 29, elected the Liberal Party and Robert Bourassa, who had been chosen as its leader in January. At first sight, this result seemed an overwhelming vote of confidence for Bourassa; he won 72 of 108 seats, with 45.4 per cent of the popular vote. But, as Jacques Parizeau commented, the Parti Québécois, which had only seven seats, garnered 23 per cent of the popular vote, such a result casting doubt on the claim that the province was a true democracy.[55] The aftermath was a summer of discontent, above all in Montreal, where Mayor Drapeau faced an election in late October. He warned of terrorism, and was taken for an electioneering alarmist.

As John English wrote,

> *Bombs punctuated the Montreal summer of 1970, and the FLQ calls for revolutionary action appeared on signposts...Rumours of kidnappings, theft of weapons and dynamite and declaration of revolutionary solidarity abounded. The Confederation of National Trade Unions (CNTU), which Marchand had led and for which Trudeau had acted as legal counsel, regularly paid the bail for the release of FLQ members, including Pierre Vallières, who used the occasion to call for a Cuban-style revolution.*[56]

On Monday, October 5, James Cross, the British trade commissioner in Montreal, was kidnapped by members of the Front de Libération du Québec. The kidnappers presented a variety of demands, the most significant of which came in their *Manifesto*: the release of twenty-three "political prisoners" from jail—all of whom had been found guilty of, or were awaiting trial for, violent crimes—$500,000, an end to police raids, and transportation for themselves to either Algeria or Cuba.[57] On Wednesday, October 7, the *Manifesto* was read over the local radio station CKAC. The following day it was read on Radio-Canada. On Saturday, October 10, a second FLQ group kidnapped Pierre Laporte, a former journalist and the popular minister of immigration and labour in the provincial government. On Friday, October 16, at the request of the Quebec government, the *War Measures Act* was proclaimed. On Saturday, October 17, Pierre Laporte was murdered. On December 3, Cross and his captors were discovered and Cross liberated. On that day, the flight to Cuba for the FLQ members already in jail was expedited by joint action of the federal and provincial governments. On December 27, Paul Rose, Jacques Rose, and Francis Simard, who were involved in the murder of Laporte, were captured, and they would be brought to trial in 1971.[58] On February 1, 1971, the federal justice minister announced that, of the 497 people who were temporarily jailed under the *War Measures Act*, 435 had been released, and 62 were charged, 32 of whom were being held without bail. The population of Montreal, at the time, was just over a million.

Roméo's account of his experiences during the crisis, from the vantage point of the PMO, reflected reactions similar to those that Pierre Trudeau, Gérard Pelletier, and Mitchell Sharp recorded in their memoirs: the general sense of disbelief that such happenings were taking place in Canada; the consensus in Ottawa that law and order should be preserved in Quebec; the determination to secure the release of James Cross, and with no concessions made to the blackmailers.[59] One of Roméo's tasks was to read, summarize, and draft replies to the flood of correspondence that arrived at the PMO during this period. As a result, he was strongly aware of the extent to which people in Montreal were appalled by events, especially by the support that students had shown the FLQ before Laporte was kidnapped. He was also aware of the way public opinion favoured the federal government after the imposition of the *War Measures Act*, which, it is generally admitted, put an end to the rising hysteria in Quebec and, more importantly, brought an end to violence against the legally constituted authorities.[60] The difference between revolutionary violence under a dictatorship and in a democracy was made clear. Roméo recalled the care with which Trudeau and Pelletier distinguished between Lévesque and the Quebec sovereigntist movement and the FLQ. Along with many others, Roméo believed that the events and consequences of October 1970 marked a defining moment in Canadian history, both for the internal politics of Quebec and for the country in general.

In personal terms, the "October Crisis" exhausted Roméo and confirmed his decision to return to New Brunswick in the summer of 1971. It was his intention to take up a teaching position at the Université de Moncton, which he saw as a return to his former teaching career. Instead, it led him directly into the life of a federal member of Parliament.

CHAPTER 7

From Backbencher to Minister

Neither Roméo nor Trudeau considered that he would remain permanently in the Prime Minister's Office. One of the terms of his appointment was that he would participate in the search for his successor. In the summer of 1970, he, along with Lalonde and the prime minister, had interviewed Peter Roberts, who was attached to External Affairs and worked with the Canadian delegation to NATO.[1] Roberts agreed to join the PMO as assistant press secretary, on the understanding that he was in line to succeed Roméo in the near future. By the time he left in July 1971, Roméo was exhausted. To return to New Brunswick with his family, to immerse himself in a society that he knew and where he was known, was to give himself much needed time and space for recollection. Throughout his life, southeastern New Brunswick was the place Roméo considered home. Its people, Acadian and anglophone, farmers and fishermen, businessmen and school teachers, poets and painters and politicians, were the people with whom he felt most comfortable. As Lalonde later remarked,

Roméo was much more at home with fishermen and farmers than in social gatherings in large cities.

On August 12, the Université de Moncton announced that Roméo had been appointed special assistant to President Adélard Savoie, and director of public relations for the institution. In an interview with the *Moncton Transcipt* the next day, Roméo remarked that he was "about to go through a period of 'decompression.'"[2] He said that he knew people identified him with the prime minister and considered that his views were a reflection of Trudeau's. He needed time away from public life, but he thought he had acquired "a knowledge of the political process, how the system works; something" he acknowledged that he would "retain for a long time."[3]

Both at the time and later, many people believed Roméo left Ottawa with a firm intention of standing for the federal Parliament in the next election. But, both at the time and later, Roméo consistently denied that this was so.[4] Throughout his life, he often referred to the years he spent teaching in Drummond (1951–1953) and at the Normal School (1955–1959) as the most productive of his life. In 1971, he had expected to be given the opportunity to teach at the Université de Moncton. It did not, however, happen. He never commented on what prevented it, except to insist, in later interviews, that he had been told that it would happen, that he had expected to teach, but that the faculty operated a "closed shop." Forty years later, it seems that a major reason for the opposition of the faculty was the imposition on the political science department, by the president, of someone, even part-time, who had not gone through the process of competing for an advertised position. There is probably some truth in this answer. Forty years ago, university faculty at many institutions began working towards more rigorous administrative control over academic decisions. By the end of the 1970s, a significant number of Canadian universities had established faculty unions

Roméo and Trudeau at the First Ministers' Conference, 1978

and enforced the idea that academic appointments were to be made with the express consent of those already on faculty.

Had there been people on the faculty willing to argue his case, it is highly likely that Roméo would have been accepted. There was, however, another factor at play in Roméo's life in 1971. He was, after all, not returning to New Brunswick as a "prodigal son," greeted with joy that he was alive and asking for sustenance from his father's house. He was returning as someone who had been successful "away." He had pursued further education not at Laval but at the Sorbonne; he had been a foreign correspondent for Radio-Canada not in Paris but in London and Washington; and he had worked not in Quebec and Montreal but in Ottawa. His political, social, and academic credentials were not those commonly offered. There were a number of faculty who considered Roméo a dangerous outsider, someone neither properly "français de France" nor a Quebec nationalist, but a jumped-up Acadian.[5] He would have to prove to many people that he was still an Acadian at heart, and that what he had achieved was of value. His decision to stand as a candidate for the federal Liberal Party in 1972 was not the result of a long-term ambition for a political career, but rather the result of a combination of factors. First, as the academic year ended, he realized that he did not want to be part of the university without teaching responsibilities. Next was the knowledge that he was no longer young, and he had a wife and growing family to support (by now Dominic was almost five, and his daughter, Geneviève, would be born on December 6 that year). Finally, there was the fact that, before he left Ottawa, Trudeau suggested to him that he consider standing for Parliament, and an opportunity to run opened in the local constituency of Westmorland-Kent.

Roméo's attachment to the Liberal Party came partly because of his family, partly from friendships, and mostly from a philosophical bent. His family had never been particularly involved in federal politics, but his father, Philéas, had worked as a stable hand for Henry Read Emmerson, the local Liberal MP. Sometime after 1936, it was Emmerson who recommended Philéas for a position with the CNR at the station at Memramcook, assistance that inclined the LeBlanc family towards the Liberals. In those days, as Roméo later remarked, political influence in local employment openings was common. The family's Liberal tendency was reinforced by the friendships he made in 1949 with Fernand Cadieux and Gérard Pelletier. These men introduced Roméo to the ideas of federal Liberals in Quebec. Admiration for Mike Pearson, which began in Roméo's early years as a parliamentary correspondent in Ottawa, developed into a genuine friendship, after he had served as Pearson's press secretary. As for political ideology, when Roméo taught at the Normal School, he came across the writings of Mackenzie King. In later years, Roméo referred to King as someone who shaped whatever formal ideas about political philosophy he possessed. For Roméo,

King's policies gave Canada important reform during his years as prime minister, from a preliminary form of old-age pensions to unemployment insurance and family allowances.[6]

Roméo's decision to run as a Liberal was simple enough, and he later described his political beliefs as clear "but not partisan." His decision to run in 1972 was equally uncomplicated. He was one of those, along with Monique Bégin and Marc Lalonde, whom Trudeau encouraged to stand for election in that year. The decision of Guy Crossman, the Liberal MP who had held the riding of Westmorland-Kent since 1963, not to run in the 1972 election opened the way for Roméo's candidacy in his home territory.[7] The riding itself had been brought together in 1966, and it would last as an entity until 1988, when it was replaced by the riding of Beauséjour. It was a large and diverse riding, though no more so than many other essentially rural constituencies. It ran 160 kilometres from the borders of Kent County in Saint-Louis-de-Kent to the Nova Scotia–New Brunswick border, the two ends tied together by a rough paved road winding through the small coastal villages. It excluded then, as later in its incarnation as Beauséjour, the city of Moncton. The total population of the riding in 1972 was roughly 55,000.[8] The parishes in Kent County were, in the 1970s, primarily but not exclusively French-speaking. Part of the constituency also included three Mi'kmaq communities, two close to Richibucto— Big Cove–Elsipogtog and Indian Island–L'nui Menikuk—and the other at Bouctouche–Puktusk. In Westmorland there was also a First Nations community near Dorchester, Fort Folly–Amlamkuk.[9] The parishes in Westmorland, closer to the Nova Scotia border, tended to have a greater number of English-speaking inhabitants, but this division is no more than an indication of the complicated linguistic mix in the riding. Roméo's command of French and English and his deep appreciation of their different linguistic strengths proved immensely valuable. He could switch easily from one to the other in mid-sentence.

Much more important in 1972 than language differences was the unifying force of the local economy. Kent County was classified in the 1960s as "the poorest county" in Canada,"[10] although there were places elsewhere that disputed the claim. Bertin LeBlanc, who managed Roméo's first campaign,[11] described the riding as one that relied to a considerable extent on the social reforms that had been introduced in the 1960s by the provincial government, when Robichaud was premier. Bertin acknowledged that the changes to the *Unemployment Insurance Act*, which the Trudeau government had passed, also helped. There was some farming, mostly subsistence, and most families had small plots where they grew their own vegetables (onions, potatoes, corn, lettuce, and tomatoes). Only around Sackville on the Tantramar Marshes was there any successful commercial farming. There was work for men in the woods as loggers, and some work in the construction industry. Above all, there was work in the fishing industry. "The women along the coast worked in the processing plants," Bertin wrote, "and fishermen worked at odd jobs outside the fishing season to help financially. Poor yes," he observed, "but in general not necessarily desperate."[12] In the villages that lay a few kilometres inland, there were families who knew harder times during the winter months. Nevertheless, there were also pockets of relative prosperity, especially in Westmorland County, where, although the fishing industry was still the major source of employment, the sale of local produce in neighbouring towns helped support the farmers.

Once Roméo agreed to run, he faced a nominating convention. His opponent was also named Roméo LeBlanc—Roméo Joseph LeBlanc—whereas the Roméo LeBlanc whose career we are following was Roméo Adrien LeBlanc. Roméo J. was a teacher, and had been active in a number of local volunteer organizations. He was a volunteer member of the board of directors of the Commission d'Aménagement Regional du Sud-Est, an organization that took fairly militant positions on the social problems in the area. Just to muddy the waters further, two of Roméo's most important helpers were also LeBlancs. Roméo remembered the convention as well-fought. It was a "delegate" convention, which is to say that the local communities across the riding sent delegates to the convention, usually four or five, and it was their votes that decided who the candidate would be. Roméo's opponent had considerably more grassroots support throughout the riding. When Roméo entered the race, he and Lyn lived in Moncton, at 146 Church Street. Moncton was not part of the riding, though his cottage in Grande-Digue was. His first task was to make himself known to possible supporters, which he did through what he called "kitchen meetings," evenings spent in the homes of men he thought would be attending the nomination convention.[13] He tended to turn up in a shirt and tie, much more formally dressed than his opponent, but his ability to listen well to people quickly became apparent. In such meetings, Roméo recalled, one learned a great deal about how people managed their lives. He more or less ignored the established power-brokers, such as the owners of fish-processing plants, who controlled access to the buildings on the wharves. He talked with those whom he considered were respected by the men in their villages. At the convention itself, he paid more attention to party workers than to the local directors of the Liberal Association, who drifted to his opponent. It was a tactic, however, that paid off. Roméo Adrien LeBlanc won the nomination with 60 per cent of the votes.[14]

Roméo realized, as he worked to win the nomination, that the local Liberal Association was due for an overhaul. He did not directly challenge those who ran it. On the same day he won the nomination, however, he renewed the board of directors, because many of those who voted for his opponent decided not to re-offer their services. It meant the loss of some of the most active fundraisers. But, as Bertin LeBlanc noted, in 1972 the federal election in Westmorland-Kent was not an expensive proposition.[15] There were no radio or television advertisements, but rather a few posters and a leaflet that went to every house. Roméo's campaign was helped by money from the provincial Liberal Association. He decided then and there that he would not accept any donation over $100, and was known to personally return cheques for larger amounts. Bertin remembers that the most common contribution was $20. Campaigning the length and breadth of the riding was exhausting. Roméo worked as hard as he had for nomination. Once more, he found the people in the villages who stood well in their own communities. Bertin found it almost impossible to get him to meetings of businessmen, such as plant owners or those who considered themselves important in the lumbering or construction industries. Roméo preferred to meet these men individually, not in arranged dinners or groups. But tell him there were forty fishermen on the wharf at St. Edouard-de-Kent who wanted to talk to him, and he was there. Given the nature of the constituency, one of Roméo's difficulties was that he aroused more enthusiasm than Trudeau. There was an undercurrent of support for the Conservative leader Robert Stanfield, whose lifestyle was more understandable to the average Acadian than was Trudeau's. Roméo believed that working people were the ones who had the most pressing problems, problems he could help solve. He also understood that these were also the people who worked the polling stations on election day and got people out to vote.

The polling stations were, and still are, vitally important in rural ridings, especially where the population is clustered in small villages. They are the federally designated voting centres. It was the custom for the parties to appoint scrutineers for each polling station. Scrutineers were party representatives who supervised voting procedures and witnessed the votes being counted when the polls closed. In 1972, scrutineers received $10 or so for their work. These positions were much valued, and people complained by letter to Roméo if they were not retained in the following election. Every poll also had one or two cars used to drive those who needed transportation to and from the polls. There was a stipend from the party to the volunteers who performed this service, to pay gasoline and meal costs. Each poll had a "poll captain" to see that the day went smoothly. Captains knew their neighbours, and their influence was considerable. It was from among the poll captains that the members of the riding associations were elected. In 1972, Roméo's election campaign cost something over $12,000, with election-day costs just over $7,000. Monique Bégin remembered that her first election campaign cost $35,000, which she raised herself.[16] On October 30, 1972, of 26,339 votes cast, 14,747 were for Roméo, 55.99 per cent of the total. This was 3,228 more votes than Crossman had received in 1968. Recalling the event, Yvon LeBlanc, who supported Roméo from the outset, remembered that, although Roméo did well among the Acadian voters, there were many anglophones in Westmorland County who also voted for him and whose support in this election was crucial. The country as a whole gave Trudeau and the Liberals 109 seats, the Progressive Conservatives won 107 seats, the New Democratic Party won 31 seats, and Social Credit won 15 seats. Roch LaSalle left the Progressive Conservative Party and ran and won his seat as an Independent. The Liberals formed the government over the next two years, in an alliance with the NDP.

Victory for Roméo brought not only celebration, but also a whole set of domestic issues that needed resolution. At the time of the election, Lyn was eight months' pregnant with their second child. She was settled happily in Moncton. Dominic was enrolled in the local Montessori school, and she enjoyed meeting the parents of other children attending classes there. Irène, Roméo's eldest sister, lived three blocks away, and Lyn found her a supportive friend. As well, Pauline Richard, a young Acadian woman from near Bouctouche, had joined the household as live-in help and a companion. Now, new living arrangements had to be contemplated, which had to take into account not only what the family needed, but also the demands of Roméo's new life. Roméo had to be in Ottawa when Parliament was sitting and, at the same time, he needed to establish not only his political head-quarters in the riding, but also some form of residence there. He and Lyn decided that the family would be based in Moncton, at least until early spring of 1973. Lyn liked the obstetrician she had in Moncton, and she would have nearby a caring sister-in law who had herself borne three children. Dominic could continue at a school he liked. Further, Roméo would come home every weekend, and the house could be put on the market. At the same time, the cottage at Grande-Digue became their formal address. Finally, Roméo set about organizing his constituency headquarters in Shediac, more or less the mid-point between Saint-Louis-de-Kent and Port Elgin.

This arrangement was no more complicated than that of most MPs whose ridings were outside Ottawa. It worked for Roméo during his first year as a MP, because, as he said in a later inter-view, he considered that the first duty of a member of Parliament was to his constituents and, for that, one needed to understand everyday life in the riding. It was a belief that led him to refuse the prime minister's offer of a position as a parliamentary secre-tary, which did not confer Cabinet rank, but was akin to being assistant to a senior Cabinet minister, and was probably the pathway to a Cabinet position. Such a refusal by a newly hatched backbencher was almost unheard of. Of course, Roméo came with more advantages than most first-time MPs. As he remarked in the *Moncton Transcript* interview, he knew a great deal about the way things worked in Ottawa, and he already had more than a casual acquaintance with the prime minister. There was not

much more to learn about the federal Liberal Party establishment, given his friendship with Marc Lalonde and others. What
he did need to do in 1972 was gain an accurate and intimate
knowledge of the politics of New Brunswick in general and how
life was lived in Westmorland County in particular. He had no
intention of being a one-term MP. To achieve re-election he
needed the solid support of his riding. He was fortunate that
Bertin LeBlanc stayed to manage affairs in the riding and quickly
became accustomed to what Roméo considered important in
coping with constituency issues.

Roméo's year at the Université de Moncton had introduced
him to the Acadia of the 1970s, after the defeat of Robichaud
by Richard Hatfield in the 1970 provincial election and after the
October Crisis. It was a much more complex Acadian world than
the one Roméo left in 1959. Then, the province had been on the
verge of a revolution that made it the first and—so far, even in
the 1970s—the only officially bilingual province in Canada. He
returned to find that many young Acadians were convinced that
the revolution had not gone far enough, and many anglophones
were convinced it had gone too far. When he had left, Acadian
political leadership had, as the historian John Reid has pointed
out, "been asserted by a middle class élite...that had striven for
reform by presenting Acadians as a hard-working, responsible
population who wished only for full participation in every facet
of provincial life."[17] While still a matter of the middle class,
Acadian politics were now important to radical students at the
Université de Moncton and its affiliated Collège de Bathurst, as
well as to the working poor in the lumber and fishing industries.
The political blindness of Leonard Jones who was Moncton's
mayor between 1963 and 1974, who refused to allow French to
be used in city business in a city one-third francophone, coupled
with the separatist movement in Quebec, led to the development of a radical nationalist stand by a number of the students

at the francophone university.[18] Their fervour might have dissipated quickly had it not been joined by the voices of the poor themselves, telling stories of the hardships they endured. Federal and provincial inquiries about poverty led to interviews at the grassroots level, particularly by the Senate Committee on Poverty. This committee was established in 1968[19] and published its report in October 1970. That same year, the "Task Force on Social Development and Social Welfare" had been set up by Robichaud.[20]

It was in the north-shore region of New Brunswick, especially in the Tracadie–Caraquet area, that destitution roused the most articulate public anger. One woman's outrage resonated throughout New Brunswick Acadian fishing villages. At a public meeting in Bathurst on January 16, 1972, attended by Jean Marchand, the federal minister of regional economic expansion, and Premier Richard Hatfield, Mathilda Blanchard accused the federal government of never doing anything other than "study and restudy the region, tell the people they were illiterate and then suggest they should move to urban areas."[21] She declared, "You've destroyed our forests! You've destroyed our oyster beds! You've ruined our farms with your property taxes! You've ruined our education system and reduced our unemployment insurance to zero by moving everything to Moncton. But we're not moving!"[22] It did not matter, as Richard Wilbur pointed out, that she "ignored such distinctions as private and public or federal and provincial jurisdictions."[23] What Madame Blanchard said was what many Acadians believed in 1972. On February 6, barely three weeks later, the formation of the Parti Acadien was announced. Acadians were "a hardworking sober people," but they were people, not cardboard puppets, and they were every bit as intelligent as people elsewhere.

Neither Madame Blanchard's anger nor the arrival of a new political party on the New Brunswick scene surprised Roméo.

Acadians in New Brunswick had a clear idea of the most memorable events of their history: their Deportation from lands they had lived on for four or five generations and their resettlement two generations later in the same region but not on ancestral lands. That resettlement had been less than five generations ago. This history was told and retold in schools and in homes by parents who said things like, "My father was Jean à Robert à Charles à Charles, and *his* father lived the exile and returned."[24] From this heritage, Roméo and all those of similar experience drew the knowledge that they were indeed a "people," with their own history, and not a simply a group derived from Quebec or France. By 1972, Acadian academics such as Muriel Roy were writing and publishing works on their own communities. Poets such as Herménégilde Chiasson were reflecting the lives of their own communities.[25] The novels of Antonine Maillet, especially *La Sagouine,* published in 1971, strikingly represented what life in poverty in a small Acadian fishing village meant during the 1940s and 1950s. Its performance as a monologue by the actress Viola Léger was a success not only in francophone, but also in anglophone Canada.[26] Whatever their economic or political situation might be, by the 1970s Acadians held a conviction that one forced exile was enough! The Acadians in the fishing villages that were the backbone of Roméo's riding might not have much formal education, but they were well aware of the conditions of their lives and how they wanted to improve.

For more than twenty years, Roméo and the friends he made in his youth who had remained in New Brunswick and worked mostly in education, journalism, or the civil service, had written to one another.[27] Theirs was a generation for whom long-distance telephone calls were rare, costly, and usually the harbinger of bad news. Their long letters, as well as his visits home, kept Roméo abreast of local politics. It was this background that prompted him to say in his nomination address that what

Westmorland–Kent needed was employment that "used the talents and energy of our people where they live. The primary occupations of farming, the fisheries, lumbering and tourism must be maintained and developed."[28]

It was also this knowledge that made him concentrate, during his first two years as an MP, on learning about the lives of fishermen. People had been economically hard-pressed in the Memramcook Valley, but few encountered the difficulties of those who did not earn enough during the fishing season to cover their costs for the rest of the year. Most fishermen took loans from the fish-processing plants to tide them over the winter, money they had to pay back at the beginning of the new season. It was the Canadian equivalent of the American lament, "I owe my soul to the company store," and was responsible for much of the anger and frustration towards federal government policies that Roméo knew existed in the small fishing villages.

The LeBlancs re-established themselves in Ottawa in the summer of 1973, renting a house in Manor Park, close to Dominic's new school. Since the Liberals were a minority government, it was clear that another election would not be long in coming. Roméo felt confident enough of his own re-election, but it seemed reasonable to hold off buying another property in Ottawa. During the following months, Trudeau reorganized his office staff, carried through a legislative program much influenced by the New Democratic Party, and brought back Keith Davey to mastermind the campaign for the inevitable election, which took place on July 8, 1974. The prime minister also introduced a program of legislation that many considered economically unsound but politically shrewd. It included an *Election Expenses Act*, the establishment of the Foreign Investment Review Agency (FIRA), and a major effort by Marc Lalonde to systemize all federal programs aimed at helping the frail and disadvantaged, thereby providing more aid to the unemployed and the elderly, and supporting the health and

Roméo and Dominic, c. 1975

education of children. The government also passed a tax cut that benefited most Canadians. After OPEC raised oil prices in 1973, the government put in place a policy that sheltered Canadians from such increases. None of this happened without opposition in the House of Commons and from the provinces.[29] During most of this time, Roméo continued to concentrate on his riding more than on the wranglings of the House of Commons. But he also learned everything he could about the way the fisheries were being managed by the government departments whose policies affected the industry.

First and foremost, Roméo came to appreciate what he had always known: that, although of major importance, the Atlantic coast was only one part of Canada's exploitation of the rich resource of its oceans. The Pacific also had an important and a highly developed fishing industry. The fact that Jack Davis from Capilano, British Columbia, had replaced Hédard Robichaud, an Acadian from Gloucester County, New Brunswick, as minister of fisheries in August 1968, had made this fact extremely clear. During the years 1972 to 1974, Roméo also came to understand that Trudeau's wish to make the civil service a more efficient servant of government policy had a considerable impact on the management of the fisheries.[30] Davis began as minister of fisheries in 1968, but on April 1, 1969, his department became Fisheries and Forestry. Barely a year later, it absorbed the Marine Sciences Directorate, which had formerly been part of the Department of Energy, Mines, and Resources. On July 11, 1971, Davis found himself the first Canadian minister of the environment, bringing together forestry, fisheries, and environmental research and management.[31] During the next two years, his empire grew, as various other activities, such as the control of hundreds of fishing wharves, originally the business of the Department of Public Works, were brought under the umbrella of the Fisheries and Marine Services divisions of Environment Canada. This process culminated in 1973, when the Fisheries Research Board of Canada, which had been an independent agency, was taken over.[32] As Roméo watched the impact these changes had on the fishing industry, he became aware of the mixture of approval and concern they aroused. While many welcomed the closer connection between management and research, others found that many of those who held senior positions in the new ministry knew more about environmental matters, and cared considerably less about the fisheries. Trudeau let it be known, during the 1974 election campaign, that Jack Davis would likely not continue as the minister.[33]

Roméo and his campaign workers did not go into the 1974 election with the idea that he would be appointed to the Cabinet, and in a position that involved responsibility for the fisheries. If he considered it a possibility, it was not something he talked about at the time or later. He began preparations for his own re-election in February, with a lengthy interview with Louis-Marie Melanson, a reporter for the daily *L'Évangéline*.[34] At the beginning

Roméo as backbencher, 1973 (second from left, back row)

and conclusion of the interview, Roméo spoke of the uncertainties of minority government, not only the tension of never knowing precisely when an election might be called, but also the heavy workload that was spread among the smaller number of MPs. He commented on an average day's workload: committee meetings, telephone calls and correspondence, meetings with civil servants about problems in the constituency, and the necessity of being available to visitors from the constituency. There was the obligatory daily attendance in the House of Commons. In the 1970s, the House still continued its business in the evenings. There were caucus meetings, which, if less well known, "were crucial. It is there," he said, "that one can emphasize the views of those who elected us to ministers, before decisions are made." The inevitable pressure to work long hours had to be controlled. Unless an effort was made to be home for the evening meal, he remarked, it was difficult to see the children. "This is why," he explained, "to the extent that it is possible, I also try to take my six-year-old son, Dominic, with me to ceremonies where it is appropriate." Further, it was also necessary to find time to read.

Turning from generalities about an MP's life to specific matters of immediate relevance to his constituents, Roméo addressed three issues, the most thorny being the question of the national park at Kouchibouguac. The agreement between New Brunswick and the federal government to create the park had been signed in 1969. Before it could open, however, people whose homes were within its proposed boundaries had, as was customary at the time, to have their properties expropriated.[35] As Ronald Rudin, a professor of history at Concordia University, has pointed out, although "residents displaced in other instances left with little signs of resistance, such was not the case at Kouchibouguac, where periodic acts of civil disobedience prevented the formal opening of the park until 1979."[36] These acts were mainly sit-ins in government offices, but there was an edge of violence, with property damage to buildings and heavy machinery. It was clear by 1974 that neither the federal nor the provincial government was handling the payments to those forced out of their homes with much sensitivity. The emergence of Jackie Vautour as an articulate leader gave the dissatisfaction coherence.[37] Some 250 families had been evicted, more than a thousand people. Roméo observed in the interview with Melanson that one of the troubles with government was that "the urgent often pre-empted the important, as was the case with Kouchibouguac." He considered that, while the matter of compensation was indeed important, the immediate need was to find stable employment for those who had lost their land and to ensure that they would benefit from establishment of the park. He pointed out that one had to distinguish between what was a matter of provincial jurisdiction—the question of expropriation and compensation payable—and what fell into the federal orbit. He stated, "I leave the provincial government to play its appointed role. As for the federal government, this matter [the issue of fishing rights and compensation for their loss] is the one on which I have spent the majority of my time."

He was able to report a considerable measure of success for his efforts. He persuaded Jean Chrétien, who was then minister for Indian affairs and northern development with responsibility for Parks Canada, to appoint an arbitrator to consider the matter fully. On Roméo's advice, Chrétien appointed Camille-Antoine Richard, a sociologist who had been in the Sociology Department at the Université de Moncton during its most tumultuous days (1968–1971).[38] His name was suggested to Roméo by people who had lived in the park, and his task was to decide who deserved compensation and how much. His report was accepted. He recommended that compensation for those who had professional fishing licences be doubled. Roméo also obtained Chrétien's agreement to reconsider all cases that had proceeded to litigation and, again, emphasized the importance of finding employment for those dispossessed. Roméo reported that more than one hundred residents found jobs. Finally, he asked Chrétien to meet with Jackie Vautour, and the minister agreed. Roméo concluded by saying that he systematically refused to make statements that would make finding any solution more complicated, something he fully intended to continue to do.

Before concluding the interview with Melanson, Roméo commented on the success of the federal government's Local Initiatives Program in Westmorland-Kent. This program was set up in November 1971 to create additional jobs during the winter months and to encourage the participation and involvement of community groups and the unemployed, for the benefit of the whole community.[39] Roméo pointed out that requests from the constituency totalled $3 million, but only $500,000 had been granted. The money was distributed by a committee of nine people, drawn from the four corners of the constituency, and he felt their judgment, however much criticized, was better than the judgment of Ottawa bureaucrats. He also dealt with the rebuilding of Route 11. He stressed that what was important about it was its convenience and safety for those who used it twice daily. He wrapped up by reviewing other federal grants that had flowed into the riding, and ended by saying that, while the government was by no means perfect, he felt there was a general desire on its part to improve Canadian lives.

Roméo fought his 1974 campaign with the same people and much the same tactics that he had used previously. The parents of Jim Taylor, Roméo's friend and former colleague, were life-long Conservatives living in Port Elgin, but they became loyal voters for Roméo. It was not affection for the friend of their son, but, in common with others of similar political views, it was the impact Roméo had when he first met them on the campaign trail. Roméo listened and never gave the impression that there was someone more important he had to rush off to meet. He treated fishermen, lumbermen, and farmers with respect, and was honest when he could not give people the help requested. Basically, he canvassed on his record as a man who considered his constituents and tried to help. Once more, he talked with people he considered opinion leaders in the small villages. It became clear to Bertin LeBlanc during the campaign that there was a distinct

Campaigning in in his constituency, Westmorland–Kent, 1974

movement of votes towards the Liberals from Roméo's opponents. The campaign cost a little more than the one in 1972,
much of the expense being for poll scrutineers on election day.
Roméo's expenses were covered by many small donations and
some financial aid from the New Brunswick Liberal Party. When
the votes were tallied, Roméo increased his majority from 55.99
per cent of the votes cast in 1972 to 62.34 per cent, receiving
16,340 votes. The Conservative candidate had 6,490, the NDP
candidate had 2,104, and the Social Credit candidate had 617
votes. On July 8, the federal Liberals returned to power with a
solid majority of 141 seats to the Conservatives' 95, the NDP
obtaining only 16, and Réal Caouette's Social Credit 11. Just over

a month later, on August 12, Roméo was appointed a minister of state with responsibilities for fisheries in the Department of the Environment.

Minister of Fishermen

The impact of the 1974 election on Roméo's life, together with his appointment as a junior Cabinet minister, was both more and less severe than the changes that had taken place on his election to Parliament in 1972. It was more severe, in the sense that the intensity of his workload increased and included a great deal more travel, not only within Canada—to the Maritimes and the Pacific Coast—but also internationally. It was less disruptive, because the move, from a rental house in Manor Park to a house he and Lyn bought on Fourth Avenue in the Glebe, was much easier than being uprooted from Moncton to Ottawa. The new home was near friends, with schools for the children within walking distance. Dominic was six years old in December, and Geneviève two. Lyn settled into Ottawa life and renewed friendships made when Roméo had worked in the Prime Minister's Office. Among these connections was Margaret Trudeau who, in the most recent volume of her autobiography, referred to Lyn as witty, intelligent, and kind.[1] In many ways, their situations were comparable but not similar. Both were young wives with considerably older husbands: thirty years between Pierre and Margaret Trudeau and fifteen years between Roméo and Lyn. Both women had married men outside their own cultural background, but Lyn had been brought up a Catholic; Margaret converted on her marriage. Neither woman had much exposure to francophone culture before marriage. Both had young children. In 1974, Justin Trudeau was three and Alexandre (Sacha) was one. Michel Trudeau was born on October 17, 1975. Margaret had lived a more flamboyant youth than Lyn, who had spent more time in study. In both cases, the husbands cherished their children. On the whole, though, the political culture of Ottawa was alien to both women. Lyn was in a more fortunate situation than Margaret, in that she and Roméo had had some years of marriage outside the fishbowl of political life. Their young children helped forge a lasting friendship between the two women, though their husbands did not become particularly close friends until after they had both left elected political life.[2]

If the changes to Roméo's personal life seemed to demand no significant adjustment, the alteration in his professional life was considerable and would eventually have an impact on his home life. It is important to note that he was not appointed as a replacement for Jack Davis, who had been the minister of the environment when the department included fisheries, as well as a host of other responsibilities. Instead, Roméo was appointed minister of state for fisheries, a position under the supervision of Environment Minister Jeanne Sauvé, a senior Cabinet appointment. This relationship lasted two years, and it was never particularly comfortable, despite their common student experience with the JEC. Quite apart from the substantive reasons, which very quickly emerged, Madame Sauvé came from a very different background than Roméo. Her circumstances were metropolitan, and she was active in the women's movement,

The Leblanc family: Roméo, Geneviève, Dominic and Lyn, 1976

while his were rural, and he had been involved in Acadian politics. Her experience as a journalist was mostly within Canada;
his had a strong international component. There was, at the outset, a lack of understanding by the senior minister of Roméo's
Acadian heritage and his belief that the power and influence of
Quebec had often been a mixed blessing for the Acadians. There
was also, on Roméo's side, a lack of understanding of the extent
to which Madame Sauvé had fought a considerable amount of
male chauvinism during her career.

Finally, there was an underlying problem for Roméo in the
very circumstances of his promotion: he was a middle-aged
backbencher, who was not particularly well-known in the inner
political circles in Ottawa, except as a journalist and a public-
relations figure. His opinions carried little immediate political
weight for the average politician and upper civil servant. This
situation was of little consequence in Roméo's mind, and he
made no particular effort to counter it. In the first place, having

been a staff member in the Prime Minister's Office for four years, he felt he had a fair knowledge of how the machinery of government actually worked. More importantly, he had a clear idea of what he wanted to achieve. When Trudeau offered him the position, Roméo took two days to consider the matter and then accepted, on the condition that "he could behave as minister 'for fishermen.'"[3] Roméo took Trudeau at his word, which meant, inevitably, conflict with those who considered that fishing was, above all, an industry centred on the needs of fish processors, and where the fishery involved matters of international waters, it should be approached first from the standpoint of Canada's international relations. It also meant that Roméo considered he could pursue his ideas without any great amount of consultation with others.

His immediate problem, however, was not a matter of policy or prestige but a question of adaptation to the change from the life of a backbencher to that of a minister of the Crown. Roméo's impression from the time he had served in the PMO that Cabinet members worked hard was about to be reinforced by direct experience. The first thing he had to accept was the extent to which his timetable was driven by unavoidable obligations. There were two kinds: those incumbent on him as member of the Cabinet and those that came from his work with his department. Cabinet meetings in the 1970s usually took place every Thursday, and lasted for two hours. A sub-series of obligations flowed from these meetings, including membership on one or more Cabinet committees, which usually met biweekly. Roméo was a member of the External Affairs and Economic Affairs Committees, 1974–1982; the Communications Committee, 1974–1984; and the Priorities and Planning Committee, 1975–1984.[4] The latter was, and still is, one of the most important of the Cabinet committees, as it acts as the executive committee of Cabinet. Committee meetings were as crucial as Cabinet meetings, but their timing could occasionally be moved from one day to the next. There was the requisite attendance at sittings of the House, "a duty" two or three times a week. Question periods were sacrosanct, as were weekly caucus meetings for the party as a whole and the meetings of one's own regional caucus. Then there were the absolutely imperative meetings with the deputy minister, often twice or three times a week. Into these engagements a constant stream of business meetings, briefing meetings, and meetings with constituents had to be inserted. Telephone calls with constituency people had to be arranged, correspondence had to be attended to, and final answers had to be overseen. Finally, at the end of the day, intergovernmental correspondence, delivered in his personal ministerial black briefcase, had to be read.[5] While this agenda was common to all ministers, those with departments that dealt with matters affecting the daily lives of Canadians were more burdened. Ministers such as Monique Bégin (health and welfare) and Roméo had more complex agendas than the ministers of justice or finance. The need to ensure that those who wrote or telephoned him received appropriate answers meant that, at the end of each day, Roméo signed off on the replies that his staff prepared for him. He read these with care because, one day, when signing some letter almost automatically, he was brought up short. As Stephen Kimber reported in his profile of Roméo, "A Newfoundland fisherman had been too ill to apply for his lobster licence before the official cut-off date and he was asking that the error be overlooked so that he could continue to earn a living. The bureaucrats' reply turned down the man's plea and said, in effect, that he should try a little harder next year."[6] Roméo had the licence sent to this fisherman and from then on took the time needed to avoid such a callous reply going out over his signature. Ever present was the need to ensure that people in his constituency felt that he was responsive to their needs, something which meant unavoidable trips to Shediac. Thanks to a committed and intelligent staff and frequent telephone calls, these trips were kept to a minimum, but he had to undertake national and international travel. There was a great benefit to having Lyn and the children living in Ottawa, but travel meant that there was less time spent with them when Parliament was in session.

There was also another matter that he had to tackle without delay: the need to understand how the Department of Fisheries actually worked and what its main areas of responsibility were. It was a government department that had changed its name and reporting line to Cabinet nine times between Confederation and 1971. Its most recent incarnation was a division within the Department of the Environment. This move was the result of the career of Jack Davis, who was appointed minister of fisheries in 1968, but whose administrative ability led to the continued expansion of his responsibilities. The last reshuffling of labels to reflect his career came about in 1973 when reorganization consolidated fisheries, oceanographic and hydrographic concerns under the title of the Fisheries and Marine Service of Environment Canada. This merger also brought fisheries research under this umbrella. In 1974, the control of fishing wharves was added, a program worth $23 million that year. The ability of fishing villages to lobby for improved wharves earned them the title among fishery officials of "Small Crafty Harbours."[7] The responsibilities of the department covered, among other matters, the development and implementation of policies in support of the seacoast and inland fisheries, the enforcement of myriad regulations, aids to navigation, and the general oversight of the conservation and sustainable use of Canada's fishing resources. The first question that Roméo had to answer as minister in the House of Commons came on October 4 from Donald Munro, regarding the development of a marina "on Saanichton Bay." It is little wonder he replied, "Mr. Speaker, I confess I have been cramming on every possible subject in expectation of a question but that one escaped me. I will take this as notice and give the hon. gentleman an answer."[8] Within the week, Roméo replied to a repeat of the question by saying that work had been halted on the marina because of concerns of the local First Nations community.[9]

In coping with all the interwoven demands of his new position, Roméo was helped immensely by the experienced senior civil servants then working in the department. One of them was Ken Lucas, who was appointed the senior deputy minister responsible for the Fisheries and Marine Service in the new Department of the Environment in 1973. His previous experience was with the British Columbia fisheries. He provided Roméo with information not only about what matters should be given immediate attention, but also about the history of previous action that had been taken in each case. This help was invaluable when substantial problems arose between Roméo and his senior minister on policy matters, on issues as fundamental as the importance of the fisheries in the Canadian economy and, as a consequence, their relative importance in relation to the other responsibilities of the Department of the Environment. Theirs was not only a disagreement about the place of the fisheries as an adjunct to the Department of the Environment, but a strong difference of opinion about the relationship between deep-sea and onshore fishing. Roméo soon made his views on the competing interests known, between the livelihood of fishermen on all coasts and the interests of the fish-processors, between the need for conservation and the right to expand the size of the catch for immediate profit. In two speeches delivered within nine months of his appointment, Roméo outlined his vision for the future of Canada's fisheries and the steps he intended to take to bring it about.

His first speech was delivered to the Atlantic Provinces Economic Council on October 24, 1974.[10] Given his audience, he began politically enough by saying that he thought "there is still room for expansion in the fisheries." But, he went on, "we need to think beyond catching the maximum amount of cod per hour per man. When fish are counted, it's people that count." He considered there were two basic ideas that had to be brought together: "on the wide scale, the idea of opportunity for development; on the individual scale, the idea of a decent life for the fishermen." To achieve these ends, he remarked, "the law gives me a strong power regarding the licensing of fishermen, and I intend to use it." He went on to say that in this and related matters, "I intend to listen closely to the bona fide fisherman, the man whose life is fishing," and pointed out that this meant fishermen "must organize. Be sure your voice is heard, and be sure that your spokesmen are properly mandated and accountable to you." He concluded: "We can't hope to manage our fish resources without the help of the fishermen. On fish stocks they have much knowledge: in any conservation policy that's to be effective, they are the caretakers and, finally, for us in the fisheries service, as for all of you with the power to influence policies, the people whose lives we affect are and will be our judges." Roméo's call for the fishermen to consider unionization startled the industry. While he never publicly endorsed unionization, he pointed out that it was an option for consideration.

His second speech, on May 5, 1975, to the Fisheries Council of Canada in Halifax, the voice of the Canadian fish and seafood industry, was also a shock to its audience.[11] He opened with a forthright reminder that, since he had last been in Halifax to talk about the fisheries, the industry had received $85 million in aid. He elaborated by underlining the investment of the government in all aspects of the fishing industry: through boatbuilding subsidies, through DREE (the Department of Regional Economic Expansion), through ports and harbours, through the Unemployment Insurance Commission (UIC), through compensation grants. "We have done so through the biologists, market analysts, product inspectors, fishing-gear technologists, and all the rest whose salaries we pay to work for you...Your claim on the attention of the state implies the participation of the state in shaping the industry's future...public funds imply public responsibility."

He intended to take control of the fisheries to ensure "a good life for the fisherman with less economic fear." These speeches provided the philosophy behind the policies that Roméo supported during his term as minister. The intellectual foundation for his vision and a detailed plan of action were presented in *Policy for Canada's Commercial Fisheries,* a departmental publication, in May 1976.

Outlining his ideas for the future of the fisheries was only one of Roméo's major focuses during the first months of his ministry. There were other matters that demanded attention. The most immediate of them was the Third United Nations Conference on the Law of the Sea, which began with a procedural meeting in New York in 1973 and would result in a final agreement in 1982.[12] Questions of the offshore rights of sovereign nations included questions not only of defence and the exploitation of mineral resources, but also, of almost equal importance, of the harvesting of fish. In this area, the federal fisheries department dominated negotiations. The groundwork for the co-operation which made this a fruitful process was laid as early as 1973 by Ken Lucas along with Alan Beesley, the head of the Canadian delegation and an outstanding senior diplomat. By 1975, Lucas had built up a good team within the department, headed by Léonard Legault, a Saskatchewan lawyer and diplomat on loan from External Affairs. As a result, the fisheries department's opinions dominated the negotiations in this area. Roméo was able to answer satisfactorily the questions put to him in the House, and his path was smoothed when he attended the proceedings in

Geneva in late April 1975 and later on in New York. The Geneva visit strengthened Roméo's understanding of the complex nature of the process of international negotiations and prepared him to speak authoritatively in answer to a question in the House about what he was doing to preserve Canada's fishing stocks. He replied that he had already laid the groundwork to reduce the quotas for offshore fishing by both Canadian and foreign fleets.[13]

There was soon to be a major confirmation that Roméo was someone who intended to act and speak about the problems facing the fisheries, especially about the actions of countries that routinely ignored quotas on fish catches to which they had earlier agreed. On July 23, 1975, he announced the closure of Canadian ports to Soviet fishing vessels and warned Spain and Portugal that the same could happen to them.[14] This action has sometimes been represented as swashbuckling and out of the blue. Certainly, as Joe Gough has pointed out, "In [the] fisheries diplomacy of the day it was a thunder-bolt."[15] But it was an obvious next step in implementing a policy aimed at gaining the necessary control of Canadian Atlantic fishing rights, something that had been pursued for several years through the International Commission for the North Atlantic Fisheries. As a result of pressure from Canada, this body tried to enforce agreed-upon quotas on the fishing fleets harvesting the North Atlantic waters, but to little avail. With the information provided by Canadian fishery patrols and National Defence surveillance, Roméo had enough evidence to act decisively, and in doing so he made national and international headlines. There was a great deal of support for his action, but it also drew some criticism. Businessmen in St. John's and Halifax deplored the loss of custom from the foreign ships and feared that the French-held islands of St. Pierre and Miquelon would profit from the closure. Others felt that historic rights of Portugal and France to the North Atlantic fishery had been overlooked. In both cases, Roméo assured the House that the countries in question supported Canada's action, and that France had informed him that St. Pierre and Miquelon did not have the resources to take up the slack.[16] It is said that he mused privately that, if they did, Canadian fuel supplies to the islands would be cut off.[17] Intense diplomacy went on before the next meeting of the International Convention for the Northwest Atlantic Fisheries, which took place in September that year in the Windsor Hotel in Montreal. This produced bilateral agreements in the spring and early summer of 1976 with the Soviet Union, Poland, Spain, and Portugal.

In less than two years, Roméo brought to successful conclusions a number of policies begun by his predecessor, and initiated some of his own. This progress was the result partly of his own clear ideas about what he wanted to do and his good relationship with the well-informed civil servants. It was also because Trudeau gave him his full support. It was not a matter of emotion for the prime minister, but the consequence of the assurance he had given Roméo on the latter's appointment to Cabinet: that he could indeed serve the needs of the fishermen. Money was found for the expansion of the offshore enforcement fleet on both coasts, the number of fisheries officers was increased, and their training was improved. Money was also found in August 1976 for changes to the unemployment provisions for fishermen. At the time, ordinary unemployment insurance lasted up to forty-two weeks, depending on the region; for fishermen it lasted only twelve weeks. As Gough pointed out, "Plant workers on regular UI often got more benefits than the fishermen who supplied them, and who might work a longer season."[18] The changes meant unemployment benefits for fishermen lasted up to twenty-seven weeks. The immediate impact was the ending of the almost unavoidable indebtedness incurred by many fishermen between the Mirimachi and Cap-Pelé during the winter. For many, lean winter months meant taking a loan from the fish-processors to

Roméo visiting the BC fishing industry, 1976

tide them over from one year to the next, which allowed the pro-
cessor to set the prices at the opening of the new fishing season.[19]

On September 13, 1976, Trudeau shuffled the Cabinet. Jeanne
Sauvé was moved to the Department of Communications, and
Roméo became minister of the Department of the Environment,
with continuing responsibility for the fisheries. His elevation to a
senior Cabinet position was partly the result of his obvious ability
to handle with firmness both domestic and international aspects
of the fisheries. It came as well because he was a bilingual francophone from outside Quebec, who was sympathetic to Quebec
grievances yet had a strong belief in Canada as a nation worth
preserving. Within two years, he went from being an unknown
backbencher to someone who was seen in Ottawa as a "bright,
tough, and forthright guy."[20] He was not afraid to make his views
known in Cabinet on matters he considered important, and it
was clear that he gathered the needed support for his policies
among the other ministers. The prime minister's backing helped,

but Roméo's own abilities were the foundation of his success. In particular, while he worked well with civil servants he respected, he had little patience with those who tried to baffle him with complicated reasoning. "Tell me," he would say, "why exactly are we doing this?" Or, alternately, "I didn't understand a word you said and I am sure nor would anyone in my constituency."[21] Both comments made speakers say clearly what they meant, and he was quick at separating theoretical verbiage from advice based on observation and an understanding of the immediate consequences of a decision. He often used a tactic that had been a standard practice among Acadian politicians fighting for power in New Brunswick during the 1950s and 1960s: that of listening to arguments but refusing to continue a debate. Instead, they (and he) would proceed to ignore the advice offered and take whatever measures were possible, without the support they had requested. Roméo made it quite clear, in such circumstances, that the decisions made were his, not those of the civil servants. He was impatient with those who tried to stall him, demanding he follow procedural rules invented for their own convenience. This was particularly true for the disbursement of government subsidies, whether these were subsidies for improvements to the wharves or the various requests for help to repair or replace small fishing vessels or for emergency aid because of a crisis in harvesting and selling a particular fish stock.[22] Again, on such occasions, he turned to Acadian examples, where support was obtained through long telephone conversations, a knowledge of what committees were involved, who should be given background material before crucial meetings, and where support on one issue might be bartered for help promised for another. Finally, if all else failed, Roméo was well aware that it was often better to act and ask forgiveness than to ask for permission and wait.

In some ways, the timing of the announcement of Canada's decision to extend jurisdiction over coastal waters to two hundred miles had a touch of this "action first—apologies later" tactic. The likelihood of declaring the new limits had been in the air since 1975, but Prime Minister Trudeau was hesitant. He considered that the "historic rights" of both the American and European fishing fleets should be taken into account. However, on November 2, 1976, Roméo and Don Jamieson, an MP from Newfoundland, who was then secretary of state for External Affairs, announced the "government's intention to act, under the authority of the *Territorial Sea and Fishing Zones Act*, to extend [Canadian] jurisdiction as of January 1st 1977." This action, which was later applied to Arctic waters, "brought 3.7 million square kilometres of ocean—the largest such zone in the world... under Canadian fisheries control. A federal publication declared that Canada was 'owner and manager' of the new zone."[23] Roméo was pleased not only that it was a great deal of hard work by his department that had "led the way," but also that the new policy was made operational with very few problems because of the excellent organization of fishery patrols at the local level. There were a fair number of criticisms that it could never be made to work. On January 1, 1977, however, fisheries vessels, aided by Coast Guard ships and support from the Navy, were patrolling the zone. There were a few incidents, but by 1978 a system was in place whereby foreign ships licensed to fish within the two-hundred-mile zone carried Canadian observers.

From the outset Roméo recognized the dangers in this success. He had already worked to silence one powerful critic with a quick trip to Russia in May 1976. He knew he would need considerable help from External Affairs to sort out problems with the United States, which had declared its intention to enact a two-hundred-mile limit as of March 1977. The American acceptance of Canada's position was guarded at best, and hostile where the boundaries between American and Canadian sovereignties met. There were several issues that demanded determined and

skilful negotiations over the next months, including the question of Canada's claim over the Arctic, given Alaska's interest
in the same waters; the British Columbia–Washington state
boundaries; as well as the rich fishing grounds on the East
Coast, especially the Georges Banks area. No matter how pressing Roméo's other concerns were, he needed to be continuously
aware of where negotiations on these questions stood. At the
same time, a serious domestic problem loomed. Even before the
two-hundred-mile limit was announced, he had been aware that
the expansion of sovereignty would be seen by many as an open
invitation to uncontrolled expansion of Canada's offshore fishery. He needed to bring about much greater management of fish
stocks by the federal government, something that would place
him in conflict with the governments of the coastal provinces, as
well as with big fishing companies and fish-processors.

Roméo's workload had greatly increased since his time as a
backbencher. It is true that his work conditions had improved.
In 1972, his salary had been $18,000 a year, plus an $8,000 non-
taxable expense allowance. Then, he had shared a secretary with
another MP and had to pay for long-distance telephone calls.[24]
In 1974, Mitchell Sharp, at that time the government House
Leader for the Liberal Party, brought in improvements to MPs'
salaries, and staffing for their offices. He did this with the full
support of the Opposition, led by Robert Stanfield. Roméo's salary rose to $25,500, with a non-taxable allowance of $45,5000.[25]
Furthermore, he had his own secretary, and long-distance telephone calls were free. But leisure time was curtailed. Having his
wife and family in Ottawa meant that he was with them at the
end of the day and on weekends. However, Westmorland–Kent
needed an occasional sighting of their member of Parliament and
he was away even more often than previously, travelling to one or
another of Canada's coasts or making a flying visit to the never-
ending Law of the Seas Conference in New York, or an equally

fleeting visit to Europe. Added to these concerns was the part he was called on to play in the general business of the government, which became more complicated on November 15, 1976, with the election of René Lévesque as head of an avowed separatist government in Quebec and a worsening economic situation in the country as a whole.

As an Acadian and the senior federal Cabinet minister from Canada's only officially bilingual province, Roméo's opinions concerning Lévesque's policies were important. On May 7, 1977, Roméo was accorded an honorary doctorate by Mount Allison University, and his speech on this occasion is a rare statement of what Canada meant to him.[26] It is a revelation of the pragmatic nature of Roméo's mind, his refusal to paint life in Technicolor, and his knowledge that there is more to human circumstances than any academic theory captures. He opened by speaking of his own experience of being an Acadian child "who learned to speak English in primary school because I had to...In my daily life there was no French radio, no magazines, few books in my native tongue...I was French. I was also poor, and rural." He recalled his surprise when, as a young adult, he discovered "others who did not share my language, or my politics, but whose preoccupations, whose objectives were mine." One of these, he went on, "was a Mount Allison graduate and the son of a Westmorland farmer...I was faced with the truth of the human condition, a condition that included poverty, illness, debt, discouragement, a condition that goes beyond language." Roméo spoke of Canada's record with other minorities, and remarked that, in his own riding, the unemployment figures for Aboriginals was "80 per cent." He was also well aware of "the resistance of good white and Christian workers to their being employed in their midst." He listed the failures of the past, including the internment of the Japanese during the Second World War and the historical treatment of peoples of the First Nations.

He spent a short time talking about the ways in which those who suffered prejudice and injustice, those whose backgrounds were not of "the majority," survived. He distinguished between survival of an individual and the preservation, in some fashion, of that individual's communal heritage. He rejected descriptions of Canada as peopled by "ships passing in the night," or as a "failed marriage," or as novelist Hugh MacLennan's perception of "two solitudes." He rejected even more strongly an idea, then currently in vogue, that Canada was a house with a landlord and tenants. "The country," he said, "is common property." All of its citizens have the right to live here and the duty to participate in its governance. "We must not leave the fate of the country," he declared "to those professionally involved."

At this point, Roméo confronted the contemporary situation in Quebec politics. He made no attempt to diminish the crisis. "The leaders of the Parti Québécois have, as their purpose, the removal of Quebec from Confederation," he said. "I do not say from Canada, " he elaborated, "because without Quebec, there will be no Canada as we know it, a nation consisting of two predominant cultural strains, with a great many allied groups of other origins, a nation that has yet to define itself as a unit." He went on to define the challenge this represented and pointed out that it was not just a movement of "a new élite, educated, and articulate," within the province, but "it was...the ordinary working people of Quebec who, through their trade unions, their cooperatives and credit unions, their dollars and their hours of work, and finally their votes, brought the PQ to power...The matter of the survival of our nation is no longer the subject of academic dissertation, of 'seminar roundtables,' or Sunday-evening news specials...It is not just Quebec which had to say yes or no to the question 'Canada? Yes or no.'"

Roméo concluded his address by outlining what the country could use to combat the crisis. There was the land itself, common to all: none could own it; the St. Lawrence was neither French nor English, but itself. There was the history of Canada, which told of failures but also of successes. He noted that New Brunswick had come to accept itself as a place where people of more than one heritage could flourish within the common polity. There were the graduates in front of him who could ensure the necessary debate, "at all levels of society," about the ways to preserve and develop the nation. It was "precisely this kind of act," the award to him of an honorary doctorate, "multiplied many times on the national scale, from the English majority to the French minority, to all minorities that will make cooperation in unity and trust." The address brought together Roméo's experience of friendship across the barriers of different languages and religious beliefs, his observation of the possibilities of solutions to disputes when situations were examined thoroughly before theories were applied. Above all, it spoke to his deep conviction, which had been nurtured by his friendship with Gérard Pelletier and Mike Pearson, that Canada should, could, and would survive. All of this was wrapped up in something that not one of these men would ever have explicitly stated: an abiding love for the country itself.

In many ways this occasion marked the end of a period of relatively easy successes for Roméo. Over the next five years, he continued to bring significant changes to the ways the department dealt with its responsibilities, but it came with an increasingly high price both politically and personally. The passage of the 1977 *Fisheries Act* was the bridge between these two phases of his career. The second reading of Bill-C38, "Fisheries Act, a measure to amend the criminal code in consequence thereof,"[27] began on May 16, 1977. The purpose of the bill was to amplify the powers, already possessed by the Department of Fisheries, to protect "the fish and man's use of fish," and to guard "the waters of fish."[28] Roméo illustrated the need for such powers by pointing out the impact of poaching, carried out with violence, especially on Atlantic rivers, where everything had been used from pitchforks to dynamite. "These vandals," he observed, "have assaulted my fisheries officers, have fired shots at them, and have threatened to burn down their homes." As for the West Coast, the loss of potential earnings there, he noted, was reckoned at $3.5 million annually, and the fines levelled on an illegal catch valued at $20,000 were no more than $200. Roméo went on to request stricter measures to deal with the pollution of Canada's oceans and rivers. To make his point here, he chose the "world's most important salmon river, the Fraser, [where] development has already destroyed 70 per cent of the estuary [that is the]...foundation of fish life."[29] The principle he enunciated was: "He who causes harm must correct." The first speaker from the Opposition benches, Lloyd Crouse, summarized the bill as dealing with "pollution, power problems, penalties, poachers, police officers, protection, politics and prohibition."[30] His speech set the tone of the discussion, and his main points were that the measure should have been adopted earlier, and minor modifications were proposed. These were made in the committee stage and greatly strengthened protection for fish habitat, making a significant improvement in Canada's environmental legislations. The bill easily passed third reading.

Between the summer of 1977 and the general election of May 1979, Roméo's professional life was concerned not only with the fisheries, but also with his responsibilities as the regional minister for New Brunswick. This role meant that he ensured that other ministers remembered New Brunswick's needs when proposing legislation or distributing monies. Obviously, support for the Trans-Canada Highway in the province and for bilingualism and educational grants received his attention, but he also spoke to and supported businessmen who needed government aid for projects. It was in his capacity as regional minister that he gave support for the development of the forestry program at Collège

Saint-Louis in Edmundston and the location of the Canadian Control Frigate Building Program in Saint John.[31] However, the fisheries continued to be his priority. He was particularly concerned with activity in three major areas: continuing efforts to give fishermen a voice in the regulation of their industry; attempts to improve conservation practices and the excellence of Canadian fish exports; and, most importantly, the effort to make Canadians and the federal bureaucracy understand the importance of the fisheries for the country. For both coasts, he used limited-entry licences, which restricted new entrants into the fishery when it began to make money. In addition, he instituted a comprehensive system of catch limits for cod, haddock, herring, and other "finfish," particularly on the Atlantic. These limits added some stability to the industry. He extensively toured not only the Atlantic fisheries, but also the inland fisheries of Saskatchewan and British Columbia. He made a quick visit to Scotland in the fall of 1978 to discuss the general health of the northwest-Atlantic fisheries. His Ottawa staff said he was easy to work with, even when he was away, because he kept in telephone communication and briefed them thoroughly on his ideas and how he thought important issues should be handled before he left; but his travels exhausted him.[32] Wherever he went, he talked with local department officials, provincial politicians, and civil servants concerned with the industry, as well as with the leaders of the fishermen's associations. In British Columbia, he often spent part of a day on board a working fishing vessel. His support of the Salmonid Enhancement Program there, which was intended to double anadromous trout and salmon production, involved a ten-year, $200-million project and brought him supporters.[33] The project also involved First Nations people working at the local level to improve conditions for salmon.

One of his innovations for improving employment prospects for fishermen was the establishment of a network of officials, in some twenty ports in the Maritimes, to help fishermen navigate the sea of regulations that controlled their lives. These officials, in Roméo's words, worked "closely with fishermen interpreting federal fisheries policy and regulations, helping them cut through red tape, and equally important, feeding in their point of view."[34] He realized that the fishermen had to deal not only with his department "in its manifold capacities—science, licensing, fishery management, small-craft harbours, development, marketing inspection, and so on—but also with the Canadian Steamship Inspection, the Canadian Coast Guard, and others."[35] The community officers helped the organizations to some degree, but, as encouraged by Roméo, they quickly gained the capacity to present their own views, and the community officers concentrated on cutting red tape. These organizations had been initiated by Davis and, with Roméo's blessing, increased in number and expanded their influence.[36] Their agenda concerned quotas and how licences were regulated. Membership in them allowed fishermen to provide their wealth of knowledge about how the fishery worked.

The twin objectives of conservation and the improvement of Canada's fishery sales presented a complexity of problems, most of which stemmed from the expansion of the fisheries during the previous five years. Roméo stated in a House debate early in 1978, "The fishery today presents a billion-dollar industry, which in the last four years has increased its production value by 55 per cent, increased its export value by 65 per cent, and taken control of 630,000 square miles of resources...Today's fisherman is earning an income 50 per cent higher, in real terms, than he could ten years ago."[37] The assertion of Canada's two-hundred-mile control over its coastal waters led to demands by the provincial governments with seacoasts and the big trawler firms, such as the Nova Scotia–based National Sea Products, for the right to exploit the new limits without restriction. The fisheries ministers of Newfoundland and Nova Scotia presented $800-million expansion plans for their fleets and processing plants, for which they wanted federal help.[38] Roméo argued that doing this, before increasing the number of fish in the water, "was like a man with an exhausted woodlot who, instead of planting new trees, spends all his money on chain-saws to cut the shrubs. Massive fleet expansion at this moment would be a Titanic undertaking, and I use the word advisedly."[39] From the outset, Roméo listened to the scientific branch of the department, which had cautioned that fish stocks were a fluctuating resource, subject to sudden variations. Above all, he considered that the fisheries should be "as attractive to the next generation as it is beginning to be to our own...a self-sustaining industry which can give to its fishermen... security of income and security of employment."[40]

To achieve this, Roméo struggled to make people understand the need for an independent government department at the federal level, devoted to the fisheries. He believed that a strong federal government presence was vitally necessary if the fisheries were to be properly managed. He was convinced of the continuing need of oversight to ensure that the life of fishermen and their families was, in every sense of the word, sustainable. His premise was: "The common property of the living resources of the sea requires federal management."[41] This view did not mean he was unwilling to consult the provinces, but he said that only "if fish grew roots" would he accept their argument for a greater role. He went on: "Some stock, for example the Atlantic salmon, migrate past five provinces [Nova Scotia, New Brunswick, Prince Edward Island, Quebec, and Newfoundland]. If we were to hand these provinces five knives—or perhaps I should say five fishing poles—to divide up that resource, I am afraid their five hooks might end up in each other's eye."[42] Roméo's view of federal authority was anything but simplistic, and he expanded ways in which he could consult with the provinces by establishing six director-generalships in the regions; they had authority to make decisions and act immediately when the situation required it. The work to establish these took time, but one of them particularly dear to his heart was that of the Gulf Region, which became fully operational as the only bilingual region in Canada in 1981. Its headquarters was in Moncton, with local area directors in Quebec City, Tracadie, Charlottetown, Antigonish, and Corner Brook. It encompassed "the waters of the Gulf of St. Lawrence and the land boundaries include[d] all of the province of Quebec and Prince Edward Island, and the headwater areas of all rivers in New Brunswick, Nova Scotia, and Newfoundland, which flow into the Gulf."[43]

Roméo was quite clear, however, that, "there will always be competing interests and objectives. The federal authority for the fisheries is the clearing house for these divergent views, the mediator for conflicting opinion and, ultimately, the decision maker." He knew that those consulted expected their views to be accepted, and when consultation led to the rejection of the views of the provinces or fish-processing companies or the fishermen's unions, many of the consulted would be angered.

Roméo campaigned for a strong federal department of fisheries because of his belief about Confederation, his belief that Canada was more than a collection of disparate provinces, an uneasy group of diverse peoples, a tiresome wrangling of the remnants of former colonies in a tense relationship with those who lived on the land before the arrival of Europeans. He believed that Canadians had established institutions of government that could change and develop as was needed, and that the ambitions of those in public life, no matter the political party, were based on a wish to improve the society they served. He as strongly believed that some ideas were better than others for the attainment of this common aim and that the unbridled pursuit of profit, the idea that the values of the marketplace should be the highest arbiter of government policy, was dangerous. The frail, whether mentally, physically, or emotionally, needed care provided by the community as a whole. These ideas came strongly to the fore when he spoke in 1979 for the establishment of the federal Department of Fisheries and Oceans. There are two places in this House speech where he summed up his position. First, he said,

> *in the disposal of this common property resource (the fisheries), which is held in trust by the government of Canada, the first interest that has to be considered— and as long as I am the minister the first interest that is considered—is the interest of the fishermen, starting with those who live in the communities that are the most isolated and whose mobility is the most limited. It was in the name of the small coastal communities and the small fishermen who could not compete with the foreign fishing fleets that we argued successfully with the rest of world that Canada should manage the 200-mile zone.*"[44]

In his other statement, made towards the conclusion of the debate, he said, "I have indicated very clearly from the time I made my public speech in Halifax that the time when fishermen arrive at the wharf and are told that the price has dropped during the trip must come to an end. I can only say that I rejoice that it is increasingly coming to an end."[45]

The bill was enacted on April 2, 1979, on the eve of the 1979 election, which was held on May 22, having been called on March 26. It took all the political skill Roméo and deputy minister Ken Lucas could muster to bring it about. Lucas had been working towards this end since 1973, when he first began at the department with Jack Davis. Once the legislation was enacted, Lucas left the federal civil service, reckoning he had used up any influence

Roméo as minister of fisheries and oceans, 1979

he accumulated.[46] John Crosbie, who had been Newfoundland's minister of fisheries from 1975 to 1976, spoke for the Opposition benches, at considerable length, against the bill.[47] There was ample infighting over what, exactly, the new department would control. In the end, "impatient with naysayers and obstacle-makers, LeBlanc went to Trudeau, who gave appropriate instructions to his Privy Council clerk."[48] Roméo was now minister of fisheries and oceans. The symbolic importance of the change was considerable, both within the country, where the rural fishermen saw their part in the fishing industry recognized, and within Cabinet, where for a number of years fisheries was considered one of the important economic issues of the country.

When the election campaign began, Roméo was physically exhausted and emotionally troubled. Bertin LeBlanc, who worked once more on this campaign, recalled that Roméo barely participated in it. People knew how hard he had worked and were aware that his relationship with his wife was in difficulty. It was general knowledge that Roméo cared deeply for his children. Dominic was nearly twelve, and Geneviève not quite five that year. It was a time when the failure of a marriage was something not accepted lightly, by either those involved or by the community at large. The impact of a breakup on the children was not only something that worried the parents, but also food for comment in the wider community. However, this personal trouble did not affect his political support, and Roméo was returned without difficulty. In fact, his plurality over his two opponents slightly increased. Roméo received 63 per cent of the votes cast (19,695).[49] Bertin LeBlanc thought that there were a number of reasons for this result. First, Roméo had earned the voters' trust by 1979, having served seven years as their MP. When he was in the riding, he attended community occasions, such as the opening of Golden Age clubs. His constituents understood his speeches, in which he talked of things they knew, the need for wharves, the question of schools, what local employment prospects there were for the children. More importantly, he ran the constituency with local people and paid little attention to the provincial Liberals or to outside federal help. Finally, as Roméo remarked to the author, in most communities he had taught at least one or more of the older teachers during his 1950s stint at Teachers' College. He was known, liked, and trusted, and if, in 1979, he looked in need of a holiday, well, he deserved it.

Roméo kept his seat but the party lost the election: the result gave the Conservatives 136 seats, the Liberals 114, the NDP 26 and Social Credit 6. Trudeau resigned as leader. He, too, had entered the election campaign exhausted and facing the end of his marriage. For both men, the brief interlude of Joe Clark's Conservative government allowed them time to take stock of their lives. The Conservatives barely had time to consider how and when they could implement their election promises before they were defeated by a combined Liberal and NDP vote on December 13, 1979.

Trudeau returned to the leadership of the Liberal Party, and the country again went to the polls on February 18, 1980. Roméo won his seat again, and again increased his plurality, receiving 21,625 votes; the Conservative candidate received 5,339; and the NDP candidate received 5,255. The Liberals won a solid majority: 147 seats out of 282, with the Conservatives at 103 and the NDP at 32. Trudeau's temper and that of the Liberal Party was very different than it had been a year earlier. Lalonde, who played a crucial role during the election, is reputed to have reminisced: "If ever we got another kick at the can we were really going to kick it."[50] Trudeau now led the government with "a hard edged approach [which] contributed to the separatist defeat in the referendum, the imposition of the interventionist National Energy Program at the heart of an aggressively nationalist economic agenda, and the repatriation of the Constitution with its charter of Rights and Freedoms."[51] The prime minister concentrated his attention on his vision of Canada and his ministers found their power and policies had to be tempered. At the same time, while the Liberals had obtained a majority, there was, both in Parliament and in the country, a strong and articulate opposition to Trudeau's ideas. There were many who were encouraged by Joe Clark's victory, even if it had been swiftly overturned, and were ready to criticize the government much more openly and harshly than they had been in 1979.

Roméo was reappointed minister of fisheries and oceans. When Trudeau spoke to him about his re-appointment, he told Roméo that the letters from fishermen asking him to do this were far more numerous than those he had received asking him to remain as Liberal leader. A crude measure of the reason for Roméo's popularity was the rise in fishermen's incomes on both the Atlantic and Pacific coasts between 1974 and 1980. In 1974, the average income of Atlantic fishermen was around $7,000 a year; by 1980 it had risen to over $12,000. On the Pacific coast, the average income had been $12,000, which had risen as high as $21,000 in 1979, but fell back again the following year to just over $12,000.[52] Such fluctuations were not unusual in the fishing industry. However, just as important as the economic improvements that had taken place was the way Roméo ensured consultation between the fishermen and the department. As he said in the House of Commons, "It does not hurt me at all to hear that people complain about my being the fishermen's minister more than the fisheries."[53] But if the improvement of the fishermen's lot had aroused little opposition by other stakeholders in the industry, Roméo's support of fishermen's associations was often sharply criticized by the fish-processing plant owners.

In fact, as he once more assumed control of the Department of Fisheries and Oceans, he faced considerable opposition. The continued emphasis he placed on conservation, the occasions on which he floated the idea of separating the fishing fleet entirely from any ownership by fish-processors, the scant sympathy he gave to the large fishing corporations that had overextended their fleets, and his continued pressure for better practices by fish exporters proved ample grounds for many in the industry to complain. Another issue was "stagflation" and the incredible rise in interest rates, neither of which were subject to influence or control by either Roméo or the fish-processors. Above all, however, the provinces' dislike of a strong federal department with excellent regional administrative management and a strong scientific component was open and bitter. Roméo irritated provincial governments "by resisting their expansion plans and generally paying little attention to them, preferring the advice of his officials and of fishermen."[54] By late 1981, the four big Atlantic corporations were in trouble and faced bankruptcy. Banks were worried about their loans. Donald Tansley had replaced Ken Lucas as deputy minister of the department in 1979. He was an extraordinarily gifted man who had worked in the New Brunswick, Saskatchewan, and the federal civil service. He proved as helpful to Roméo as Ken Lucas had been. He and Roméo worked to produce plans to resolve the problems on the Atlantic coast. These involved an ever-greater expansion of federal power and were rejected by Trudeau and his advisers in December 1981. In January 1982, the Prime Minister's Office announced that Michael Kirby, then a top official in the Federal-Provincial Relations Office, would replace Tansley, and a Task Force on the Atlantic Fisheries would be set up. In the fall, Trudeau moved Roméo to public works and made Pierre de Bané minister of fisheries and oceans.

There were a number of reasons for Trudeau's decision to move Roméo from fisheries and oceans to public works. On the surface, it can be accounted for because of the number of enemies Roméo had made, who pressured the prime minister to get rid

of him. The Fisheries Council of Canada and influential provincial politicians, including some from Quebec, wanted Roméo
dismissed. He had also annoyed bureaucrats in the government's central agencies—Finance, Treasury Board, and the Privy
Council—with his political skill in circumventing their obstruc-
tion of his plans, which seriously upset their view of their own
power.[55] There were other reasons, both political and personal.
Politically, Roméo became deeply involved in the repatriation
of the Constitution and the Charter of Rights. His commitment
to the Department of Fisheries and Oceans was tempered by his
realization that he had probably achieved as much as he could,
and perhaps new ideas were needed. He knew that the restruc-
turing of the department in the federal civil service was unlikely
to be undone. The very strength of opposition from some fishermen's associations to his policies for conservation of fishing
stocks and his demands that they look at better ways of processing fish made him feel he had enabled them to make their views
known. He never completely accepted Joe Gough's view that he
had influenced "fisheries history more than any other minister since Peter Mitchell at Confederation."[56] However, Roméo
knew that decisions he made, such as that which settled the
jurisdictional lines between Quebec and the Maritimes for the
exploitation of a number of fish stocks, would last well into the
future. In his last speech before the Fisheries Council of Canada,
Roméo said that he only wanted equality for the fisherman, and
he had forced the industry to take a major step in that direction.

He was not unhappy to move on. His personal reason for
so doing made the change more acceptable to him. Lyn and he
had come to terms and signed a separation agreement in 1981.
There was little or no publicity about it. Geneviève and Dominic,
as well as Lyn, have spoken of the lack of recrimination with
which arrangements for the family were made and carried out.
Nevertheless, the failure of his marriage was a bitter experience

for Roméo. He made clear to the prime minister, whose own experience made him sympathetic, his immediate need to cut down on his travelling in order to be available for Dominic and Geneviève, who were fourteen and nine years old. Trudeau suggested Indian affairs, but Roméo was happier in public works, a ministry where he was be able to work with minimum publicity on a number of questions that had become important to him. So, he left fisheries and oceans with few regrets. Roméo remains the longest-serving minister in charge of Canadian fisheries, and his reputation among inshore fishermen has not diminished.

CHAPTER 9

From Elected to Appointed Office

During Roméo's last two years as minister of fisheries and oceans the temper of public life in Ottawa was radically different than it had been when he was first appointed to Cabinet in 1974. The election of that year continued Trudeau's hold on power with a majority government, which was then lost in the 1979 defeat and followed by the short Joe Clark government. The election of February 1980, after Trudeau had both resigned and come back as leader, returned the Liberal Party with a majority.

The economy, however, was starting to deteriorate, and continued to do so over the next two years. In 1974, Trudeau had thought separatism was an issue that could be controlled and had set out to implement policy changes, aided by Michael Pitfield, who served as clerk of the Privy Council and secretary of the Cabinet. However, less than three months after the 1980 election, on May 20, Trudeau faced the prospect of the first referendum in Quebec on separatism. The question presented to the Quebec electorate had been released in December 1979, and read:

The government of Quebec has made public its proposal to negotiate a new agreement with the rest of Canada, based on equality of nations.

This agreement would enable Quebec to acquire the exclusive power to make its laws, administer its taxes and establish relations abroad—in other words, sovereignty—and, at the same time to maintain with Canada an economic association including a common currency.

Any change in political status resulting from these negotiations will be submitted to the people through a referendum.

On these terms, do you agree to give the government the mandate to negotiate the proposed agreement between Quebec and Canada?[1]

Eighty per cent of Quebec's 4.4 million voters cast their ballots: 59.5 per cent "no" and 40.5 per cent "yes."[2] Trudeau worked hard, as John English has pointed out, "to enhance the federal presence and create a stronger national government."[3] The referendum over, the next eighteen months saw the politics of the country dominated by the battle to "patriate" the constitution, with an attached Charter of Rights.

The priority given to the issue was a reflection of Trudeau's determination to bring about a lasting change in Canada's constitutional structure and, perhaps, defeat the separatist movement in Quebec. It was a time when he used not only the members of cabinet, but also the majority of the Liberal members of Parliament, as well as every other means he could imagine, to carry the argument. He led an increasingly bitter fight with the provinces. Rulings from the Supreme Court were sought on the federal right to act; provinces lobbied in London to protest radical constitutional change, and were helped there by the remnants of imperial nostalgia among the British. First Nations peoples also added their pleas to the provincial lobbying in the British capital. At the same time, the prime minister confronted considerable opposition from the media. The electorate as a whole was often bored and sometimes hostile. If he got much less from the eventual constitutional agreement than he wanted, that he got an agreement at all was extraordinary.[4] As Edward McWhinney has pointed out, the achievement was not and could not have been the work of just one man, or even of one brief period. Quoting the nineteenth-century political scientist Jeremy Bentham, who believed that such changes demand a company to achieve, McWhinney wrote, "The constitutional company includes federal and provincial ministers, Parliamentarians, and senior civil servants, professors, publicists and editorial writers (francophone and anglophone), specialists in the constitutional question. It is a relatively small company, linked by professional and sometimes personal friendship, extending over the many years of constitutional debate."[5] This is not the place to list all those who played a major part in the making of the Canadian constitution. In his recollections, however, Roméo remembered the crucial work of Michael Pitfield, as well as that of Jean Chrétien, minister of justice, and Marc Lalonde, minister of energy. All three men used their influence and talents to shape and sell the package.

As for his own involvement in the process, Roméo recalled one matter of general policy about which he had felt very strongly at the time—and still did. There were also two particular issues the resolution of which he considered he had a significant impact. There was no doubt in his mind that the patriation of the constitution needed to be done, and he strongly supported a national Charter of Rights. He fully endorsed Trudeau's reply to the premier of Manitoba, who had warned him "that his course of action would 'tear the country apart.'" Trudeau had answered, "If the country is going to be torn apart because we bring back from Britain our own constitution after 115 years of Confederation and after more than fifty years of fruitless discussions, and because we have asked for a Canadian charter of rights, when most of you already have provincial charters, then the country deserves to be torn up.'"[6] Roméo was never overtly either anti-British or anti-monarchist, but when a committee of the British House of Commons, the Kershaw Committee, began to advance legal claims over Canada and its constitution, he was outraged. When then–High Commissioner to Canada Sir John Ford announced publicly that "he believed the British should not and would not pass the patriation bill,"[7] Roméo was one of the many who, shocked and angered, applauded Jean Chrétien when the latter said in the House of Commons, "The age of being taught from England is past."[8]

Roméo was joined in his belief in the rightness of patriation by the Conservative premier of New Brunswick, Richard Hatfield, along with the Conservative premier of Ontario, Bill Davis. They brought their talent and their influence to bear to help shape the *Charter of Rights and Freedoms*. All three were consummate working politicians, accustomed to using conversation to persuade others of the importance of a political action. Richard Hatfield and Roméo were united in their concern about two issues. In Part I, Sections 16 to 23, which deals with Canada's official languages, both men argued for provisions that would take into account not only New Brunswick's particular needs but also the needs of minority language groups elsewhere in the country. Hatfield took the lead in seeing that, in the final draft, English and French were recognized as the official languages of New Brunswick.[9] At the same time, he supported Roméo in his struggle to ensure that, in Part I, Section 23, minority education rights were excluded from the "notwithstanding clause."[10] Roméo believed he had considerable influence on this decision. He was also convinced, again with Hatfield's support, that he had helped ensure that, in Part II, Section 31, the commitment to the constitutional principle of economic equalization and the correction of regional economic disparities within Canada were included. In looking back on the tumultuous events of those years, Roméo also considered that the questions of Aboriginal and women's rights had received some needed attention, even if, along with a number of other questions, much more needed to be done.

Roméo did not publicly comment on the refusal of the government of Quebec to accept the decision by nine other provinces and the federal government on the morning of November 5, 1981.[11] But he regarded Premier Lévesque's refusal to sign the accord as regrettable. His view was grounded in his belief in the ability of Canada to adjust its traditions to the evolving circumstances that the country would inevitably confront in the years to come. This belief came partly from his own experience as an Acadian, watching his province bring significant, almost revolutionary, change during the 1960s, change cemented by the actions of an anglophone premier, Richard Hatfield, in the 1970s. It came from his experience in seeing the change in the place given to francophones at the federal level, both as politicians and civil servants during the 1970s. It also came from his friendship with Mike Pearson, whose love for Canada had been rooted in Ontario, but embraced Quebec as an essential part of his country. Roméo not only saw possibilities for growth in the Canada he knew, but also believed that the fragmentation of states into small ethnic enclaves was a step backwards. He was convinced that, however difficult it might be to forge a just society out of more than one culture, it was the rational path to take. He had felt bitter about the situation of Acadians in New Brunswick when he was a young man, but he had come to appreciate that, while knowledge of past injustices was necessary to understand the present, it was not in and of itself a blueprint for the future.

While knowledge of the Deportation required the recognition of historical injustice, in Roméo's opinion, this past wrong was insufficient as a basis for the development of present policies. He spoke often of a need for a clear analysis of what the "now" demanded. What were the characteristics of Acadian heritage, of Quebec, of francophones elsewhere in the country, that should be preserved? What customs should be supported by social policies? When thinking about language needs, how should educational policies, from to kindergarten to universities, be structured? How should the cultural treasures of artists and writers, of musicians and actors, be carried from generation to generation? The past should be a base for growth, not a stultifying reiteration of grievance. There was, as well, in Roméo's mind and in the minds of Acadians in general, the question of the survival of their way of life should Quebec separate. A myriad of questions were in the air about possible developments, from the necessity of transport links between Ontario and New Brunswick, to whether a union of Prince Edward Island, Nova Scotia, and New Brunswick could emerge—in which the Acadian population would be almost a negligible minority—to whether the future of northern New Brunswick would be as part of Quebec. All these queries presented possibilities that had no appeal for Roméo and no great attraction for the majority of Acadians in New Brunswick. Throughout the remaining years of his political life, during which time the possibility of Quebec separatism was a continuing issue, Roméo spoke, whenever it was appropriate, of Canada as a state worthy of service to and by all its citizens, capable of development and growth when needed. The new *Constitution Act, 1982* was proclaimed by Elizabeth II on Parliament Hill, April 17, 1982.

At the end of September that year, Trudeau made a number of changes to his cabinet, and among them, he moved Marc

Roméo at an event in his constituency, 1981

Lalonde to finance and Roméo to public works. This position was not Trudeau's first choice for Roméo, which had been the Indian Affairs portfolio. Roméo and Lyn had decided to separate. Their marriage had been in difficulties for the past three years, to some extent caused by their age difference. This decision meant new living arrangements for the children. Dominic turned fourteen in December 1981, and Geneviève had her tenth birthday on December 6, 1982. Roméo wanted a position with much less travel, since he intended to see as much of the children as he could. An amicable arrangement was reached between Roméo and Lyn: Dominic would live with his father during the week, and see his mother most weekends, and Geneviève would live mostly with her mother, and see her father on weekends. Dominic and Geneviève recall the arrangement as one that worked, and Lyn remembered that Roméo made a considerable effort to ensure that it did.[12] Given his own marital history, Trudeau was sympathetic to

Roméo's family situation and appointed him as minister of public works on September 30, 1982, after the Constitution was signed in April. In retirement, Roméo spoke not regretfully but wistfully that he had not seen his way to accepting the Indian affairs portfolio.

Public works meant responsibility for a truly astonishing collection of government business. First of all, there was what might be expected: matters pertaining "to the design, construction, improvement, repair, maintenance and demolition of buildings and facilities of the government of Canada," everything from the construction and design of the National Gallery and the Museum of Civilization to marine works and harbour developments, construction and renovations on Indian reserves, and projects that fell under the Special Recovery Capital Costs Program (SRCPP)."[13] He was also responsible for the National Capital Commission and the Canada Mortgage and Housing Corporation. The change from minister of fisheries and oceans meant a major change in lifestyle, in the type of work demanded, and in the impact he had on Canadian lives. Roméo had carried through major reforms in the management of Canada's fisheries, whereas now he had to run an ongoing concern efficiently. It was, to a large extent, a question of seeing people carry out policies already established, and deciding priorities within established guidelines, but it involved a great deal less travel. The work week, when Parliament was sitting, was a little shorter, as a result of recent parliamentary reforms—there were no more evening sessions—and, except for constituency visits, Roméo was most often in Ottawa during this time.

If this particular appointment came about because of Trudeau's sympathy for the demands of Roméo's domestic life, it was also the result of the reputation Roméo earned for honesty in handling government monies and career opportunities when he was minister of fisheries. The position he had taken when he was first nominated—that he would raise campaign funds through small contributions from the many rather than large donations from the few, set the tone for his political life. People who sought favours from him with a discreetly offered *quid pro quo* were quickly and firmly turned down. Bertin LeBlanc and Yvon LeBlanc, who worked for him during his election campaigns, remember very clearly rebuffing such individuals.[14] In matters of temporary government appointments, Roméo was ready to receive recommendations from Liberals, Progressive Conservatives, or New Democrats, those who knew something about what the position in question demanded and could speak to the skills of the individual they nominated. Of two equally qualified candidates, it was true that he would often support the Liberal, but the individual had to be qualified and acceptable to the permanent staff. In terms of work contracts, for wharves for example, a call for bids was almost always required. As far as large federal government programs that were administered by other departments were concerned, Roméo made certain that New Brunswickers, of whatever political stripe, knew about them, and knew how, where, and when to apply, and he ensured that the granting authorities were aware of New Brunswick interests.[15]

Personal circumstances and a political reputation for non-partisan fairness and honesty were important factors in appointing Roméo as minister of public works, but there was also a question of Liberal Party politics. Trudeau was aware that Roméo had no intention of running in the next election and was keeping his own counsel about who he would support as successor to the leader of the Liberal Party. His appointment as minister of public works was the least controversial that Trudeau could make.

Roméo's first speech in the House of Commons in his new post made his priorities clear. He emphasized the part of his portfolio that dealt with the federal housing programs. The

federal government had played an increasingly important role
in housing since the Task Force on Housing Development and
Urban Planning had reported in 1968, under Paul Hellyer, then
minister of public works.[16] In this, Roméo again showed the
same care for the average person, caught in the financial crisis of
the early 1980s, that he had demonstrated as "minister of fishermen." He said that his first concern was with "the ability of
Canadians to become home owners and that rental accommodation be available...I am deeply concerned about the housing
conditions of native Canadians and of low-income families in
rural areas as well as in cities and towns."[17] It was his responsibility for the Canada Mortgage and Housing Corporation that
allowed him to bring his ideas to bear on these issues—and
where he was faced with the most challenges, because dealing
with it involved an understanding of the relationships among an
alphabet soup of housing programs established by previous governments. In 1974, the federal budget introduced the Registered
Home Ownership Savings Plan (RHOSP) and the Multiple Unit
Residential Building (MURB) tax provision. The Residential
Rehabilitation Assistance Program (RRAP) and the Rural and
Native Housing Program (RNHP) were established. In 1978, the
Urban Native Housing Program (UNHP) and the On-Reserve
Housing Program (ORHP) were established. In 1981, the fed-
eral budget introduced the Canadian Mortgage Renewal Plan
(CMRP), the Canadian Home Ownership Stimulation Program
(CHOSP), and the Canadian Rental Supply Program (CRSP).
Roméo was minister of public works for nineteen months, and it
gave him just enough time to exploit the good will towards both
himself and his department of finance minister, Marc Lalonde.

The bitter economic storm that swept the country in 1982
arrived, it seemed, without any warning. As John English has
written, "Unemployment soared into double digits, housing
prices dropped, car lots were crammed with unsold vehicles,

mortgage interest rates stood at an incredible 22 per cent in August 1981."[18] The budget of November 12, 1981, did little to improve the situation, and many, including the prime minister and the eminent Canadian economist Richard Lipsey, were uncertain as to what remedies to apply.[19] For Roméo, there was the prospect of immediate action, with the passage of an amendment to the *National Housing Act.* The bill had been prepared during the time of his predecessor, Paul Jones Cosgrove. Its major provision was to provide "home owners who find, on renewing their mortgages, that their monthly payments will exceed 30 per cent of their household incomes... grants amounting to as much as $3,000."[20] Roméo urged the House of Commons to pass the legislation speedily, since grants had already been approved for 6,000 families, but the money could not be sent until the legislation was passed. By November 25, cheques were in the mail, thanks, Roméo noted, to unpaid overtime on the part of staff.

Roméo not only moved quickly to implement this short-term help, but also worked with Marc Lalonde to provide long-term remedies, through more generalized support to the housing industry. Lalonde, who was named minister of finance in the Cabinet shuffle of 1982, provided Roméo with considerable funds. Lalonde's intentions were signalled early in 1983 with a pre-budget demand for supplementary funding in February.[21] Roméo opened the debate for the government on the second reading of the bill, saying that he wished to "emphasize the importance of these proposals which are aimed at maintaining adequate funding to stimulate the housing industry...Each 10,000 unit increase in housing starts creates over 25,000 person-years of employment." Summing up funding for housing in this budget, Roméo reported that "a total of $335 million in additional resources over the next 18 months has been allocated...this being in addition to over $1 billion which has been channelled into housing measures over the past year and above the regular CMHC budget of some \$2 billion."[22] By the end of the debate, questions of support for the provision of non-profit housing, low-cost housing, and social housing, as well as housing on reserves, were being raised.

The budget itself was brought down on April 29, and it was one that rejected the economic path chosen by both the United States and the United Kingdom. Speaking in its defence, Roméo said, "this government has not removed the social program protection for those who need help the most." He went on to "welcome the measures which strengthen our traditional social programs and make special provision to assist low-income families."[23] He related in detail where the more than \$220 million to his department would be allocated, pointing out the impact the funding of the various programs would have on the construction industry. "Employment," he said, "related to residential construction will increase from about 176,000 to approximately 354,000 [jobs]"[24] in the coming year, and some 20,000 person-years had already been added, because of the renovation programs. He continued, "it is easy to talk about housing measures in terms of units and dollars...but these measures affect real people, real households, in a direct way."[25] He made particular mention of the \$6.70 million to be spent in 1983 and the \$20 million that would be spent in 1984 on rural and Native housing programs. In many ways, this was Roméo at his most pragmatic, persuading Lalonde and Trudeau in particular, and the cabinet in general, of the necessity to make shelter a major area for government action.

Roméo was one of those ministers who paid attention to his correspondents, and letters from low- and middle-income Canadians, asking for help as they struggled with the economic ills of the country, filled his mailbox. There was little that Roméo could do except work through his officials and make sure that the replies sent out were not abrupt or unsympathetic.[26] Bertin

LeBlanc, who joined his office staff for a year in 1982, reported that Roméo worked an eighty-hour week.[27] If shelter was Roméo's primary concern, he also looked after other matters, including subvention for building projects in Quebec and New Brunswick or elsewhere in the country.

The usual flurry of odd issues also came through his hands, one of which had an ironic twist he found amusing. It concerned the piano of Canada's internationally renowned pianist Glenn Gould. On Gould's death, Roméo decided that the artist's piano would be a fine artifact for Rideau Hall. He knew that Gould had modified its interior and covered its outside with cigarette burns and watermarks. In Roméo's mind, it would be transported to Rideau Hall in this condition as a memorial to the brilliant and eccentric artist. It was indeed transported to Rideau Hall and is still there. On the way, however, it was cleaned up, polished, and rebuilt by the well-meant attention of those who undertook the task for Public Works.

In 1981, a forty-two-day-long postal strike, 11 per cent unemployment, and a record-breaking spike in mortgage interest rates set the tone for a summer of discontent. The Liberal government battled the prevailing ills of the country in the early 1980s by strengthening popular social programs. In particular, it paid attention to national health services. The minister responsible was Monique Bégin, "popular, articulate in both official languages and ready to fight the conservative establishment."[28] On July 25, 1983, she introduced the *National Health Act* to prevent extra billing, something that received immediate and wide public support. The Opposition in Parliament was led by Brian Mulroney, who had been elected leader of the Conservative Party on June 11, 1983. He rallied his party to give the *Health Act* full support, an action that removed a strong reason for people to vote Liberal. At the same time, the National Energy Program, for which Lalonde was considered responsible, was bitterly fought by

Alberta and caused widespread resentment throughout western Canada. The deficit, moreover, reached a record high. By the end of the year, it was obvious that an election was looming. Trudeau resigned as leader of the Liberal Party on February 29, 1984, and John Turner was elected leader at the Liberal convention on June 16. He succeeded Trudeau as prime minister on June 30. The day before, Trudeau had appointed Roméo to the Senate.

Roméo's decision not to run in the 1984 election, which Turner called on July 9, had been made before his appointment to the Senate. He was fifty-seven years old, had been twelve years in elected political life, and for ten of those years was a minister of the Crown. For those ten years, his life had been dominated by the demands of his position. In the last months of Trudeau's time in power, Roméo spoke with him about his future, and he later remembered these conversations with both pride and affection. Roméo, while liked and respected by his colleagues, did not make many close friends in Ottawa, and his relationship with Trudeau was one that became closer after they had left elected political life. Roméo recalled that Trudeau offered him a number of options at this time, including appointments to various international positions as Canada's representative. Roméo said that he accepted the Senate because it allowed him to remain in Ottawa and be a presence in his children's lives, to learn how the Senate functioned, and, at the same time, to continue to be of use there to both New Brunswick and Canada.[29]

He had certainly been of service to both his province and the country, over and above the work he had done with the departments he headed. Most cabinet ministers worked in much the same manner, helping small towns find the route to funds to rebuild themselves. In Roméo's case, he had given support to local development plans, such as the revitalization of Moncton's core and the development of Market Square in Saint John.[30] Another common way cabinet ministers provided help to their own constituencies and to the ridings of others in their region was assistance for firms seeking major government funding for work that lay outside the purview of their own responsibilities. One such project that Roméo worked on was to help the Saint John Dry Dock and Shipbuilding Company obtain the contract to build ships for the Canadian Control Frigate program. This company had been bought by K.C. Irving in the 1950s. By the late 1970s, it was the centre of a flourishing conglomerate of companies with major interests in forestry, shipbuilding, oil, and newspapers. He ran his companies as private family concerns, helped by his sons Arthur, born in 1928; James, born in 1931; and Jack, born in 1932. Arthur and James met with Roméo in 1979, asking for his advice in preparing a bid on what they learned could be considerable work for their shipyards. He gave them ideas about who was experienced in preparing such bids, who needed to be aware of their interests, and how they should present their ideas. He also said he would support their bid, as and when it was appropriate for him to do so. There was little further contact between the family and Roméo at this time. Probably in 1980, Roméo pointed out to Elsie Wayne, who had been elected to the Saint John municipal council in 1977, that he would have difficulty in continuing his support for the Irving bid for the frigate project if she continued to oppose funding for a French school and community centre in that city. This kind of pressure was a normal part of the politics of government for both parties when in power, and its impact was commensurate with the personality of the individual addressed. Sometimes it marked a turning point in the deal; in this case; it was probably important but not crucial. In March 1982, an agreement was signed between the federal and New Brunswick governments to build a school and a community centre for the francophone population of Saint John. The school opened its doors in 1984, and the community centre in 1985. Meanwhile, in August 1983, the Canadian government announced that Saint John had been awarded the contract. It was the largest single shipbuilding order issued in Canadian history to that time. The first of these frigates, HMSC *Halifax*, was launched in 1988. A total of twelve ships were built in all, most during the next decade.

The centre of Roméo's House of Commons life and duties had always been his constituency and Canadian fishing interests. But his work on various cabinet committees and subcommittees had woven in another complex tapestry of activities. His lifelong dislike of undue publicity, his lack of ambition for public recognition—other than that strictly necessary for the work he did—meant that he was often overlooked. Yet he had had a very considerable influence on the development of Liberal Party policies and politics, both inside and outside Parliament. His membership on the crucial Priorities and Planning Committee was only one such place where his influence had an effect. He was also a member of the cabinet committees on Economic Regional Development, Government Operations, Social Development, and Political Planning, as well as the Committee on Communications and the Information Sub-Committee, on which he served as chair.[31] The minutes of these committees reveal the extent to which he was seen by members of the party, both in and out of Parliament, as someone with significant influence on the direction of Liberal policies. His activities often took him well outside his official mandate.[32] While the needs of his family were paramount, it was these aspects of his life as an MP that reconciled him to leaving elected office for the Senate. He knew he would be able to continue in his role as a senior member of the Liberal Party, one whose advice was often sought and very often acted upon.

His participation in the Liberal Party convention, held in mid-June 1984, which chose Trudeau's successor, John Turner, was not much more than peripheral. Turner then called an election

Roméo LeBlanc and K.C. Irving, 1981

on June 9 for September 4. It was fought, brilliantly by Mulroney and bitterly by Turner, on the Liberal record. The Liberals retained one seat in Manitoba and one in British Columbia, all other western ridings going to the Tories. The Liberals were elected in 14 ridings in Ontario and 17 in Quebec. Roméo's old riding. Westmorland–Kent in New Brunswick, which had elected him with 21,625 votes in 1980, returned the sole Liberal from that province, Fernand Robichaud, with 14,709 votes. Prince Edward Island also returned a single Liberal to the 33rd Parliament; Nova Scotia, two; and Newfoundland and Labrador, three. Mulroney and the Progressive Conservatives received 50 per cent of the popular vote and 211 of the 282 seats.

Roméo spent much of the summer of 1984 with his children at Grande-Digue, the property that had been a summer cottage for an order of nuns from Montreal, which he had bought in 1969. It stood on a bluff along the coast between Shediac and Cocagne and had been improved and partially winterized over the years.

Its most endearing features were the large kitchen and dining area, its marvellous views of the sea, its ample land. Over the next years, Roméo planted potatoes, tomatoes, and zucchini, as well as savory, an herb much used in Acadian cooking. The cottage's disadvantages were the small bedrooms, which had been built for the minimum privacy and comfort requirements of the nuns. In 1984, its water came from a well and electricity was temperamental. Visits from friends and relatives made the days pass quickly enough. Roméo's brother and sisters often came for visits. Here, Roméo took some time to recover not only from ten years as a minister of the Crown, but also from what, at that time, was the worst defeat for a governing party at the federal level.

Roméo and his children were back in Ottawa for the opening of the school year in 1984. Geneviève turned twelve on December 2 and Dominic was seventeen on December 14. When Parliament was in session, Dominic was accustomed to walking up Parliament Hill to his father's office when his school day ended, and later in life he recalled this routine with great pleasure. Genevieve remembers with equal pleasure the times her father took her to riding lessons, though he was never fond of horses and tended to stand back from the animals. By the spring of 1985, much of Roméo's energy had returned. He was appointed in 1984 to the Senate Standing Committee on Internal Economy, Budget and Administration, which dealt then, and deals now, with the finances and administration of the Canadian Senate. He took an increasing interest in a number of the questions that the body dealt with, particularly those concerning the Senate library.[33]

In 1985, the *De Novo Journal* came into being. It was seen as a new venture to promote the spread of Liberal ideas across the country. While Roméo played no official role in its production, his correspondence for the period between spring 1985 and fall of 1987 show that he was a moving force in the philosophy of the

At the LeBlancs's summer cottage, Grande Digue

journal.[34] He spent a fair amount of time giving advice to young Liberals, as the *De Novo Journal* was primarily the voice of the younger members of the party. This involvement reawakened his love of teaching. He accepted the offer of a visiting fellowship in the Institute of Canadian Studies at Carleton University. Dr. Richard Clippingdale, who was the director of the institute at that time and a committed "red Tory," had no hesitation in seeking out Roméo, and less difficulty in persuading the dean of the faculty, the author, to accept his appointment. The initiative taken by Carleton University was followed by Concordia University and the Université de Moncton. He gave occasional lectures at both institutions. After Dominic enrolled in the University of Toronto as an Ontario Scholar in the fall of 1985, Roméo was willing to give more time to the affairs of the Liberal Party.

In 1986, he had become a member of the Senate Foreign Affairs Committee, and perhaps it was this responsibility that made him take particular notice of an event that occurred in Nova Scotia the following year: the arrival on July 12, offshore from the tiny fishing village of Charlesville, of the *Amelie*, a Chilean-registered cargo ship from Rotterdam. On board were 173 Sikh refugees: 172 men and one woman. They had paid various sums of money to sail on the ship, some as much as $5,000. They were dropped into the water and most of them were able to swim to shore, some helped with flotation devices. There they met confused local people and an RCMP officer. One or two of the refugees spoke some English. All were quickly disabused of the notion that it was possible to take a taxi to Toronto. Instead, they were taken to the village hall and fed peanut butter and jelly sandwiches. Rosalie Stoddard, a villager who knew the Sikhs were bound for Halifax and needed food and drink before they left, said, "We knew they would probably be vegetarian and we figured...they could probably eat that."[35] Officials acted with speed and these particular refugees were all admitted to Canada and later became citizens.[36] Some of them still return to Charlesville to thank those who helped. For Roméo, the reception of these refugees by the villagers was the essence of Canada—no hysteria, no guns, no imprisonment, no media hype, just neighbourliness and immediate appropriate help. It was a story he told over and over during the next twenty-five years. Roméo maintained they were offered toothbrushes. If this claim was a little airbrushed, its essence was indeed true.

The finalization of the legal separation between Lyn and Roméo occurred in 1987. Dominic recalls that it was achieved without bitterness. By the election of 1988, Roméo was once more following politics with a passion, reading every daily newspaper available to him. The election took place on November 21, and brought him back, along with many Canadians, to a fascination with federal politics. While the Free Trade Agreement, which had been initialled in Washington on October 4, was by no means the sole issue, it was John Turner's passionate arguments against it that set fire to the election. The English-language television debate on Tuesday, October 25, meant the Liberals moved from looking at one more bitter defeat to a respectable second-place finish. Mulroney and Turner both spoke eloquently, but it was generally considered that Turner won the debate. He argued that the Liberals:

> built a country east west and north. We built it on an infrastructure that deliberately resisted the continental pressure of the United States. For one hundred years we have done it. With one signature of a pen, you have reversed that, thrown us into the north-south influence of the United States, and will reduce us, I am sure, to a colony of the United States, because when the economic levers go, the political independence is sure to follow.[37]

The other important issue that caused problems for the government was the Meech Lake Accord, an agreement that had had been reached by Prime Minister Mulroney and the ten provincial premiers on April 30, 1987. As historian Michael Bliss explained, "Its terms...included the recognition of Quebec as a distinct society and various limitations on Ottawa's power to control the federation."[38] Because it changed the amending formula for the constitution, it needed the consent of all provincial legislatures, as well as the federal legislature, within three years. While the agreement seemed at first to be generally accepted, it soon became clear that it faced a mounting wave of criticism. Quebec decided the accord did not go far enough in recognizing its unique status and Manitoba thought it had gone too far. Trudeau spoke strongly against it. Many people felt it was an agreement reached by "eleven men in suits," deciding the future of Canada, without any real consultation about its provisions with its citizenry. It became a growing issue during the election campaign. In the end, however, the Progressive Conservatives won 169 seats, 42 fewer than they had previously held, with 43.2 per cent of the popular vote. The Liberals more than doubled their seats, from 40 to 83, with 31 per cent of the popular vote.

This result was encouraging for Roméo. For the past four years he had given time and attention to Senate matters. In 1989, he was made the chairman of the Senate Internal Economy, Budgets and Administration Committee, of which he had been a member since 1984. He was interested not only in the well being of senators, but also of their staff. Questions of the reclassification and salaries of senators' secretaries as well as the allowable budget for the hiring of researchers and consultants had his attention.[39] In addition, he took part in the debates over the legislation surrounding Bill C-72, which amended the *Patent Act*. The amendments guaranteed patent owners greater freedom, something Roméo thought unwarranted.[40]

However, now that there was the possibility of a Liberal resurgence, he became much more involved in the daily life of the party. He considered the differences between the policies of the Liberals and the Progressive Conservatives more than a matter of rhetoric. He thought the Free Trade Agreement was a matter of continuing concern because, regardless of the way it was interpreted, it would be of huge importance to the Canadian economy. The importance of the Meech Lake Accord was a question of even greater concern to him. He was unsure that it was the best way forward, but he considered that its success or failure would be of great significance for the country as a whole.

In May 1989, Turner announced that he was stepping down as leader, and Roméo attended the convention to choose his successor, held in Calgary in early June 1990. A superficial reading of its result—the selection of Jean Chrétien on the first ballot, with 56 per cent of the votes cast—seemed to signify a united party. However, Paul Martin, Jr., who had been elected in 1988 for the riding of LaSalle–Émard in Montreal, received 1,176 votes, or 25.19 per cent. He and his supporters had fought bitterly against Chrétien. The failure of the Meech Lake Accord to gain the requisite agreements from the provinces was confirmed the day before the convention vote. Elijah Harper, an Aboriginal member of the Manitoba legislature, drove the final nail in its coffin with a speech in the provincial legislature, outlining the total lack of adequate participation and recognition of Aboriginal people in the development of the accord. This led to a noisy confrontation between the two Liberal candidates and Chrétien faced cries of "Judas" and "sell-out" from the floor, because he would not unequivocally pronounce himself for or against it. He was convinced Martin had inspired the hecklers. The rivalry between the two men and their supporters endured until the defeat of the Martin government by the Conservatives on February 6, 2006. Roméo had supported Chrétien in his first bid for the leadership in 1984. He had no enthusiasm for Turner as leader and he saw no reason to change his mind six years later. Chrétien was already a Cabinet minister when Roméo became an MP and both men considered themselves lifelong friends.

During the remaining months before Prime Minister Mulroney called for an election in 1993, Roméo divided his time between caring for his children, his duties in the Senate, and acting as a influential senior member of the Liberal Party. He also renewed his acquaintance with Diana Fowler, who had shared an apartment with Lyn in London. Roméo had stood in for Diana's father at her wedding when she married her first husband in the 1960s. She was now a widow with two children, and lived in London. Their friendship would flourish over the next few years. He still lived in the house on Fourth Avenue in Ottawa, spending as much of the summer as possible at Grande-Digue. Dominic went to the University of New Brunswick on a Canadian Bar Association scholarship in 1989 and graduated with a Bachelor of Law degree in 1992. Geneviève graduated from Lisgar High School in Ottawa in 1991 and went on that year to the University of Toronto to work towards a B.A. It was during this period that Roméo began to feel financially pressed. Throughout his life he was generous to members of his extended family, and now, with two children, one in mid-university career and one just beginning university studies, he began to worry about money. In the first months of 1984, his last year as a Cabinet minister, his income was $92,000 with a $16,000 non-taxable living allowance. In September of that same year, his first year as a senator, his income was $52,800—a drop of $40,000—and his non-taxable allowance was $8,600—a drop of $7,400. The adjustment was considerable, but he managed. Now he was concerned about the amount of help he could give his children over the next years.

He found his life in the Senate became more interesting than it had been, partly because, in 1992, he became a member of

In the office of Prime Minister Jean Chrétien, 1995

the Canada–France Parliamentary Association, established in 1965, and the International Association of French-speaking Parliamentarians, which had first seen the light of day in Luxembourg in 1967. The growth of international co-operation among the 150 million francophones throughout the world, and the development of agencies to facilitate it, had expanded from 1986, when the first conference of the "Heads of State and Government of Countries Using French as a Common Language" took place.[41] With Quebec seeking international recognition, attendance at such organizations, especially the parliamentary associations, was a matter of major importance for Canada. The year 1992 also saw Mulroney attempt to deal with the rising discontent with the federation in Quebec, which was, in part, caused by the failure of the Meech Lake Accord. In 1991, two reports were produced in Quebec: the "Allaire Report" sponsored by the Liberal Party of that province, and the report of the Bélanger–Campeau Commission, which the Quebec government established. Both documents underlined the widespread discontent in the province with the way the federation operated. The federal government established its own commission, generally known as the Spicer Commission, which also reported in 1991. With these inquiries as background, Mulroney set about creating another agreement to solve the constitutional problems of the country. The Charlottetown Accord was presented in August 1992 and the country was asked to vote for its adoption in a referendum on October 26. It was defeated nationally by a vote of 55 per cent to 45 per cent.

Ever since the end of the Liberal convention in 1990, Roméo had been involved with the party's preparation for the next election. This planning began with a "thinkers' conference held in Aylmer, Quebec, in 1991, to decide what the platform should be and how to deal with the issue of free trade, on which they had fought the Conservatives in the 1988 election. It was from this conference that the "Red Book" took shape, which explained the Liberal aims and ambitions to the voters during the election year.[42] Its official title was *Creating Opportunity: The Liberal Plan for Canada*. Paul Martin, Jr., and Chaviva Hošek directed its preparation, and thousands of copies were distributed. It was one of the first attempts at a "contract with the public" political campaign, and much of its specificity would come back to haunt the Liberals. Roméo was one of those consulted during its preparation. He was to play an important part in the 1993 election, which would be held in the fall that year when the five-year term of Parliament ended in September. Prime Minister Kim Campbell, who succeeded Brian Mulroney as leader of the Progressive Conservatives in June, asked Governor General Ray Hnatyshyn to dissolve Parliament on September 8, and the election took place on October 25.

Campbell had little time to consolidate her position and organize her team for the election. The Liberals immediately swung into campaign mode, not only with the "Red Book" and new faces among their candidates, but also with a strong support team, headed by John Rae, the brother of Ontario MPP Bob Rae. John was a long-time supporter and friend of Jean Chrétien, whose business it was to counter Progressive Conservative claims and arguments. Roméo was part of this group, which became known as the "War Room." They were particularly effective in responding to the attack ads produced by Progressive Conservative campaign strategists, in particular one that emphasized Chrétien's partial facial paralysis, which had resulted from a childhood illness. When the ad appeared, its insensitivity and tastelessness produced an instant negative reaction. Roméo agreed strongly with Chrétien that no major response from the Liberal Party should be made. Chrétien himself, speaking in New Brunswick, merely said, "God gave me a physical defect, that I've accepted since I was a kid." Roméo did, however, suggest that Liberal supporters should ask their Conservative friends what they thought of the ad. The extent to which it affected the final vote has been debated. It certainly lost the Conservatives support among women voters who were active in volunteer work helping the physically frail.[43] The defeat of the Progressive Conservative government was cataclysmic. The party, which had won 43 per cent of the popular vote and 169 seats in 1988, was reduced to 16 per cent of the vote and two seats. The root cause of this defeat, however, went further back than the weeks of the campaign. As Michael Bliss noted, "The Conservatives had actually built up more new debt in their nine years than all the previous governments combined...[the] annual deficit adding about $40 billion a year to Canada's mountain of debt."[44] Within six years, Paul Martin, Jr., as minister of finance, with the continuous strong support of the prime minister, would bring the country a budgetary surplus.

One of the immediate appointments the prime minister asked the governor general to make was that of Roméo as speaker of the

Senate. He was so named on December 7, 1993. Like the speaker of the House of Commons, the speaker of the Senate must have the confidence of all parties, since he or she has the duty of presiding over debates and keeping order in the chamber. However, while the speaker of the Senate is expected to act without bias, he or she is also expected to represent the views of government and has the right to cast an original vote, rather than only breaking a tie. Unlike the position of speaker of the House of Commons, this position holds no management or administrative duties. Such a role is carried out by the chairman of the Senate Standing Committee on Internal Economy, Budgets and Administration, the position Roméo held from 1989 to 1991. One of the most important differences between the roles of the two speakers is that, in order of precedence, the speaker of the Senate is qualified to represent Canada at official state functions both at home and abroad. For Roméo, the appointment meant the end of financial worries, since the salary was $95,000, plus a non-taxable living allowance of $14,000 and a car allowance. Taking inflation into account, the compensation brought him back to what he had earned as a Cabinet minister five years earlier. He enjoyed his time in this position. He knew the temper of the "Red Chamber," the pace of discussion, and the work done in its corridors. He was particularly aware of the way in which its members played a part in influencing the government of the day. He very much enjoyed the occasions when, the governor general being otherwise engaged, he accepted the credentials of new diplomats on their arrival in Canada. These were occasions for conversations with a diverse range of people. But his tenure as speaker was short. On November 24, 1994, the Prime Minister's Office announced that he would be the next governor general of Canada.

In an interview after his retirement, Roméo recalled that his first reaction when Chrétien asked him to assume the position was that he already had "un bon job," and had no desire

Page-274 body.

Roméo as speaker, c. 1993

whatsoever to leave it.[45] But the prime minister knew what he wanted: someone who could speak about Canada with authority and ease in both official languages and, should complex constitutional issues arise, deal with them knowledgeably.[46] He drew on all his powers of persuasion when he interviewed Roméo, telling him that Canada had never had a governor general from the Atlantic

Provinces, certainly not an Acadian, and that, in the present circumstances, it would be particularly valuable to have a francophone from outside Quebec—"hors du Québec—so named. It would, Chrétien considered, send "a message to all Canadians about the vitality of the French-speaking community outside Quebec."[47] The prime minister's final strategy was to point out the need of the country and the wishes of an old friend. When Roméo asked for time to think about the post, Chrétien pushed him for his decision. Roméo accepted, and immediately also announced that "he [would] marry his partner, Diana Fowler." Roméo and Lyn's divorce had been finalized in June 1992.[48] He and Diana were married in a private ceremony in early November 1994 in Moncton, New Brunswick. He was installed as the 25th governor general of Canada on February 8, 1995.

Roméo had had no ambition to be governor general of Canada, and he had not expected to be appointed to the position. It meant a revolution in his and Diana's life, one which neither had expected. Roméo had accepted both a request of his old friend and the request of the prime minister, which he felt he could not refuse without an overwhelming reason. Diana herself had agreed. Both were stunned, however, by the change from relative privacy to lives where others were present virtually twenty-four hours a day. For many years, Roméo's working life was controlled by a timetable based on government schedules and the oversight of secretaries. Now his life was a matter of nearly inescapable official obligations, and to secretaries were added a household staff and security personnel. There were aspects of living in Rideau Hall that he enjoyed from the beginning, especially the greenhouses. The burden of a structured existence was also helped by the professionalism of his staff. They were aware of the difficulties he faced and appreciated his habit of thanking them personally for what they did, which eased the transition to the life of governor general. The Right Honourable

Roméo and Diana, at his installation as governor general, 1995

Ramon Hnatyshyn, the outgoing governor general, cautioned Roméo about the heavy workload which awaited him.

Few Canadians have a clear idea about what this position involves, except for the duty of opening Parliament and setting elections in motion. It is a life that combines an exhausting round of public appearances in small communities with ceremonial duties of state in the capital; of journeys to the edges of Canada and overseas visits to other countries; of constantly meeting new people with little relief of time with family and friends. It demands an ability to reflect the complexities of Confederation to Canadians, to mirror both its challenges and its achievements, to find ways to encourage those who serve it, and yet to talk of what must be renewed. It involves physical strength, as well as intellectual and emotional courage. A consideration of some crude statistics gives pause: during the four years that they lived at Rideau Hall, Roméo delivered 791 speeches and Diana 104. Mostly together, they accepted 1,852 invitations to events throughout Canada. During the same 48 months, they hosted the visits of 19 heads of state to Canada, and, at the request of the Canadian government, made nine state and official overseas visits.

In spite of these rigorous official demands, Roméo made an individual contribution to the traditions of the office. He had considerable experience in the corridors of power, and his international experience as a journalist and minister of fisheries stood him in good stead where diplomatic niceties were concerned. Once he accepted the appointment, Roméo thought about both what was possible to do and what he wished to do with the opportunities it provided. There were three issues which, above all, he wanted to address: the place of Aboriginal Canadians in the country's history; recognition of the strength of Canadians to face problems which they confronted; and Canadians' knowledge of their own history and culture. He consistently made all three issues themes in his many speeches and, at the same time,

The royal visit: HRM Queen Elizabeth and Roméo, 1997

took practical measures to illustrate their importance to him. He referred often to the long history of Aboriginal life in Canada and, on June 21, 1997, National Aboriginal Day, he unveiled an Inukshuk on the grounds of Rideau Hall. It had been created in Cape Dorset by Kananginak Pootoogook and shipped to Ottawa, where it was rebuilt. In his speech at the unveiling, Roméo stressed that it was five hundred years since John Cabot landed on Canada's Atlantic coast, nearly a thousand years since the Vikings arrived in Newfoundland; but the first peoples had "already been here for more than ten thousand years."[49] He was determined to find ways to make the experiences of Aboriginals a known part of history for Canadians.

It was not just knowledge of Aboriginal history that Roméo wanted Canadians to understand. It was also the full, complex history of Canada. As a foundation for this aim, in October 1996, Roméo established the Governor General's Award for Excellence in Teaching Canadian History. This award, administered by the Canadian National History Society, is awarded annually. He also completed the work that Governor General Ray Hnatyshyn had begun—of making Rideau Hall relevant to the people of Canada and not just an expensive lodging for "Their Excellencies." During Roméo's years in office, the number of visitors tripled, to an estimated 125,000 a year. An official Visitor Centre was opened, and more than 65,000 attended summer concerts during these years. Roméo told those he had the opportunity to meet that it was "their house and gardens." He was just a passing tenant.

It was his own sense of the country's past that led him to defy both federal and provincial governments at the end of 1996 and hold the governor general's New Year's levée, on January 1, 1997, at La Citadelle, the governor general's residence in Quebec City. The federal government thought it unwise. The result of the second referendum about whether Quebec should secede from Canada had taken place less than fifteen months earlier, on October 30, 1995. The narrow margin of victory for the federal government, 50.58 per cent against and 49.42 per cent for, had seriously shaken Ottawa. It was feared that riots and hostile demonstrations might result if the governor general decided to spend part of the holiday season in his official residence in Quebec. Lucien Bouchard, who had become the premier of Quebec on January 26, 1996, on the resignation of Jacques Parizeau, made it clear that he thought such a visit unnecessary and unwelcome.

Furthermore, both federal and provincial governments informed Roméo that no one would come to the levée. Roméo was vindicated: no riots occurred and 3,000 attended.

On this visit to Quebec, Roméo accepted the invitation of Pierre Maison to appear on his live call-in television show. It might have proved disastrous, but Roméo's old skills as a journalist surfaced and allowed him to put his own ideas forward on his role as governor general.[50] The first questioner asked how he could bring himself to be governor general, a useless position that was a hangover from colonial times. Roméo replied that, until the country was democratically changed to another system, he had as much right as any other Canadian to hold the position. The second questioner took more time and asked her question with considerable hostility. "You are an Acadian," she began, "and your acceptance of this position shows you as a traitor to your people and your history. How can you defend what you have done?" Roméo replied that there were two options for someone who felt betrayed by the way things had happened in the past: the first was to try to replay history and make it come out differently the second time around. This option, Roméo said, almost never worked. The second option was to think first about what there was in the past that one needed to preserve, what heritage should be cherished, and, second, to consider what now, in the present, must and could be done to achieve that end. The interview ended fairly quickly after this, as Roméo went on to emphasize that the world in the late twentieth century was very different from the world of the eighteenth, and that Acadians had managed to move with the changes that had taken place since then. Roméo made an official visit to Quebec City each year and received approximately 3,000 visitors on each occasion. He also held the New Year's levée in Winnipeg in 1998 and in St. John's, Newfoundland, in 1999.

The most consistent activity for Roméo during his years in office were the travels he and Diana made throughout Canada. The speeches he made on these occasions were short and centred on the history of the locality and the achievements of the community. His ambition was to help Canadians understand the worth of their country and the tools they had at hand to develop its strengths. He knew that neither the major media outlets nor the large urban centres had much interest in the activities of the governor general. When he met with his monthly planning group, the people who worked on his schedule, he set out to select two kinds of events to attend: visits to smaller towns and communities, which had not seen a governor general in the past ten years, and celebrations of volunteer organizations that worked for the needs of the frail in society. Roméo travelled from one end of the country to the other, from Hay River in the Northwest Territories to Baie-Saint-Paul and Rothesay, from small towns in the Prairie provinces to fishing villages in British Columbia. He told stories of local history and linked them to present-day events, and he listened when the young and the old told him their stories. It was this aspect of his work that was behind his establishment of the Canadian Caring Award, which recognizes the everyday courage and dedication of ordinary people, caregivers, and family members who have made extraordinary contributions to their families or communities. Since its inception more than 500 people have received this award.

To a great extent, Diana Fowler LeBlanc accompanied her husband on his travels, but she also had her own sphere of activity. She had spent the years from 1969 to 1980 working in London in various medical and legal fields. From 1980 to 1989, she was much involved in a number of educational and research projects for the British and international societies for the Prevention of Child Abuse and Neglect. When she returned to Canada, she registered for a degree in Social Work at McGill

LeBlanc and his wife in Calgary, c. 1996

University, which she completed in 1996. During their lives as the vice-regal couple, Diana spent some of her time and turned her attention to an independent program of events, centred upon questions of palliative care and Aboriginal issues. She established the Diana Fowler LeBlanc Aboriginal Social Work Scholarship, tenable at recognized universities and colleges across Canada. For husband and wife, the contact with thousands of Canadians, even if for only brief periods, remained most strongly in their memories.

They also never forgot the fascination—and exhaustion—that attended the entertaining of foreign dignitaries at Rideau Hall or the foreign travel, undertaken at the request of the Canadian government. Into this round of duties came a steady stream of international visitors and reciprocal travel to other countries. Apart from the opening of Parliament, these occasions, whether at home or abroad, were among the most tightly structured events in which the governor general took part. Governed by protocol and precedent, they were an important part of the foreign policy of Canada. The governor general and his wife could call on professional help from the Prime Minister's Office and External Affairs, but in the main, Their Excellencies and the Rideau Hall staff had but one crucial task to perform: to be the perfect hosts. In March 1995, the president of the United States, Bill Clinton, and his wife, Hillary Clinton, were the first such guests to be welcomed by the LeBlancs. The outgoing personality of the president made this not only a pleasant but a relaxed occasion. The majority of such visits were more the necessary social occasions of a country's diplomatic relations. However, the visit of His Excellency Nelson Mandela, president of the Republic of South Africa, and Madame Graça Machel in September 1998 stood out in Roméo's memory. It was memorable partly because Roméo appointed Mandela a Companion in the Order of Canada, the first foreign national so honoured. But it remained so vivid mainly because of the stature of the man who had spent twenty-eight years in prison as part of his struggle against apartheid, and who never became embittered. In his speech at the banquet for President Mandela, Roméo said, "The world has long known that South Africa is a land of rich resources, it is a land of gold, of diamonds and of natural wonders. But your life, sir, has shown the world a different richness, the wealth of the heart."[51]

Keeping Roméo on a tight leash was a reasonable task when he was in Ottawa, but a far less simple matter when he was abroad. He tended to depart from the text that he and his staff had prepared for the occasions, explaining some major point with an anecdote. The most difficult task for his staff, however, was to keep him talking to government officials, rather than ordinary members of the public. He had an unerring ability to forsake the one and cultivate the other in any gathering. Despite misgivings, however, External Affairs officials were impressed with his capacity to establish friendly relations with even the most punctilious of his hosts. He was the first Canadian governor general to visit India on a state visit in March 1998. He also paid such a visit to Africa in the early spring of 1999, where he visited Côte d'Ivoire, Tanzania, Mali, and Morocco. On these travels, he and Diana made it a point to talk to the non-governmental aid groups from Canada, which were working to help the poorest and the destitute. On their return to Ottawa, they followed up such conversations by finding out ways in which they could support such groups from within Canada.

By the summer of 1999, Roméo knew that he did not want to be governor general during the celebrations of the millennium in 2000. Life as governor general had begun to exhaust him, and the round of celebrations that he would need to attend appalled him. He talked to the prime minister about the timing of his resignation, and the latter persuaded him to do one more major event: presiding over the meeting of the Francophonie in Memramcook, New Brunswick, in September. This gathering proved to be, for both men, not only a demonstration of support for their general aspirations, but also an affirmation of a certain success. For the prime minister, it marked a turning point in the attitude of the French government towards Canada. Jean Chrétien believed that the then-president of France, "Jacques Chirac was finally converted to the virtues of Canadian federalism by the Francophone summit in Moncton...The existence of an old and vibrant French-speaking community outside Quebec was an eye-opener for him and the other leaders, all of whom were genuinely surprised by and impressed with the story of the Acadians."[52] For Roméo and the Acadian community in general, there was a much deeper satisfaction, and he had no hesitation in making it perfectly plain to many in his audience who had consistently doubted there was an Acadian people with an identity separate from that of Quebec and France. In his welcoming speech he said,

> *The decision to welcome you to Memramcook was no accident. The Société Nationale de l'Acadie wanted to greet you here for reasons connected with our collective history. Our national association came into existence in this very place in 1881, when 5,000 Acadians from the three Maritime provinces and representatives from Quebec gathered at this spot. The modern Acadia was born here when it affirmed its distinct identity and its determination to stand unbowed. Today none can doubt that it has succeeded, for the president of France is enshrining the fruits of our tenacity by honouring us with his presence."*[53]

The prime minister had achieved the recognition from France of Canada as a viable nation and the governor general had received acknowledgement of the reality of an Acadian identity from a significant international gathering.

By the year's end, Roméo and Diana had left Rideau Hall and returned to the house on the shore of New Brunswick. They left Ottawa by train, seen off by a crowd of well-wishers, and arrived in Moncton to be greeted by an equally large assembly to welcome him home. Recalling this occasion, he remembered how exhausted he felt and how refreshing it was to walk in his garden by the sea. He also remembered that many had told him he had helped people, in small ways and large, to value Canada as a country that cared for its citizens and a country that listened to its own people. This, he felt, was reward enough.

Epilogue

The change from life in Rideau Hall to private life meant a considerable adjustment for the LeBlancs, but one that was much different from the move in 1995. In the first place, Roméo and Diana, and their children, had had several months to plan, rather than just the few weeks they had in 1995. This time it was a change from a life of work in the public eye to private life in retirement. They now had the freedom to put themselves and their children first. It was a return to the familiar, to a pattern that had been established before 1995, of time split between Grande-Digue and an apartment in Montreal. It was also an arrangement which reflected their different pasts and different tastes: Diana had been living in Montreal since she returned to Canada, and her mother still lived there, as did many of her friends. Her life had been spent in big cities, London and Paris. Roméo's attachment to Grande-Digue had begun thirty years before, and his surviving brother lived fairly close. For Roméo, Montreal meant, above all, Diana and baseball. For Diana, Grande-Digue meant Roméo

In retirement at Grande Digue, 2000

and summers by the sea. The two dwellings allowed a reasonable compromise between partners who had come together late in life.

Both were exhausted as the year 2000 began, but it became clear that Roméo's exhaustion was reason for concern. He was still in his seventies, but during the last years he had worked a punishing schedule. He had asked the prime minister to accept his resignation before his term was complete because he felt that he would not be able to cope with the demands that would be made on the governor general during the millennium year. There was apparently nothing particularly seriously wrong, but increasing deafness made public life difficult and back trouble diminished his energy. During this first summer of his retirement, he adapted, with great pleasure, to a routine which included the collection of as many daily newspapers as possible, visits to and from his relatives as well as old friends, gardening, and the organization of the house.

His continued interest in political life was heightened by Dominic's political ambitions. These had not been discouraged by his father, but Roméo had been extremely proud of his son's attainments at law school and thought that he would be a successful lawyer. Dominic did indeed practise law successfully, adding to his qualifications with an LL.M. from Harvard Law School in 1997, and worked with the firm of Clark, Drummie in Moncton from 1997 to 2000. His ambition, however, was to be a politician. Jean Chrétien had encouraged him and employed him as a special assistant in the PMO from 1993 to 1996. Dominic ran for election for the first time in the 1997 election and was defeated. In the 2000 federal election, held on November 27, he ran again in Roméo's old riding of Beauséjour and won decisively against three other candidates—those of the Progressive Conservatives, the Canadian Alliance, and the New Democratic Party—collecting 47 per cent of the votes cast.

By the end of 2000, Roméo had recovered much of his strength. The division of their lives between Montreal and Grande-Digue worked for both him and his wife. He was chosen by the Université de Moncton as its chancellor, and was pleased that a university that had denied him a teaching position in 1972 and rejected his candidacy for its presidency in 1985 now wished him to be its chancellor. He watched the political life of the country all the more closely because of Dominic's involvement. His son made sure that Roméo went to Florida to watch the Montreal Expos during spring training, for he had been a lifelong fan of that baseball team. Dominic also managed in these years to take his father once more to Paris. Geneviève, who values her privacy and has as much discretion as her father, had graduated from the University of Toronto and had begun to build a career with the

Roméo and Geneviève at Rideau Hall, c. 1997

federal civil service. She also often made the journey from Ottawa to see him. His everyday social life tended to revolve round visits with his brother Léonard, who lived in Memramcook, and his nephew Charles, the son of his eldest brother, who lived in Moncton. Dominic was frequently at his father's house on weekends as he followed his father's advice and got to understand the needs of his constituency. Otherwise, old friends, such as Donald Savoie, dropped in for coffee. Roméo hosted small dinner parties for four or five friends, Claude Bourque, Robert Pichette, and Murielle Roy, among others. Lobster and wine were usually on the menu, and guests brought salads. Talk ranged over past politics and present crises. Dominic's marriage in June 2003 to Jolène Richard, a lawyer who later became a provincial court judge, was the occasion for major rejoicing. Her father is Guy Richard, who has served as chief justice of the Court of Queen's Bench in New Brunswick.

However, Roméo knew his energy was less than it had once

been. During a long conversation with me at his home in Grande-Digue in the fall of 2000, Roméo talked at length about how fortunate he was with his children. He also touched on his belief in the strength of Acadian identity and his love for France, his admiration for the British legal system and his equally strong admiration for the capacity of the United States to govern itself, particularly recalling the defeat of McCarthy and the success of the civil-rights movement. He spoke of the intricacies that complicated life for Canadian politicians. At the very end of the evening, over the last coffee, he said that he did not regret his growing inability to read new books, he was satisfied with the newspapers and television. His words had the echo of Robert Louis Stevenson's lines: "Here he lies where he longed to be / Home is the sailor, home from the sea, / and the hunter home from the hill."

This was one of the last lengthy talks I had with him for, by the end of 2003, it was clear that he was struggling with Alzheimer's disease. During the course of that year, he made his last visit to Parliament Hill for the unveiling of his portrait as speaker of the Senate. The then-speaker of the House of Commons, Peter Milliken, teased him, telling him he could now only refer to his son "as the Honourable Member from Beauséjour."[1] Roméo turned seventy-six in December that year, and by the end of 2004 he needed twenty-four-hour care at his Grande-Digue home. Friends continued to call—making short visits—among them his early campaign manager Bertin LeBlanc and Robert Pichette, who had served New Brunswick well as a senior civil servant. By late 2007, there was just an occasional smile of response for such visitors. Until his death on June 24, 2009, his family lived with his slow but unremitting decline. In an interview with Mike de Souza, a reporter for the *National Post*, the day after Roméo's death, Dominic commented on the last four years of his father's illness. "I lived it like any other child seeing his father or mother

Friends in retirement at Grande Digue: Roméo and Chrétien, 2003

stuck with such a difficult illness," he said. "I saw someone with an enormous capacity to express himself in both French and English...who at the end was no longer able to communicate."[2]

The media coverage of Roméo's death was extensive. It was covered not only in the major newspapers of the Atlantic region, of Quebec, and of Ontario, but also those of the Western provinces. The emphasis was similar in newspapers across the country, with most quoting Prime Minister Harper's comment that LeBlanc was "a passionate Canadian who served his country with distinction and honour."[3] Roméo would have appreciated the fact that Harper mentioned his establishment of an award "that recognized volunteer and community work among Canadians." Governor General Michaëlle Jean's comment would have pleased him. She said, "He was a proud and tireless defender of la francophonie, both at home and abroad. He carried in him a love of the French language, in particular the accents, colours and rhythms of his Acadian roots, where he took his last breath, facing the ocean that cradled him in his youth."[4] Roméo would also have enjoyed the tributes paid to him by many long-term colleagues, among them Monique Bégin, Don Boudria, and Marc Lalonde. For Monique Bégin, Roméo was, above all, someone who cared for his constituents, whether he was a backbencher or a Cabinet minister. For Don Boudria, who was elected to the House of Commons in 1984 as Roméo was appointed to the Senate, he was the governor general who visited isolated farmers who had been struggling for days to cope without electricity during the ice storms of 1998.[5] For Marc Lalonde, who had known him since he was twenty years old, Roméo "was a very effective politician and a very good one. He was unflappable and a pleasure to work with, either in the Cabinet or the PMO. He had no enemies that I knew of."[6] Donald Savoie, the holder of the Canada Research Chair in Public Administration and Governance at the Université de Moncton, believed that Roméo's contribution to public life was founded on the basic elements of Canada "whether it was English/French, urban/rural, the working poor." Roméo, for Savoie, remained loyal all his life, whether as a backbencher, a Cabinet minister, or the governor general, to the belief that these elements matter.[7]

But the tribute that was paid by Dominic LeBlanc to his father is the one which brought together the feelings of friends and colleagues in the most fitting manner. This was the way in which Dominic, employing every ounce of his inheritance as an Acadian—the characteristic which led the Québécois to coin the phrase "stubborn as an Acadian"—had his father's state funeral take place in the parish church of Memramcook, New Brunswick, rather than in a cathedral in Moncton or Ottawa. He was helped by the fact that the church in question, St. Thomas, could seat up to 1,500 people. This was the small village that was home to St. Joseph's, the college that gave Roméo a bilingual education, strong enough for him to do graduate studies at the Sorbonne.

This was the river valley where Acadians and anglophones helped one another in time of need. And, on July 7, 2009, this was the place where the Canadian political elite and local people came together to bury a man both groups wished to honour. The occasion was part state ceremonial and part an expression of sorrow, from family members and neighbours, for a man they had known and loved. The staff work by Kevin Fram, who had been a friend of the family since meeting Dominic in the 1980s, kept officialdom to the minimum, while ensuring that the necessary security presence could do its work.

The ceremonies began with a slow procession through a grey drizzle from the old building where Roméo had taken classes and edited the student newspaper to the church. A guard of one hundred, provided by the Department of National Defence, and a military band preceded the draped casket in its hearse. Thirty-two honorary pallbearers—from former Prime Minister Jean Chrétien and his wife to assorted old friends—followed. They walked for some ten minutes along the tree-lined route, watched from both sides by members of Fisheries and Oceans Canada.

In the church, the funeral mass was embellished by the musical talent of Dominic's wife, Jolène, who not only wrote some of the music herself, but also arranged much of the music for the small number of local musicians involved. Phil Fontaine, the national chief of the Assembly of First Nations, read a passage from the book of Sirach (also known as Ecclesiasticus) with great conviction, as if he himself were its author. The three eulogies were brief and heartfelt: Jean Chrétien spoke first, and his observations appear in the foreword of this book; the author spoke next, having the honour to represent the wide circle of Roméo's many friends. Dominic was the last speaker, and his words recalled Roméo as a beloved father who passed on his belief in the common bonds that encompassed humanity. Dominic made his thoughts on this matter the more vivid by thanking the caregivers who had looked after Roméo in his last years of life. The concluding monition was given by the parish priest, Father Arthur Bourgeois, who spoke of Roméo's life as one illuminated by compassion and the desire to help the frail. The burial in the cemetery behind the church was a private matter, but there was a reception in Old College that began almost immediately.

This hospitality was something at which Roméo would have been very much at home. And he would have found it amusing. The entrance doors to the rooms where it took place were guarded by young RCMP personnel, whose duty it was to check invitation cards. It was a hopeless task. Small bustling Acadian women, who had known Roméo all their lives, were not going to be denied their right to attend the occasion. A few uniformed RCMP officers, however well trained, were no match for the much older women and men, at least some of whom had invitations. The people from the length and breadth of the surrounding area felt that this was their funeral. During the next couple of hours, people reminisced, told stories of pranks played and acerbic remarks made, and finally went out into the soft rain of a summer night, sad but with the immense satisfaction of knowing that a good man had been given his due. As one of the villagers from Memramcook remarked to a reporter, "He's from down home, he's a good man, he's one of us."[8] But, as the portrait that was painted of him as governor general so poignantly shows, at the end of his life there was no "them and us," just suffering humanity.

Acknowledgements

I have been fortunate to enjoy the generous support of Roméo's family while I worked on this book. His son, Dominic, arranged access to for me to his father's papers and introduced me to people who had been important in his father's life. His daughter, Geneviève, talked to me about his presence in her life. His first wife, Joslyn Carter LeBlanc, remembered their time in Washington in the mid-sixties and their years in Ottawa in the seventies. She searched for photographs of these years and generously allowed me to use some of them. Diana Fowler Leblanc, his second wife, remembered the years when he was speaker of the Senate and governor general and also searched out other photographic records. Roméo's nephew Charles LeBlanc and his mother Mélindé, Roméo's sister-in-law, also provided me with many details.

Many of his friends and colleagues made time to talk to me about his life and his work. It would be invidious to place their testimonies in any sort of order except alphabetical but the book owes a very great deal to the following: Monique Bégin, Claude Bourque, Rita Cadieux, Paul-Émile Carrier, Herménégilde Chiasson, Jean Chrétien, Marshall Crowe, Winnifred Dionne, Kevin Fram, Herb Gray, Joe Gough, Marc Lalonde, Bertin LeBlanc, Yvon LeBlanc, Nelson Lynch, Robert Pichette, Murielle Roy, Donald Savoie, and Jim Taylor.

As well I owe much to the encouragement and support I received from the Université de Moncton, both financial and intellectual. Donald Savoie read the book in manuscript form and provided travel funds, and his administrative assistant, Ginette Benoit, gave me much encouragement. Maurice Basque made certain that I was aware of new works by Acadian scholars relevant to this work. André Duguay helped with work in the local archives and by bringing together a collection of photographs. Two other young scholars, Tim Krywalak of Carleton University and Shawna Quinn of the University of New Brunswick, were a major help with Library and Archives Canada and the New Brunswick Provincial Archives respectively. Nor must I forget to thank the staff of LAC in general for courteous and helpful service.

I was also helped by a number of people whose professional experience was relevant to an understanding of Roméo's life: in particular, Ed Broadbent and Monique Bégin for their view of the life of an elected politician; Derek Burney and Torrance Wylie for federal politics in general; Peter Dobell for the changes in Canada's parliamentary system since 1963; Thomas Delworth, Michael Kergin, Claude Laverdure, and Basil Robinson for their view of Canada's diplomatic relations; Marshall Crowe, Blair Seaborn, and Max Yalden for their view of the interaction between deputy minister and Cabinet ministers; and Clark Davey, David Halton, and Don Newman for commentaries about the life of journalists. Monique Bégin, Herb Gray, Claude Bourque, Sheila Brown, Margaret Conrad, Winnifred Dionne, and Donald Savoie read the full manuscript, and Charlotte Gray almost all of it. Their comments considerably improved it and it would never have been completed without their encouragement. I also owe many thanks to Sandra Barry, who took an ill-typed manuscript and made it presentable for the publisher.

And I want to conclude by thanking Nancy Sewell, Diane Young, and James Lorimer himself, all of Formac/Lorimer, who were determined to get this book out this year.

Endnotes

Chapter 1 – From Memramcook to Rideau Hall

1 MacKinnon, *The Crown in Canada*, 96.
2 Delacourt, *The Globe and Mail* (November 23, 1994), 1.
3 Stewart, "Viceroy Choice Stirs Fuss on Hill," *The Toronto Star* (November 23, 1994), 23.
4 *The Toronto Star* (November 24, 1994), 27.
5 McWhinney, *Chrétien and Canadian Federalism*, 22.
6 *The Globe and Mail* (November 23, 1994).
7 *The Toronto Star* (November 23, 1994).
8 Ibid.
9 *The Vancouver Sun* (November 23, 1994).
10 Ibid.
11 Robichaud, "Il est hautement qualifé avec toute la dignité et la compétence que la poste commande," *Le Soleil* (November 23, 1994).
12 LeBlanc, "Roméo LeBlanc, Parrain d'Acadie," *La Presse* (November 23, 1994).
13 Lavoie, "Un beau geste de Roméo LeBlanc," *Le Soleil* (November 24, 1994).
14 Michel Vastel, "Chrétien serait-il déloyal envers le Québec," *Le Soleil* (November 25, 1994).
15 *The Toronto Star* (November 23, 1994), 3.
16 Boutros-Boutros Ghali, "Address," in *Le Congrès mondial acadien: L'Acadie en 2004*, 18.
17 *Le Soleil* (December 18, 1994), 46; *Le Droit* (December 14, 1994), 28.
18 Duguay, *Le Moniteur Acadien* (February 25, 1995).
19 *The Globe and Mail* (February 9, 1995), 4.
20 *The Toronto Star* (February 9, 1995), 12.
21 *The Globe and Mail* (February 9, 1995), 4.
22 *La Presse* (February 9, 1995), A1.
23 *Le Soleil* (February 9, 1995), A13.
24 *Le Devoir* (February 9, 1995), A5.
25 *The Toronto Star* (February 9, 1995).
26 Graham, *All the King's Horses*, Epilogue, 224–54.
27 MacKinnon, *The Crown in Canada*, 138.

Chapter 2 – Cormier's Cove

1   Landry and Lang, *Histoire de l'Acadie*, 137.
2   Forbes, "The 1930s: Depression and Retrenchment," 274.
3   Cited in Savoie, "L'Enseignement en Acadie," 437.
4   Université de St. Joseph/University of St. Joseph. [*Calendar*], 1941–1942, 39.
5   Kimber, "Misfit Among the Mighty," *The Financial Post* (October 29, 1977).
6   Pelletier, *The Years of Impatience*, 101.
7   Essential reference works for the history of the Canadian development of both the JOC and the JEC are Clément, *Histoire de L'Action Catholique au Canada français,* and Hamelin, *Histoire du Catholicisme Québécoise.* For more recent scholarship, see also Meunier and Warren, *Sortir de la "Grande Noirceur."*
8   Pelletier, *The Years of Impatience*, 101.
9   *La Presse* (June 25, 1945).
10 See Cuplinskas, "Guns and Rosaries," 7–28.
11 Lettre du R.P. Bélanger, s.j. in *Archive*, American Academy of Religion, *Dossier Action Catholique*, 1940.
12 See Pelletier, *The Years of Impatience*, 103–5.
13 Cited in Juneau, "60ième anniversaire de la J.E.C. internationale," *La Presse* (September 9, 2006).
14 Pelletier, *The Years of Impatience*, 104.
15 Mounier, *L'affrontement chrétien* and [Mounier], *Be Not Afraid: Studies in Personalist Sociology*, 1954.
16 *JEC* 1, no. 7 (1941): 2.
17 Juneau, "60ième anniversaire de la J.E.C. internationale."
18 Ibid.
19 Roméo LeBlanc, *Liaisons*, 1947.
20 Ibid., *Liaisons*, 1948.
21 Letter from Roméo LeBlanc to Marguerite Michaud, April 1948, MG35A, vol. 138, no. 295, Roméo LeBlanc Papers (hereafter RLP). Library and Archives Canada (hereafter LAC).
22 RLP, MG35A, vol. 135, no. 296. LAC.

Chapter 3 – Transitions and Interruptions, 1948–1955

1   Kimber, "Misfit Among the Mighty," 4–9.
2   The 1941 census gives Canada's population as 11,507,000; that of 1951, 13,648,000.
3   Morton, *A Short History of Canada*, 192.
4   Ibid., 204.

5   Bothwell et al., *Canada Since 1945*, 109–10.
6   Morton, *A Short History of Canada*, 216.
7   Ibid., 82–3.
8   Bothwell et al., *Canada Since 1945*, 82.
9   Statistics Canada, "Population Growth (1851–2001 Censuses)," <www40.statcan.ca/101/cst01/demo03.htm>.
10   Statistics Canada, "Population Urban and Rural, by Province and Territory," <www40.statcan.ca/101/cst01/demo62a.htm>.
11   Kimber, "Misfit Among the Mighty," 5.
12   Cited in ibid., 5.
13   "Dont les mentalités different autant que le nombre des Provinces," MG 35A, vol. 138, no. 292, RLP, LAC.
14   Kimber, "Misfit Among the Mighty," 5.
15   Pelletier, *The Years of Impatience*, 103.
16   Madame Cadieux to N.E.S.G., August 2008, [private conversation].
17   Pelletier, *The Years of Impatience*, 103.
18   Pelletier and Trudeau were thirty, and Marchand was thirty-one. Their friendship lasted for the rest of their lives.
19   English, *Citizen of the World, Vol. I: 1919–1968*, 199.
20   The owners were an American company, and, it was said, none of those at the managerial level spoke French.
21   The following is pieced together from an interview with Léonard and memories of other family members, including those of his nephew, Charles, the son of his brother Antoine, as well as from Roméo's own recollections.
22   Madame Cadieux to N.E.S.G., private conversation.
23   More than 50 per cent of the potato crop today is sold for processing to McCain Foods Ltd., and 45 per cent is destined as seed potatoes for markets outside the province. Cereals such as wheat, barley, and oats are grown mainly as part of the crop-rotation cycle.
24   "Académie Notre Dame de Drummond," 4.
25   Belliveau, "Acadian New Brunswick's ambivalent leap," 64.
26   Two of the French-speaking Conservative members were from Quebec, and were frequently referred to by the Opposition as "invaders." See Wilbur, *The Rise of French New Brunswick*, 183.
27   New Brunswick Department of Education, *Annual Report*, 1946, 4; ibid., 1953, 10.
28   Ibid., 1952, 10.
29   "Brief presented by l'Association Acadienne d'Éducation."
30   See the biography of A.M. Sormany by Alexandre J. Savoie, *Un demi-siècle d'histoire acadienne*. For personal memoirs of men who gave leadership in this area, see Calixte F. Savoie, *Mémoires d'un nationaliste*

acadien, and Alexandre J. Savoie, *Un siècle de revendications scolaires au Nouveau Brunswick.*

31 The Collège du Sacré-Coeur was developed by the Eudist fathers on the foundation laid down by Father Prosser LeBastard in 1899. It received its charter as a university in 1941. See Tremblay, *50 ans d'éducation 1889–1949.*

32 In 1969, this association became l'Association des Enseignants Francophones de Nouveau Brunswick, with the same rights and privileges as the New Brunswick Teachers' Association.

33 L'Association des Instituteurs Acadiens, *Les instituteurs acadiens de Nouveau Brunswick.*

34 LeBlanc, *Les Acadiens*, 50.

35 The best analysis of the issue is by Snow, *Les droits linguistique des Acadiens de Nouveau Brunswick.*

36 Interview 3, MC778, Armand St. Onge Papers, PANB.

37 "Six-pâtes" is based on layers of at least six meats: pork, veal, chicken, beef and/or venison, and often partridge and pheasant, cooked in a kettle with pastry between each meat.

38 These scholarships had been established after the Second World War by Robert Picard, a French citizen, later consul for France in Halifax and Quebec City. In 1953 only one scholarship was awarded each year.

39 Letter from Roméo LeBlanc to Gloria David, December 1, 1953, MG35A, vol. 138, no. 295, RLP, LAC.

40 Rousseau, *Émile.*

41 Letter from Roméo LeBlanc to Gloria David, December 1, 1953, MG35A, vol. 138, no. 295, RLP, LAC.

42 Talbott, "Vichy and Resistance France," 208.

43 Anyone interested in further reading on Vichy France should start with Paxton, *Vichy France.* The magisterial study of Amouroux, in ten volumes, *La grande histoire des Francais sous l'occupation,* is still unsurpassed. The last two volumes were published with the general title of *La grande histoire de la France après l'occupation.*

44 The statistics for casualties and deaths in the Second World War are constantly being revised, but the above are within the parameters of the data published in 2007. In terms of percentage loss of population, France lost 1.35 per cent, 697,000 out of not quite 42,000,000; Germany over 10.47 per cent, 7,293,000 out of a population of 69,623,000. See Knapton, *France: An Interpretive History,* 517.

45 Ibid., 525–6.

46 Ibid., 518.

47 Talbott, "Vichy and Resistance France," 216. Fewer than 3,000 returned.

48 Siefer, *The Church and Industrial Society*, 4.
49 Boon and Doyle, "Secularly Employed Clergymen," 325–45. See also Amal, *The History of the Worker Priests*. In explaining his own feelings about these men, Roméo advised a friend to read Cesbron's novel *Les saints vont en enfer*. The most accurate portrayal of the movement is Loew, *Journal d'une mission ouvrière 1941–1959*.
50 Letter from Roméo LeBlanc to Gloria David, March 11, 1954, MG35A, vol. 138, no. 295, RLP, LAC.
51 Ibid.
52 Letter from Roméo LeBlanc to N.E.S.G., 1955, private correspondence.
53 Letter from Roméo LeBlanc to Gloria David, December 1, 1953, MG 35A, vol. 138, no. 295, RLP, LAC.
54 Letter from Royal Society of Canada to Roméo LeBlanc, May 14, 1954, MG 35A, vol. 138, No. 295, RLP, LAC.
55 This periodical began in 1945 and continues publication today. Its aim has been to encourage dialogue among the young, and it has been credited with playing a fundamental role in the reconciliation of Germany and France after the war.
56 Letter from Roméo LeBlanc to Gloria David, December 1, 1953, MG35A, vol. 138, no. 29, RLP, LAC.
57 Preston, Wise, and Werner, *Men in Arms*, 331.
58 Judt, *Post War*, 282–3.
59 Ibid.
60 Preston, Wise, and Werner, *Men in Arms*, 343.
61 Davidson, *Vietnam at War*, 163.
62 These figures are approximate. The numbers of dead, wounded, and captured on the French side has to be augmented by the toll taken by south Vietnam. See Windrow, *The Last Valley*.
63 Vietnam was only part of what had been known as French Indo-China, which also included Laos and Cambodia. (Laos gained its full independence in December 1954 and Cambodia negotiated a similar arrangement in 1955.)
64 Letter from Roméo LeBlanc to Gloria David, March 22, 1954, MG 35A, vol. 138, no. 295, RLP, LAC.
65 Letter from Roméo LeBlanc to Gloria David, April 16, 1954, MG 35A, vol. 138, no. 295, RLP, LAC.
66 The conclusion to this letter was written in English. She later married an American and spent the rest of her life in the United States. Letter from Gloria David to Roméo LeBlanc, n.d., MG 35A, vol. 138, no. 295, RLP, LAC.

67 Covering more than 2,381,741 square kilometres, four times the size of Texas, Algeria is bordered by Morocco and Western Sahara on the west, and by Tunisia and Libya on the east. The Mediterranean is to the north, and to the south are Mauritania, Mali, and Niger. The Saharan region, which is 85 per cent of the country, is, at the opening of the twenty-first century, still almost completely uninhabited. The other two French North African colonies, Morocco and Tunisia, had difficult but far less violent paths to independence, which came to Morocco in 1956 and to Tunisia in 1957.

68 Judt, *Post War*, 285.

69 There is still controversy over the number of dead related to the war. Algerian sources put the total at a million, French sources at less than half a million. At least two million Algerians fled the country to France, Morocco, and Tunisia, and there was also "a settling of accounts" in the independent country after 1962. See Connelly, *A Diplomatic Revolution*; Horne, *A Savage War of Peace*.

70 Letter from J.-Gérard De Grâce to Roméo LeBlanc, 1955, MG 35A, vol. 138, no. 291, RLP, LAC.

71 Ibid.

Chapter 4 – Teacher to Journalist: Fredericton to Ottawa and Beyond

1 Léonard, the middle brother, was self-supporting at this time, but his wages did not allow him to help the family.

2 Letter from Rhéal Guadet to Roméo LeBlanc, Hull, April 29, 1955, MG 35A, vol. 138, no. 294, RLP, LAC.

3 Letter from New Brunswick Civil Service Commission to Roméo LeBlanc, May 27, 1955, MG 35A, vol. 138, no. 291, RLP, LAC.

4 His reported income for that year after deductions was $1,716. Roméo's income tax return for 1955 is RLP, LAC.

5 Allain and Basque, *Une presence qui s'affirme*, 106.

6 In 2009, even though New Brunswick had become the only official bilingual province in Canada in 1969, the question of French language rights continued to be a lively political, social and cultural issue.

7 Canada's population in 1953 was 14,886,000; in 1955 it was 15,736,000. In 1953, the birth rate was 27 per thousand, one of the highest in the world. Immigration in 1954 brought 154,227 people to Canada, and in 1955, 109,946 arrived.

8 In particular, see Innis, *The Bias of Communications*.

9 Bothwell et al., *Canada since 1945*, 142.

10 Kilbourn, "The 1950s," 320.

11 In 1956, a deal was struck with the provinces to co-operate on this project. When the final segment was opened in November 1956, it had cost $924 million, of which the federal government had paid $567 million. Bothwell et al., *Canada since 1945*, 143.

12 Massey became Canada's first native-born governor general in 1952. Other members of the commission were Norman A. MacKenzie, Georges-Henri Lévesque, and Arthur Surveyer.

13 The eight principal headings of the *Report* are: Broadcasting (Radio Broadcasting and Television); National Film Board, Other Federal Institutions (The National Gallery, National Museums, Federal Libraries, Public Records and Archives, Historical Sites and Monuments); Aid to Universities; National Scholarships; Scientific Research under the Federal Government; Information Abroad; A Council of the Arts, Letters, Humanities, and Social Sciences.

14 Quoted in Bothwell et al., *Canada since 1945*, 152.

15 In particular, see the articles in Beaulieu, ed., *L'Évangéline 1887–1982*, and articles published during this decade in the *Educational Review*, the voice of the New Brunswick Teachers' Association.

16 There are a number of analyses of this event. In English, see Belliveau, "Acadian New Brunswick's Leap into the Canadian Liberal Order" and Wilbur, *The Rise of French New Brunswick*, 182–200. In French, see Hautecoeur, *L'Acadie du discours pour une sociologie de la culture acadienne*, 92–101.

17 What follows is a summary of his analysis, the key sentence being: "Il faut revenir, en 1953, sur le Déportation pour marquer officiellement et collectivement la nouveauté de la situation des Acadiens dans les années cinquante…repeater le meme pour éclore le nouveau." Hautecoeur, *L'Acadie due discours*, 94.

18 Cormier was the president of St. Joseph's University when Roméo studied there.

19 Roméo LeBlanc to N.E.S.G., 2001, private conversation.

20 It became the Société Nationale des Acadiens in 1957.

21 Belliveau, "Acadian New Brunswick's Ambivalent Leap," 65.

22 *Debates*, New Brunswick Legislature, February 18, 1955, 64. See Wilbur, *The Rise of French New Brunswick*, 159–181, for an insightful analysis of this period.

23 Roméo LeBlanc to N.E.S.G., 2001, private conversation.

24 In an interview recorded for Radio-Canada, Moncton, just after he had retired from being governor general.

25 Jones, *Fredericton Flashbacks*, 66.

26 Ibid., 68.

27 Picot, *A Brief History of Teacher Training in New Brunswick*, 121.

28   Jones, *Fredericton Flushbacks*, 69.
29   The terminology here follows the practice of the time, when a distinction was customarily made between those born or brought up in New Brunswick with Acadian ancestry, and francophones who had migrated to the province from elsewhere.
30   Picot, *A Brief History of Teacher Training in New Brunswick*, 105.
31   Rural schools had 80 per cent of the students and 60 per cent of the available funding.
32   Letter to Angéle Godin, October 12, 1955, 31.1.Y, Fonds de l'Association des Instituteurs Acadian, Centre d'Etudes Acadiennes (hereafter CEA), Université de Moncton.
33   Picot, *A Brief History of Teacher Training in New Brunswick*, 120.
34   Ibid., 102.
35   Roméo LeBlanc to N.E.S.G., 2001, private conversation.
36   Ibid., 2000, private conversation.
37   Jones, *Fredericton Flashbacks*, 66.
38   Ibid., 68.
39   These letters have been organized in Correspondence, Mikan #3916360, RLP, LAC. In particular, see section 2 and the letters of "Pape" Cyr and Joyce Walker.
40   Letter from Rhéal Gaudet to Roméo LeBlanc, December 10, 1957, MG 35A, vol. 138, no. 295, RLP, LAC.
41   Interview with Roméo LeBlanc, undated, labelled "journalism," Centre d'Études Acadiennes archives, Université de Moncton.
42   The correspondence makes this conclusion very probable, but since I have not been able to trace the lady in question I prefer not to use her name.
43   Roméo LeBlanc to N.E.S.G., 2001, private conversation.
44   Duffy, *Fights of Our Lives*, 194.
45   It has been remarked that this election, and its successor in 1958, have been argued about over the past decades by political scientists and historians alike: "Why did a government that had ruled for so long, and generally so well, with such a minimum of fuss and bother, suddenly collapse?" Bothwell et al., *Canada since 1945*. The reader that wishes to follow the story more fully should consult Duffy's *Fights of Our Lives* and the many excellent biographies and memoirs that have appeared in the last thirty years of those who were in public life at the time.
46   Duffy, *Fights of Our Lives*, 226.
47   Smith, *Rogue Tory*, 275.
48   Ibid., 277. The ethics of using a confidential report of a previous government are discussed here.

49   Kilbourn, "The 1950s," 358.
50   Sevigny, *This Game of Politics*, 93.
51   Duffy, *Fights of Our Lives*, 228.
52   Bliss, *Right Honourable Men*, 213.
53   The Canadian Press Gallery has existed since 1916, and is a loosely
      knit association of journalists. Physically, it is the place overlooking
      the floor of the House of Commons where political journalists are
      allowed to congregate, to watch, and later to report on parliamentary
      proceedings. While the actual association has the major role in
      accepting someone as a member, the Speaker has the final word on
      access.
54   Clark Davey to N.E.S.G., private correspondence. Davey kindly sent
      me his recollections of his time in the parliamentary Press Gallery of
      the late 1950s and early 1960s.
55   There are a number of sources for Roméo's work as journalist. See
      papers in Mikan #3845647, RLP, LAC. Recordings of most of his
      broadcasts from 1959 to 1966 can be found at the Radio-Canada
      archives in Montreal.
56   La Revue de l'Actualité, CBC/Radio-Canada Archives (hereafter CBC/
      RCA).
57   La Revue de l'Actualité, CBC/RCA.
58   Women were granted the right to vote in federal elections in 1918.
      Manitoba women received the right in January 1916; Saskatchewan
      women in March of that year; and Alberta followed suit. In 1917,
      British Columbia and Ontario acted similarly; Nova Scotia did so in
      1918; New Brunswick in 1919; Prince Edward Island in 1922; and
      Newfoundland in 1925.
59   Roméo LeBlanc, November 17 and 20, 1961, CBC/RCA.
60   See Brunet and Côté, *Le patriote: Marcel Chaput.*
61   Roméo LeBlanc, October 31 and November 1, 1961, CBC/RCA.
62   Ibid., December 23, 1961, CBC/RCA.
63   Roméo LeBlanc, October 18, 1962, CBC/RCA.
64   MG 35A, vol. 138, no. 294, RLP, LAC.
65   MG35, A138/291: 1962, RLP, LAC.
66   Roméo LeBlanc, Le décè de Dag Hammerskjold, September 23, 1961,
      CBC/RCA.

Chapter 5 – Foreign Correspondent: London and Washington
1   Roméo LeBlanc to N.E.S.G., 1956, private conversation.
2   Letter from Ed Higginson to N.E.S.G., February 2, 2010, private
      correspondence.

3   Ibid., January 29, 2010.
4   Roméo LeBlanc to N.E.S.G., 1956, private conversation.
5   I am indebted to David Halton for knowledge of the life of a foreign correspondent. [See biographical note.]
6   Roméo Leblanc, October 13, 1962, CBC/RCA Montreal.
7   The First French Republic was established in 1792; the Second in 1849; the Third lasted from 1870 to 1940, when the Vichy regime was established. In 1945, France narrowly avoided civil war, as those who had supported the Vichy government, which had signed a peace treaty with Germany, and those who fought in the Resistance battled, in some places literally, to shape the future of the country.
8   Yes: 12,809,363; No: 7,932,695; Abstentions: 6,280,297.
9   For a quick survey of events, see the *United Nations Year Book, 1962*, 104–9. For a more lengthy account, see Stern, *The Week the World Stood Still.*
10 In particular, see Kennedy, *Thirteen Days.*
11 Roméo LeBlanc, October 27, 1962, CBC/RCA Montreal.
12 Letter from Ed Higginson to N.E.S.G., 2009, private correspondence.
13 The gradual development of this group over the next thirty-one years resulted in the present-day European Union of twenty-seven member states. Its population is over 500 million.
14 Roméo LeBlanc, "L'Année 1962 dans le Monde: L'aspect économique," CBC/RCA Montreal.
15 De Gaulle, *De Gaulle parle, 1962–1966.*
16 Interview with Roméo LeBlanc, n.d., CBC/RCA Moncton.
17 In particular, see the reports of the celebration of the 40th anniversary of the treaty in 2003, a celebration which led to the creation for the first time of a common Franco-German history course book to be used in both countries and foster a "shared vision" of their past.
18 Roméo LeBlanc, April 8, 1963, CBC/RCA Montreal.
19 Ibid., April 27, 1963, CBC/RCA Montreal.
20 Roméo LeBlanc, May 8, 1963, CBC/RCA Montreal. This and the following interview from Brussels on the May 10 were radio, not television broadcasts.
21 Ibid., May 10, 1963, CBC/RCA Montreal.
22 See the Moncton tapes, in which he recalled the details of the British election that took place in 1964. Interview with Roméo LeBlanc, n.d., CBC/RCA Montreal, copies of tapes in RCA Moncton. See also Roméo LeBlanc, July 31, 1963, CBC/RCA Montreal.
23 Ibid., title/document, October 27, 1963, CBC/RCA Montreal.
24 Interview with Roméo LeBlanc, n.d., CBC/RCA Moncton.
25 Letter from Ed Higginson to N.E.S.G., February 2, 2010, private correspondence.

26 Bothwell et al., *Canada Since 1945*, 258.
27 Roméo LeBlanc, November 22 and 25, 1963, CBC/RCA Moncton.
28 Letter from Roméo LeBlanc to Gérard Pelletier, November 30, 1963, MG 35A, vol. 138, no. 294, RLP, LAC.
29 Ibid.
30 Roméo LeBlanc, January 26, 1964, CBC/RCA Montreal.
31 Ibid., March 1, 1964, CBC/RCA Montreal.
32 The history of this issue has been written about at length. For a short account, see Girard, *Canada in World Affairs*, 286–303.
33 Roméo LeBlanc, May 17, 1964, CBC/RCA Montreal. See also commentary in Hilliker and Barry, *Canada's Department of External Affairs*, 379–80.
34 Ibid., May 24, 1964, CBC/RCA Montreal.
35 The journalists in question were Jacques Fauteux, Raymond Guernier, Roméo LeBlanc, Gilles Loiselle and Jacques Ouvrard.
36 She told me that she accepted various spellings, but this was the legal spelling of her name. She has been most often called Lyn. N.E.S.G. private conversation with Lyn Carter LeBlanc.
37 Interview with Roméo LeBlanc, n.d., CBC/RCA Moncton.
38 Roméo LeBlanc, "La Grande Bretagne," October 11, 1964, CBC/RCA Montreal.
39 For a study of the importance of this election and its immediate result, see Marr, *A History of Modern Britain*, 224–31.
40 Roméo LeBlanc, "Canada: Les Elections Brittaniques," October 16, 1964, CBC/RCA Montreal.
41 Ibid., "Canada: Déchirement au sein de la Communauté économique européene," December 13, 1964, CBC/RCA Montreal.
42 Ibid., "Canada: Analyse des événements de l'année 1964," CBC/RCA Montreal.
43 Those chosen for inclusion in this account were about matters which Roméo later remembered as being of particular significance for him. Roméo LeBlanc to N.E.S.G., 2001-2004, private conversation.
44 Roméo LeBlanc, "Visite de Krouchtchev en Egypte," May 24, 1964; ibid., "Krouchtev visite Denmarke, Suède et Norvège," July 5, 1964; ibid., "Rodésie du Sud-Indépendance," November 15, 1964, CBC/RCA Montreal.
45 Letter from Jean Boucher, Civil Service Commission of Canada, to Roméo LeBlanc, March 26, 1964, MG 35A, vol. 138, no. 294, RLP, LAC.
46 Letter from Roméo LeBlanc to Alphonse Ouimet, April 4, 1965, MG 35A, vol. 138, no. 294, RLP, LAC.
47 Roméo LeBlanc, "De Gaulle-ONU-Allemagne," February 7, 1965; ibid., "Elections Municipale-France," March 21, 1965; ibid., "Grande-

Brétagne Politique extérieure," April 18, 1965, CBC/RCA Montreal.

48   Ibid. to N.E.S.G., 1984, private conversations.

49   See Mikan #33845647, RLP, LAC.

50   English, *Citizen of the World*, 396.

51   Ibid.

52   Interview with Roméo LeBlanc, February 25, 1965, BBC home service transcription, MG 35A, vol. 138, no. 29, RLP, LAC.

53   *La semaine à Radio-Canada* XV, no. 44 (July 1965): 2. *La semaine à Radio-Canada* was a weekly bulletin of information put out by the corporation.

54   Roméo LeBlanc, "La Revue de la Semaine," June 17, 1965, CBC/RCA Montreal.

55   For a general overview of the question, see Woodhouse, *Modern Greece*. See also Kondratyev, "The Aspida Affair and the Reactionaries," 92–3.

56   E-mail from Ed Higginson to N.E.S.G., March 2010, private conversation.

57   Roméo LeBlanc, "Grèce," August 8, 1963 CBC/RCA Montreal.

58   Lyn Carter LeBlanc to N.E.S.G., February 2010, private conversation.

59   Kimber, "Misfit Among the Mighty," 6.

60   Lyn Carter LeBlanc to N.E.S.G., February 2010, private conversation.

61   English, *Citizen of the World*, 416.

62   Roméo LeBlanc, "Campaign électorale fédérale," September 27, 1965, CBC/RCA Montreal.

63   Ibid., "Roméo LeBlanc fait le point sur la campagne électorale, à cinq semaines due scrutin fédérale," October 3, 1964; "Pierre Nadeau et Roméo LeBlanc font le point sur le campagne électorale des deux principau chefs du parties fédéraux le liberal Lester B. Pearson et le conservateur John Diefenbaker," October 24, 1964; "La campagne électorale fédérale vue par les correspondents," November 1964, CBC/RCA Montreal.

64   Knowlton Nash to N.E.S.G., 2009, telephone conversation.

65   *La semaine à Radio-Canada* XV, no. 44 (July 24–30, 1965): 2.

66   Roméo LeBlanc, "Conference de Presse due President de Radio-Canada," January 11, 1966, CBC/RCA Montreal.

67   Cited in Nash, *The Microphone Wars*, 316.

68   The report and its reception has been analyzed in detail in Nash, *The Microphone Wars*, 314–19.

69   Roméo LeBlanc to N.E.S.G., 2002, private conversation.

70   Roméo LeBlanc, "Égalité – Noirs – États Unis," June 14, 1965, CBC/RCA Montreal.

71   Ibid., "Droit Civique – Senant – États Unis," September 10, 1966,

CBC/RCA Montreal.

72 Hickey, *Window on a War*, 350.

73 As well as his television special, "Morley Safer's Vietnam—A Personal Diary," see also Safer, *Flashbacks: On Returning to Vietnam.*

74 Roméo LeBlanc, "Guerre due Vietnam: mission de paix," January 24, 1966; ibid., "L'Aggravation de la crise vietnamienne," January 30, 1966; ibid., "Tour de l'horizon des divers évènements entourent la guerre de Vietnam," February 13, 1966, CBC/RCA Montreal.

75 Debates about the Vietnam war have burgeoned in the years since it ended. I have relied on Demma, "The U.S. Army in Vietnam," for factual information.

76 Roméo LeBlanc, "Compte rendu de la conference de presse du secrétaire de la Défense Robert McNarra de porter la guerre aux abords de Hanoi; division du congrès américain face à ces bombardements," July 3, 1966, CBC/RCA Montreal.

77 Ibid., "Revue de la semaine," October 1, 1966, CBC/RCA Montreal.

78 Ibid., "Parti travailliste-election—Grand-Bretagne," March 19, 1966, CBC/RCA Montreal.

79 Ibid., "21ième Assemblée des Générale des Nations Unies," September 22, 1966; ibid., "La revue de la semaine—Extrait du bilan dressée par le présidente sortant (Fanffani d'Italie)…coloré par les frustrations engendrées par la guerre de Vietnam," September 24, 1966, CBC/RCA Montreal.

80 Ibid., "Parti Republicaun – Guerre du Vietnam," October 4, 1966; "Proces Jack Ruby," October 5, 1966; "Noveau developments sur la guerre du Vietnam," October 8, 1966, CBC/RCA Montreal.

81 Dallek, "Three new revelations about LBJ." Dallek is an American historian specializing in American presidents. See his two-volume life of Johnson, *Flawed Giant.*

82 Roméo LeBlanc, "Évènements relies à guerre du Vietnam cette semaine," October 22, 1966, CBC/RCA Montreal.

83 Ibid., "Derniers Développements sur la guerre due Vietnam," October 29, 1966, CBC/RCA Montreal.

84 Ibid., "Reportage de Roméo LeBlanc sur la visite do Lyndon B. Johnson en Nourvelle Zélande, Australie, Phillipines, Vietnam, Thailande et Malasie," November 11, 1966, CBC/RCA Montreal.

Chapter 6 – An Unexpected Path to Political Life

1 Even this second, common enough term for the events of the deportations of 1755–1763 modifies the idea that Acadian life in some way extinguished the Acadian people.

2   Interview with Roméo LeBlanc, No. 3: "La vie politique," CBC/RCA Moncton.
3   Kimber, "Misfit Among the Mighty," 4.
4   Cited in ibid.
5   Interview with Roméo LeBlanc, "Les Coulisses de l'Actualité," February 13, 1967, CBC/RCA Moncton. Translation and précis by N.E.S.G.
6   Letter from Roméo LeBlanc to CBC Accounting Department, June 30, 1967, MG 35A, vol. 138, RLP, LAC.
7   Roméo LeBlanc, "Le Vietnam du Nord," February 27, 1967; ibid., "Robert Kennedy Guerre du Vietnam," March 2, 1967; ibid., "General Westmoreland-Vietnam," April 28, 1967; ibid., "Guerre de Vietnam—Lyndon B. Johnson," May 3, 1967; ibid., "Voyage de Kossyguine aux Etats-Unis," June 24, 1967; ibid., "Recontre-Kossyguine-Johnson á Washington," June 26, 1967, CBC/RCA Montreal.
8   The Privy Council itself is made up of the prime minister, the ministers of the Crown, and the clerk of the Privy Council. The most intelligent and elegantly written guide through the maze of Canadian government organizations are the two books by Savoie, *Governing from the Centre* and *Court Government and the Collapse of Accountability in Canada and the United Kingdom*.
9   Stursberg, *Lester Pearson and the Dream of Unity*, 499.
10   Kimber, "Misfit Among the Mighty," 4.
11   Memorandum, Office of the Prime Minister, April 1968, MG 35A, vol. 138, box 296, RLP, LAC.
12   In particular, see letters such as that from his sister Emily in Boston, March 27, 1965, MG 35A, vol. 138, box 291, RLP, LAC.
13   Munro and Inglis, *Mike: The Memoirs of the Right Honourable Lester B. Pearson*, 239.
14   Ibid., 238.
15   The Conservatives had won eight seats and Social Credit had won twenty.
16   The FLQ was founded in February 1963. Its first bombs exploded at the Canadian Army barracks, March 7–8, 1963. William O'Neill, aged sixty-five, a night watchman, was killed in a bombing on April 27, 1963.
17   Munro and Inglis, *Mike: The Memoirs of the Right Honourable Lester B. Pearson*, 242.
18   Cited in Bothwell et al., *Canada since 1945*, 281.
19   An analysis of the developing tensions between France and Canada at this time is in Hilliker and Barry, *Canada's Department of External Affairs, Vol. II*, 292–400.

20   Letter from Halstead to the under-secretary of state, December 2,
     1966; cited in ibid., 396.
21   Munro and Inglis, *Mike: The Memoirs of the Right Honourable Lester B.
     Pearson*, 263–4.
22   Just over 600,000 Canadians fought in the First World War, out of a
     population of just over eight million. In all, 59,544 were killed. The
     historiography of Vimy Ridge is considerable. Two major works are
     Hayes et al., *Vimy Ridge: A Canadian Reassessment*, and Barris, *Victory
     at Vimy Ridge.*
23   Munro and Inglis, *Mike: The Memoirs of the Right Honourable Lester B.
     Pearson*, 264.
24   Cowley and Cowley, *One Woman's Journey*, 155–6.
25   See Munro and Inglis, *Mike: The Memoirs of the Right Honourable
     Lester B. Pearson*, 268–9, for the prime minister's personal account of
     these events.
26   The full text of de Gaulle's speech can be found in de Gaulle, *Discours
     et Messages*, 186–90. A lengthy excerpt from the Montreal speech is
     found in English, *The Worldly Years*, 341–2.
27   A long argument ensued as to whether de Gaulle's words had been a
     deliberate indiscretion or a mistake in a moment of euphoria. See the
     discussion about this in Pelletier, *The Years of Choice*, 243–6.
28   Munro and Inglis, *Mike: The Memoirs of the Right Honourable Lester B.
     Pearson*, 268.
29   Ibid., 169. See also the autobiography of Gordon Robertson, the Clerk
     of the Privy Council, *Memoirs of a Very Civil Servant*, 235.
30   Morton, *A Short History of Canada*, 243.
31   Cited in Hillmer, ed., *Pearson: The Unlikely Gladiator*, 13.
32   Bégin, "Continuity," 165.
33   For details see Bothwell, et al., *Canada since 1945*, 273–4.
34   For a short account of this debacle, see ibid., 304–5. Mitchell Sharp,
     finance minister at the time, offers his own account in his memoirs,
     Which Reminds Me, 159–60.
35   Westell, "Trudeau's television success trims Parliament's power," 8.
36   Pelletier, *The Years of Choice*, 281.
37   Roméo LeBlanc to N.E.S.G., 2003, private conversation. Confirmed by
     Marc Lalonde to N.E.S.G., summer 2010.
38   Duffy, *Fights of Our Lives*, 240.
39   Trudeau, *Memoirs*, 87.
40   Robertson, *Memoirs of a Very Civil Servant*, 254.
41   Trudeau, *Memoirs*, 106.
42   An elegant and detailed account of the election is given by English in
     Citizen of the World, Vol. II, 1–32.

43 Trudeau, *Memoirs*, 109.
44 Robertson, *Memoirs of a Very Civil Servant*, 255–6.
45 Ibid., 259.
46 Trudeau, *Memoirs*, 123.
47 Robertson, *Memoirs of a Very Civil Servant*, 261.
48 Marshall Crowe to N.E.S.G., Fall 2007, private conversation.
49 Doyle, *The Premiers of New Brunswick*, 71.
50 The act creating the university was passed in 1963. The opening of the campus in Moncton took place in 1965.
51 The act passed on April 18, 1969, two months before the federal act.
52 The best place to begin reading about this venture is Cormier, *L'Université de Moncton Historique*.
53 Robertson, *Memoirs of a Very Civil Servant*, 261; Sharp, *Which Reminds Me*, 193.
54 Ibid.
55 Saywell, *Quebec 70: A Documentary Narrative*, 22–3.
56 English, *Just Watch Me*, 79.
57 The published documentation on the crisis is immense. For quick reference, Saywell's *Quebec* is excellent, as is a more recent work by Tetley, *The October Crisis 1970*. Tetley was a member of the Bourassa cabinet during the crisis.
58 The names and the sentences of the FLQ members involved in the October Crisis are found in Tetley, *The October Crisis 1970*, Appendix 4, 234–5.
59 Robertson, *Memoirs of a Very Civil Servant*, 261; Sharp, *Which Reminds Me*, 193.
60 Tetley, *The October Crisis 1970*, 147.

Chapter 7 – From Backbencher to Minister

1 Roberts, *Raising Eyebrows*, 94.
2 *Moncton Transcript* (14 August 1971), 11.
3 Ibid.
4 In particular, see Kimber, "Misfit Among the Mighty," 6; and the post-retirement radio interview, CBC/RCA Moncton.
5 For a longer discussion of the situation of the Université de Moncton at this time, see Wilbur, *The Rise of French New Brunswick*, 227 et seq.
6 Roméo read King's writings with interest, in particular *Industry and Humanity: A Study in the Principles of Underlying Industrial Reconstruction*, first published by Thomas Allen in 1928.
7 The riding consisted of that part of Kent County that included the parishes of Dundas, Harcourt, Richibucto, St. Charles, St. Louis,

St. Paul, Weldford, and Wellington, and that part of Westmorland County that included the parishes of Botsford, Dorchester, Sackville, Shediac, and Westmorland, the towns of Sackville and Shediac, and the village of Port Elgin. Moncton, Dieppe, and the Miramichi formed part of other ridings.

8   The boundaries of the riding did not follow the boundary of Westmorland County, and the excision of Moncton meant that its edges were imprecise. See *Census of Canada: Population: Census divisions and sub-divisions (Atlantic Provinces)*, Vol. I, pt. 1: 92–704, 1971.

9   In 2010, the population of Elsipogtog was 3,014, Puktusk was 89, and L'nui Menikuk was 160. Mi'kmaq Resource Centre, Cape Breton University.

10   Savoie, *I'm from Bouctouche, Me*, 3.

11   Bertin LeBlanc to N.E.S.G., October 10, 2010.

12   Ibid., October 12, 2010.

13   R.L.B. to N.E.S.G., 2003, private conversation.

14   Bertin and Yvon LeBlanc to N.E.S.G., September 19, 2010 private conversation.

15   Bertin LeBlanc to N.E.S.G., October 11, 2010.

16   Monique Bégin to N.E.S.G., 2009, private conversation.

17   Reid, "The 1970s: Sharpening the Sceptical Edge," 478–9.

18   See Savoie, *I'm from Bouctouche, Me*, 96–106.

19   It was a Canada-wide enquiry.

20   Published by the Queen's Printer, Fredericton, NB, 1971.

21   Wilbur, *The Rise of French New Brunswick*, 247.

22   *Telegraph Journal* (17 January 1972).

23   Wilbur, *The Rise of French New Brunswick*, 347.

24   A generation is generally considered to be thirty years, from birth to parenthood. However, living memory can stretch from grandfather to grandchild, which makes the span of oral history often considerably longer. This tradition was told to me by a number of Acadians who were in their sixties in the 1970s.

25   Chiasson, *Mourir à Scoudouc*.

26   It affirmed for many, but not all, Acadians a particular sense of their history. For some Acadians, however, the life story of someone who had been a prostitute at one point was unacceptable as a representative of the Acadian people.

27   This correspondence has been organized by LAC as LeBlanc Papers, Correspondence (1948–1999) Mikan #3916360.

28   Nomination speech, private collection of Bertin LeBlanc.

29   English has a clear summary of the difficulties Trudeau faced from

Alberta and from the members of his own party in *Citizen of the World*, 212–30.

30   See Robertson, *Memoirs of a Very Civil Servant*, 254–9.

31   Joe Gough has been, in conversations and e-mails and through his definitive scholarly study, *Managing Canada's Fisheries from Early Days to the Year 2000*, a crucial aid in my writing about the fisheries. In what follows, the dance of footnotes will show my indebtedness to his eminently readable scholarship.

32   For a detailed account, see Gough, *Managing Canada's Fisheries*, 290–2. See also Anderson, "The Demise of the Fisheries Research Board of Canada," 151–6.

33   Gough, *Managing Canada's Fisheries*, 292.

34   Louis-Marie Melanson, *L'Évangéline* (February 15, 1974), 7.

35   See MacEachern, *Natural Selections: National Parks in Atlantic Canada, 1935–1970*.

36   Rudin, "Kouchibouquac in Acadian Memory," 1.

37   Jackie Vautour, now in his late seventies, continues to battle for the restoration of his rights. Whatever else he did or did not achieve, his struggle fundamentally changed the way the government dealt with the establishment of national parks.

38   See Warren and Massicotte, "La fermeture du department de asociologie de l'Université de Moncton."

39   For a general survey of such programs, see Arin and Wong, "Direct Job Creation Programs: Evaluation Lessons on Cost-effectiveness," 161–9.

Chapter 8 – Minister of Fishermen

1   Margaret Trudeau, *Changing My Mind*, 72.

2   Dominic LeBlanc to N.E.S.G., 2010, private conversation.

3   Gough, *Managing Canada's Fisheries*, 292.

4   *Canadian Parliamentary Guide, 1996*, 18.

5   I am much indebted to Monique Bégin for her reminiscences of life as a minister. Her personal record-keeping was much more meticulous than Roméo's.

6   Kimber, "Misfit Among the Mighty," 6.

7   Gough, *Managing Canada's Fisheries*, 291.

8   *Commons Debates*, 1974–1976, 124.

9   Ibid., October 8, 1974, 204.

10   Cited in Gough, *Managing Canada's Fisheries*, 308.

11   Ibid., 309–10.

12   For an overview of the importance of these meetings, see "United Nations convention on the Law of the Sea, Montego Bay, December

10, 1982. (http://untreaty.un.org.codavl/ha/uncls/uncls.html). Gough provides a detailed chronological account of events in Part V of *Managing Canada's Fisheries.*

13   *Commons Debates,* May 9, 1975, 5635.
14   For a blow by blow account of this and related events, see Gough, *Managing Canada's Fisheries,* 297 et seq.
15   Ibid., 297.
16   *Commons Debates,* July 23, 1975, 1053–55.
17   Gough, *Managing Canada's Fisheries,* 297.
18   Ibid., 312.
19   Bertin LeBlanc and Yvon Leblanc to N.E.S.G., 2010, private conversation.
20   Cited in Kimber, "Misfit Among the Mighty," 6.
21   Former staffers to N.E.S.G., 2008, private conversations.
22   Gough, *Managing Canada's Fisheries,* 298.
23   Ibid.
24   I am indebted to the Hon. Monique Bégin for these details.
25   Sharp, *Which Reminds Me,* 236–7.
26   Roméo LeBlanc, address to Mount Allison University graduating class, May 7, 1977.
27   *Commons Debates,* May 16, 1977, 5667–99.
28   Ibid., 5667.
29   Ibid., 5668.
30   *Commons Debates,* 1670.
31   Ibid.
32   Bertin LeBlanc to N.E.S.G., 2010, private conversation.
33   See Gough, *Managing Canada's Fisheries,* 369.
34   *Commons Debates,* May 11, 1978, 5325.
35   Gough, *Managing Canada's Fisheries,* 345.
36   Ibid., 319 et seq.
37   *Commons Debates,* May 11, 1978, 5326.
38   *Canadian Fishing Report,* July 1979.
39   Roméo LeBlanc, Speech to the Fisheries Council of Canada, Quebec, May 3, 1978.
40   *Commons Debates,* May 11, 1978, 5327.
41   Ibid., 5326. (R.L.B. speaking.)
42   Ibid.
43   Government of Canada, *Information Gulf Region du Golfe.* I am indebted to Terence Booker, who sent me a collection of Government of Canada publications on the creation of the region.
44   *Commons Debates,* January 24, 1979, 2535.
45   Ibid., 2537.

46   Gough, *Managing Canada's Fisheries*, chap. 4, 293, note 4. He went on to the Food and Agriculture Organization of the United Nations.
47   See *Commons Debates*, February 16, 1979, 3314–20.
48   Gough, *Managing Canada's Fisheries*, 293. Based on his private conversation with Roméo.
49   History of federal riding since 1967, <http://www2.parl.ge.ca/lop/ HFER/hfer.asp?/Language=E&Search=Det&Include=Y&>.
50   Duffy, *Fights of Our Lives*, 301.
51   Ibid.
52   Gough, *Managing Canada's Fisheries*, 360.
53   *Commons Debates*, May 8, 1980, 835.
54   Gough, *Managing Canada's Fisheries*, 333.
55   Bertin LeBlanc to N.E.S.G., private conversation. See also Gough, *Managing Canada's Fisheries*, 333.
56   Gough, Managing Canada's Fisheries, 292.

Chapter 9 – From Elected to Appointed Office

1   Cited in McWhinney, *Canada and the Constitution*, 29–30.
2   Ibid., 35.
3   English, *Just Watch Me, Vol. II, 1968–2006*, 446.
4   Details of these tumultuous years have been told elsewhere. See Sheppard and Valpy, *The National Deal*, for a contemporary account; Simpson, *Discipline of Power*, 238–372, offers some interesting observations; and, above all, English, *Just Watch Me, Vol. II, 1968– 2006*, 428–555, gives an authoritative account of the events.
5   McWhinney, *Canada and the Constitution*, viii–ix.
6   Cited in Bliss, *Right Honourable Men*, 267.
7   English, *Just Watch Me, Vol. II, 1968–2006*, 500.
8   When Sir John went further, and gave a press conference to elaborate on his views, British Prime Minister Margaret Thatcher immediately recalled him. Canada, *Commons Debates*, February 6, 1981.
9   McWhinney, *Canada and the Constitution*, 59.
10   This clause gives provincial governments the right to opt out, under certain conditions, of those sections dealing with fundamental freedoms, legal rights, and equality rights, providing that the opting-out provisions be re-enacted by the province in question not less frequently than once every five years. See ibid., 97.
11   On December 2, 1981, the House of Commons voted to accept the final revised constitutional resolution by a vote of 246 to 24. It came into force on April 7, 1982.

12 Lyn LeBlanc, Dominic LeBlanc and Geneviève LeBlanc to N.E.S.G., 2008–2010, private conversations.
13 These headings are used in the catalogue of Library and Archives Canada to describe the section of the Roméo LeBlanc fonds, for the period of his career as minister of public works.
14 Bertin LeBlanc and Yvon LeBlanc to N.E.S.G., summer 2010, private conversations.
15 For a general discussion of the issues of patronage, see Simpson, *Spoils of Power*. For a personal analysis of the issue, see Savoie, *I'm from Bouctouche, Me*, 165–9.
16 For an overview see Hulchandski and Grieve, *Housing Issues and Canadian Federal Budgets*.
17 Canada. *Commons Debates*, October 29, 1982, 20203.
18 English, *Just Watch Me, Vol. II, 1968–2006*, 539.
19 Ibid., 542.
20 Canada. *Commons Debates*, November 17, 1982, 20746.
21 Ibid., February 28, 1983, 23116.
22 Ibid., May 2, 1983, 25056.
23 Ibid.
24 Ibid.
25 Ibid., 25057.
26 See correspondence in LAC, LeBlanc Papers, minister responsible for Canadian Housing and Mortgage Corporation, Mikan #382695.
27 Bertin LeBlanc to N.E.S.G., March 29, 2011, private correspondence.
28 English, *Just Watch Me, Vol. II, 1968–2006*, 553.
29 Taped conversations after his retirement, CBC/RCA Moncton.
30 LAC, LeBlanc Papers, New Brunswick Special files, Mikan #3806313.
31 Ibid., Committees and Cabinet Documents (1983–1987), Mikan #3808247.
32 Ibid.
33 Ibid., Senator, Mikan #3827217.
34 Ibid., MP and member of the Liberal Party (1968–1997), Mikan #3845693.
35 Keller, "Sikh Refugees who Landed on NS Beach." See also Thompson, "Bystander Assistance during Emergencies in Rural Coastal Shelburne County, Nova Scotia."
36 The incident prompted a national debate on what to do about illegal immigrants.
37 Cited in Duffy, *Fights of Our Lives*, 345. Duffy's summary of the election in general, but particularly of the TV debate, is excellent reading.
38 Bliss, *Right Honourable Men*, 293.

39   LAC, LeBlanc papers, Senator (1973–1995), Mikan #3827217.
40   Smith, Land and Government Division, Government of Canada, "Patent Protection for Pharmaceutical Products in Canada."
41   Mason, "La Francophonie: Structures, Organization, and Philosophical Underpinnings," 2.
42   Grady, "The Liberal Red Book," <http://globaleconomics.ca/redbookhtm>.
43   This observation comes from my own experience at the time interviewing women living in Western Canada who were associated with the volunteer organizations and members of the National Council of Women.
44   Bliss, *Right Honourable Men*, 315.
45   Interviews with Roméo LeBlanc, n.d., CBC/RCA Moncton.
46   Chrétien, *My Years as Prime Minister*, 247.
47   Ibid.
48   The certificate was issued on June 8, 1992.
49   <http://archive.gg.ca/media/doc.asp?lang=e&DocID=92>.
50   Attempts by Dominic LeBlanc and I to procure copies of the broadcast have been to no avail. I have checked my recollections of the broadcast with Bertin LeBlanc and there is general agreement as to the sense of what Roméo said.
51   LeBlanc, Rideau Hall speech, September 24, 1998. <http://archive.gg.ca/media/doc.asp?lang=e&DocID=126>.
52   Chrétien, *My Years as Prime Minister*, 141.
53   "Governor General LeBlanc's speech…during the Sommet de la Francophonie." <http://archive.gg.ca/media/doc.asp?lang=e&DocID=52>.

Epilogue

1   Noted by Dominic LeBlanc in a record of an interview he gave in office, June 3, 2009: no record of interviewer.
2   *National Post*, June 25, 2009, A2.
3   Souza, *Edmonton Journal*, June 25, 2009, A7; Delacourt, *Toronto Star*, June 25, 2009, A19.
4   Delacourt, *Toronto Star*, June 25, 2009, A19.
5   Spencer, *Toronto Sun*, June 25, 2009, 26.
6   Martin, *Globe and Mail*, June 26, 2009, R5.
7   Cited in ibid.
8   Bryden, *Daily Gleaner* (Fredericton), June 25, 2009, A1.

Bibliography

Primary Sources

When I first began working on the LeBlanc Papers, they had just been sent to Library and Archives Canada, and were in a number of unsorted files that had been placed in boxes and roughly catalogued. The catalogue was created using the MG35 reference numbers. When LAC began the process of a more elaborate system, Victor Chabot had the courtesy to consult me on the way in which the reference system which I had used could be used as a guide to the more sophisticated system being created—the Mikan system. We agreed that if I gave both the date and subject of the document cited, plus the reference to the catalogue I used, there should be no difficulty to those working later on. This is what I have done.

Archives

"Lettre du R.P. Philippe Bélanger, s.j.," in *Archive*, American Academy of Religion, *Dossier Action Catholique*, 1940.

Armand St. Onge Papers. Interview 3, MC778. Public Archives of New Brunswick.

"Brief presented by l'Association acadienne d'éducation to the Honorable Premier...in support of a Bilingual Teachers'College." RS116B3K, 1954, Public Archives of New Brunswick.

Fonds de l'Association des Insituteurs Acadiens. Correspondence. 31.1.Y. Centre d'Études Acadiennes, Université de Moncton.

LeBlanc, Roméo. Address to Mount Allison graduating class, May 7, 1977, typescript Ministry of Fisheries and Environment, author's personal copy.

Mi'kmaq Resource Centre, Cape Breton University. <http://www.uccb.ns.ca/nbcouncils.html>.

Roméo LeBlanc Papers. Correspondence, 1948–1999. MG 35, A138/291–296. Library and Archives Canada. Mikan #3916360/#3845647.

Government Documents

New Brunswick Department of Education Annual Reports, 1946, 1952, 1953.

Canadian Fishing Report, July 1979.

Census of Canada, 1941.

Census of Canada: Population: Census divisions and sub-divisions (Atlantic Provinces). Vol. I, part I, 92–704, 1971.

Commons *Debates,* 1974–1976.

New Brunswick Legislature, *Debates,* 1955.

History of federal riding since 1967, <http://www2.parl.ge.ca/lop/HFER/hfer.asp?/Language=E&Search=Det&Include=Y&>.

Information Gulf Region du Golfe.

Statistics Canada. <www40.Statcan.ca/101/cst01/demo62a.htm>.

United Nations Convention on the Law of the Sea, Montego Bay, December 10, 1982, <http://untreaty.un.org. codavl/ha/ uncls/uncls.html>.

Books

Allain, Greg, and Maurice Basque. *Une présence qui s'affirme: La communauté acadienne et francophone de Fredericton, Nouveau Brunswick.* Moncton, NB: Les Éditions de la Francophonie, 2003.

Amal, Oscar. *The History of the Worker Priests.* New York: Paulist Press, 1986.

American Military History. Washington, DC: Center of Military History, United States Army, 1989.

Amouroux, Henri. *La grande histoire des français sous l'occupation.* 10 vols. Paris: Robert Laffont, 1993.

L'Association des Instituteurs Acadien. *Les instituteurs acadiens de Nouveau Brunswick: Un manuel de reseignements,* 1950.

Barris, Theodore. *Victory at Vimy Ridge: Canada Comes of Age, April 9–17, 1967.* Toronto: Thomas Allen, 2007.

Beaulieu, Gérard, ed. *L'Évangeline, 1887–1982: Entre l'élite et le peuple.* Moncton, NB: Éditions d'acadie, 1997.

Bégin, Monique. "Continuity," in *Pearson: The Unlikely Gladiator,* Norman Hillmer, ed. Montreal and Kingston: McGill-Queen's University Press, 1999, 163–7.

Belliveau, Joel. "Acadian New Brunswick's Ambivalent Leap into the Canadian Liberal Order," in *Creating Postwar Canada: Community, Diversity, and Dissent, 1945–75,* eds. Magda Fahrni and Robert Rutherdale. Vancouver: University of British Columbia Press, 2008.

Bliss, Michael. *Right Honourable Men: The Descent of Canadian Politics from Macdonald to Chrétien.* Toronto: HarperCollins, 2004.

Bothwell, Robert, Ian Drummond, and John English. *Canada Since 1945: Power, Politics, and Provincialism.* Toronto: University of Toronto Press, 1989.

Bruneau, Charles. *Petite histoire de la langue française.* Paris: Colin, 1955–1958.

Brunet, Jean-Marc, and Jean Côté. *Le patriote: Marcel Chaput et son époque*. Montréal: Editions de l'Ordre Naturiste Social de Saint-Marc l'Évangeliste, 2006.

Canadian Parliamentary Guide, 1996. Toronto: Greyhouse Publishing Canada, 1996.

Careless, J.M.S. and R. Craig Brown, eds. *The Canadians, 1867–1967.* Toronto: Macmillan of Canada, 1968.

Cesbron, Gilbert. *Les saints vont en enfer.* Paris: Paderborn Schöningh, 1965.

Chrétien, Jean. *Straight from the Heart.* Toronto: Key Porter Books, 1985.

————. *My Years as Prime Minister.* Toronto: Knopf Canada, 2007.

Chaisson, Herménégilde. *Mourir à Scoudouc.* Moncton, NB: Éditions d'Acadie, 1974.

Clément, Gabriel. *Histoire de l'Action catholique au Canada français.* Montréal: Éditions Fides, 1972.

Le Congrès mondial acadien: l'Acadie en 2004: Actes des conférences et tables rondes. Moncton, NB: Éditions d'Acadie, 2004.

Connelly, Matthew James. *A Diplomatic Revolution: Algeria's Fight for Independence and the Origins of the Post–Cold War Era.* New York: Oxford University Press, 2002.

Cormier, Clément. *L'Université de Moncton: Historique centre d'études acadiennes.* Moncton, NB: Université de Moncton, 1975.

Cowley, Deborah, and George Cowley. *One Woman's Journey: A Portrait of Pauline Vanier.* Ottawa: Novalis, 1992.

Daigle, Jean, ed. *Les Acadiens des Maritimes: Études thématiques.* Moncton, NB: Centre d'Études Acadiennes, 1980.

Dallek, Robert. *Flawed Giant: Lyndon Johnson and His Times, 1961–1973.* 2 vols. Oxford, UK: Oxford University Press, 1991, 1993.

Davidson, Philip. *Vietnam at War.* New York: Oxford University Press, 1988.

de Gaulle, Charles. *Discours et messages: Vers le terme: Janvier 1966–Avril 1969.* Paris: Plon, 1970.

——— . *De Gaulle parle, 1962–1966.* Paris: Fayard, 1970.

Demma, Vincent H. "The U.S. Army in Vietnam," in *American Military History.* Washington DC: Center of Military History, United States Army, 1989.

Doyle, Arthur T. *The Premiers of New Brunswick.* Fredericton, NB: Brunswick Press, 1983.

Duffy, John. *Fights of Our Lives: Elections, Leadership, and the Making of Canada.* Toronto: HarperCollins, 2002.

English, John. *Citizen of the World: The Life of Pierre Elliott Trudeau, vol. I: 1919–1968.* Toronto: Alfred A. Knopf Canada, 2006.

——— . *Just Watch Me: The Life of Pierre Elliott Trudeau, vol. II: 1968–2000.* Toronto: Alfred A. Knopf Canada, 2009.

——— . *The Worldly Years: The Life of Lester Pearson, vol. II: 1949–1972.* Toronto: Lester & Orpen Dennys, 1992.

Forbes, E.R. "The 1930s: Depression and Retrenchment," in *The Atlantic Provinces in Confederation,* eds. E.R. Forbes and D.A. Muise. Toronto: University of Toronto Press, 1993.

Forbes, E.R., and D.A. Muise. *The Atlantic Provinces in Confederation.* Toronto: University of Toronto Press, 1993

Girard, Charlotte S.M. *Canada in World Affairs, vol. XIII: 1963–1985.* Toronto: Canadian Institute of International Affairs, 1980.

Gough, Joe. *Managing Canada's Fisheries from Early Days to the Year 2000.* Sillery, QC: Éditions de Septentrion, 2006.

Graham. Ron. *All the King's Horses.* Toronto: MacFarlane, Walter and Ross, 1995.

Hamelin, Jean. *Histoire du catholicisme québécoise.* Montreal: Boréal Express, 1984.

Hautecoeur, Jean-Paul. *L'Acadie du discours: Pour une sociologie de la culture acadienne.* Quebec City: Presses de l'Université Laval, 1975.

Hayes, Geoffrey, Andrew Iarocci, and Mike Bechthold, eds.

Vimy Ridge: A Canadian Reassessment. Waterloo, ON:
Wilfrid Laurier University Press, 2007.

Hickey, Gerald. *Window on a War: An Anthropologist in the
Vietnam Conflict.* Lubbock: Texas Tech University Press,
2002.

Hilliker, John, and Donald Barry. *Canada's Department of
External Affairs, vol. II: Coming of Age, 1946–1968.*
Ottawa: Canadian Public Administration Series # 20, 1995.

Hillmer, Norman, ed. *Pearson: The Unlikely Gladiator.* Montreal
and Kingston: McGill-Queen's University Press,
1999.

Horne, Alistair. *A Savage War of Peace: Algeria, 1954–1962.*
Harmondsworth, UK: Penguin, 1979.

Innis, Harold J. *The Bias of Communication.* Toronto:
University of Toronto Press, 1951.

Jones, Ted. *Fredericton Flashbacks: Stories and Photographs
from the Past.* Halifax, NS: Nimbus Publishing, 2003.

Judt, Tony. *Post War: A History of Europe since 1945.*
London: Penguin, 2005.

Kennedy, Robert F. *Thirteen Days: A Memoir of the Cuban
Missile Crisis.* New York: Norton, 1969.

Kilbourn, William. "The 1950s," in *The Canadians, 1867–
1967,* eds. J.M.S. Careless and R. Craig Brown. Toronto:
Macmillan of Canada, 1968.

Knapton, Ernest John. *France: An Interpretive History.* New
York: Charles Scribner's Sons, 1971.

Landry, Nicolas, and Nicole Lang. *Histoire de l'Acadie.* Sillery,
QC: Éditions de Septentrion, 2001.

LeBlanc, Emery. *Les Acadiens.* Montréal: Les Éditions de
l'Homme, 1963.

Lévesque, Réné. *Attendez que je me rappelle.* Montreal:
Québec Amérique, 2007.

Loew, Jacques. *Journal d'une mission ouvrière, 1941–1959.*
Paris: Éditions du Cerf, 1959.

MacEachern, Alan. *Natural Selections: National Parks in*

Atlantic Canada, 1935–1970. Montréal and Kingston: McGill-Queen's University Press, 2001.

MacKinnon, Frank. *The Crown in Canada.* Calgary, AB: Glenbow-Alberta Institute/McClelland & Stewart West, 1976.

Marr, Andrew. *A History of Modern Britain.* London: Macmillan, 2007.

McWhinney, Edward. *Chrétien and Canadian Federalism: Politics and the Constitution, 1993–2003.* Vancouver: Ronsdale Press, 2003.

Meunier, E. Martin, and Jean-Philippe Warren. *Sortir de la "Grande noiceur": L'horizon "personaliste" de la Révolution tranquille.* Sillery, QC: Éditions de Septentrion, 2002.

Morton, Desmond. *A Short History of Canada.* Edmonton, AB: Hurtig Publishing, 1983.

Mounier, Emmanuel. *L'Affrontement Chrétien.* Paris: Seuil, 1945.

———. *Be Not Afraid: Studies in Personalist Sociology.* Toronto: Harper, 1954.

Munro, John A., and Alex I. Inglis. *Mike: The Memoirs of the Right Honourable Lester B. Pearson, vol. 3: 1957–1968.* Toronto: University of Toronto Press, 1975.

Nash, Knowlton. *The Microphone Wars: A History of Triumph and Betrayal at the CBC.* Toronto: McClelland & Stewart, 1994.

Paxton, Robert O. *Vichy France: Old Guard and New Order, 1940–1944.* New York: Alfred A. Knopf, 1972.

Pelletier, Gérard. *The Years of Choice, 1960–1968.* Alan Brown, trans. Toronto: Methuen Publications, 1987.

———. *The Years of Impatience, 1950–1960.* Alan Brown, trans. Toronto: Methuen, 1984.

Picot, J. Ernest. *A Brief History of Teacher Training in New Brunswick, 1848–1973.* Fredericton, NB: Department of Education, 1974.

Preston, Richard, Sydney F. Wise, and Herman O. Werner.

Men in Arms: A History of Warfare and Interrelationships with Western Society. 4th ed. New York: Holt, Rinehart and Winston, 1979.

Reid, John. "The 1970s: Sharpening the Sceptical Edge," in *The Atlantic Provinces in Confederation*, eds. E.R. Forbes and D.A. Muise. Toronto: University of Toronto Press, 1993, 478–9.

Roberts, Peter. *Raising Eyebrows: An Undiplomatic Memoir.* Ottawa: Golden Dog Press, 2000.

Robertson, Gordon. *Memoirs of a Very Civil Servant: Mackenzie King to Pierre Trudeau.* Toronto: University of Toronto Press, 2000.

Rousseau, Jean-Jacques. *Émile, ou De l'éducation.* 1792.

Safer, Morley. *Flashbacks: On Returning to Vietnam.* New York: Random House, 1990.

Savoie, Alexandre J. *Un demi-siècle d'histoire acadienne,* Moncton, NB: author, 1976.

——— . "L'Enseignement en Acadie," in *Les Acadiens des Maritimes—Études thématiques*, ed. Jean Daigle. Moncton, NB: Centre d'Études Acadiennes, 1980.

——— . *Un siècle de revendications scolarie au Nouveau-Brunswick, vol. I: Français au compt gouttes, 1871–1936.* Moncton, NB: author, 1978.

Savoie, Calixte F. *Mémoires d'un nationaliste acadian.* Moncton, NB: Éditions d'Acadie, 1979.

Savoie, Donald J. *Court Government and the Collapse of Accountability in Canada and the United Kingdom.* Toronto: University of Toronto Press, 2008.

——— . *Governing from the Centre: The Concentrations of Power in Canadian Politics.* Toronto: University of Toronto Press, 1999.

——— . *I'm from Bouctouche, Me.* Montreal and Kingston: McGill-Queen's University Press, 2009.

Saywell, John. *Quebec 70: A Documentary Narrative.* Toronto: University of Toronto Press, 1971.

Sévigny, Pierre. *This Game of Politics.* Montreal and Toronto: McClelland & Stewart, 1965.

Sharp, Mitchell. *Which Reminds Me: A Memoir.* Toronto: University of Toronto Press, 1994.

Siefer, Gregor. *The Church and Industrial Society.* London: Danton, Longman and Todd, 1964.

Smith, Denis. *Rogue Tory: The Life and Legend of John G. Diefenbaker.* Toronto: MacFarlane, Walter and Ross, 1995.

Snow, Gérard. *Les droits linguistiques des Acadiens du Nouveau-Brunswick.* Quebec City: Government of Quebec, 1981.

Stern, Sheldon M. *The Week the World Stood Still: Inside the Secret Cuban Missile Crisis.* Stanford, CA: Stanford University Press, 2005.

Stursberg, Peter. *Lester Pearson and the Dream of Unity.* Toronto: Doubleday Canada, 1978.

Talbott, J.E. "Vichy and Resistance France," in *The Transformation of Modern France: Essays in Honor of Gordon Wright,* ed., William B. Cohen. Boston and New York: Houghton Mifflin Co., 1997.

Tetley, William. The *October Crisis, 1970: An Insider's View.* Montreal and Kingston: McGill-Queen's University Press, 2007.

Tremblay, Marc. *50 ans d'éducation, 1889–1949.* Bathurst, NB: L'Université du Sacré-Coeur, 1949.

Trudeau, Margaret. *Changing My Mind.* Toronto: Harper-Collins, 2010.

Trudeau, Pierre Elliott. *Memoirs.* Toronto: McClelland & Stewart, 1993.

United Nations. *Yearbook of the United Nations, 1962.* New York: Author, 1962.

Université de Saint-Joseph/University of St. Joseph. [*Calendar*], 1941–1942. Memramcook, NB: Author, 1941.

Westell, Anthony. *The Inside Story: A Life in Journalism.* Toronto: Dundurn, 2002.

——— . *Paradox: Trudeau as Prime Minister.* Scarborough,

ON: Prentice Hall, 1972.

———. *Reinventing Canada*. Toronto: Dundurn, 1994.

Wilbur, Richard. *The Rise of French New Brunswick*. Halifax, NS: Formac Publishing Company, 1989.

Windrow, Martin. *The Last Valley*. London: Wiedenfeld and Nicolson, 2004.

Woodhouse, C.M. *Modern Greece: A Short History*. London: Faber and Faber, 1998.

Journals and Newspaper Reports

"Académie Notre-Dame de Drummond (1949–1999)—La planification et la construction de la première école centrale de Drummond." *La Cataracte* (October 6, 1999), Section B4.

Anderson, Francis. "The Demise of the Fisheries Research Board of Canada: A Case Study of Canadian Research Policy." *Journal of the History of Canadian Science, Technology and Medicine* 8, no. 2 (1984): 151–6.

Arin, Roy, and Ging Wong. "Direct Job Creation Programs: Evaluation Lessons on Cost-effectiveness." *Canadian Public Policy–Analyse de politiques* 26, no. 2 (2000): 161–9.

Boon, Robert L., and Ruth T. Doyle. "Secularly Employed Clergymen: A Study in Occupational Role Recomposition." *Journal for the Scientific Study of Religion* 13, no. 3 (1974), 325–45.

Cuplinskas, Indre. "Guns and Rosaries: The Use of Military Imagery in the French-Catholic Student Newspaper *JEC*." Canadian Catholic Historical Association, *Historical Studies* 71 (2005), 7–28.

Dallek, Robert. "Three New Revelations about LBJ." *Atlantic Monthly* (April 1998).

Duguay, Henri-Eugène. "Les déportés de Grand-Pré envahissent Ottawa." *Le moniteur acadien* (February 2, 1995).

Kimber, Stephen. "Misfit Among the Mighty: Fisheries Minister Roméo LeBlanc has taken a Unique Route to Ottawa's Corridors of Power." *Financial Post* (October 29, 1977), 4–8.

Kondratyev, V. "The Aspida Affair and the Reactionaries." *International Affairs* 12, no. 12 (1966), 92–93.

Pelletier, Gérard. "Utiliser au besoin la farce, la traité et la nouvelle, pour mettre en marche les inactifs, aider ceux qui peinent, redresser les jugements faux," *JEC* 1, no. 7 (1941), 2.

Rudin, Ronald. "Kouchibouguac in Acadian Memory." Paper presented at a meeting of the Canadian Historical Association, University of British Columbia, Vancouver, June 2008, 1.

Safer, Morley. "Morley Safer's Vietnam—A Personal Diary." CBS, 1967.

Stewart, Edison. "Viceroy Choice Stirs Fuss on Hill." *Toronto Star* (November 23, 1994), 23.

Warren, Jean-Philippe, and Julian Massicotte. "La fermeture du département de sociologie de l'Université de Moncton: Histoire d'une crise politico-épistélogique." *Canadian Historical Review* 87, no. 3 (September 2006), 463–96.

Westell, Anthony. "Trudeau's Television Success Trims Parliament's Power." *Toronto Daily Star* (April 15, 1970), 8.

Biographical Sketches

Chapter 2 – Cormier's Cove

Joseph Cardijn was born into a poor working-class family in 1882. His father was a coal miner. Ordained in 1906, he was sent to a parish in a poverty-stricken district of Brussels in 1912. His early efforts at establishing what was, in essence, a lay apostolate, met strong resistance from the bishops and he was branded a Communist. However, he was supported by Pius XI and, in 1965, he was made a cardinal by Pope Paul VI. Joseph Cardijn died in 1967.

Jacques Maritain (1882–1973) was the pre-eminent French political thinker and philosopher of the time. His writings influenced General de Gaulle and the establishment of the constitution of the Fourth French Republic in 1946. Maritain was also instrumental in the pronouncements on human rights put forward by the United Nations in 1948, and influenced the Canadian *Charter of Rights and Freedoms*. He had spent 1940–1945 in the

United States, and between 1948 and 1957 he taught at a number of American universities, including Princeton. He returned to France permanently in 1960.

Emmanuel Mounier was born in Grenoble in 1905 and died in 1950. A graduate of École Normale Supérieure in Paris, by the 1920s he had become known for his support of co-operative forms of economic management. His work quickly became the touchstone for Catholic social action in France, where his work inspired not only those already committed to the progressive youth movements but also the French Confederation of Democratic Labour and, after 1945, the worker priests. It also spread to the United States, where it was Mounier's ideas that inspired the organization of the Catholic Worker movement. In 1932, he founded the journal *Esprit*, which became, and continues to be, an influential forum for progressive Catholic thought in Europe.

One of *Georges Bernanos*'s (1888–1948) most influential works was *Journal d'un curé de campagne* (1936), for which he won the Grand Prix de l'Académie Française. The central character in the novel is an enthusiastic and idealistic young priest sent to a desperately poor parish in northern France, who dies of cancer, worn out by his efforts to make the Catholic faith a reality to his indifferent flock.

Marguerite Michaud (1903–1982) was born in Bouctouche, NB. She was one of the first Acadian women to graduate from a university, receiving her B.A. from Acadia University in 1923. She received a diploma in French literature from the Sorbonne, an M.A. from Columbia University, New York, and, in 1947, a Ph.D. from the Université de Montréal. She became an important friend of Roméo's when they were both teaching at the Normal School in Fredericton from 1955 to 1959.

Chapter 3 – Transitions and Interruptions, 1948–1955

André Malraux was born in Paris, France on November 3, 1901. He died in the same city on November 23, 1976. His novel *La condition humaine* (*Man's Fate*) drew on his experiences in Asia in the 1920s. It won the Prix Goncourt in 1933. He fought in Spain in 1936 and in the French Resistance during the Second World War, and was de Gaulle's minister of information in 1945–1946. He was also minister of state for de Gaulle in 1958–1959, and France's first minister of cultural affairs, from 1959 to 1969.

Emery LeBlanc (1918–1987) was the editor-in-chief of *L'Évangéline* from 1943 to 1973. His editorials during those years and his book *Les Acadiens* (Montreal: Éditions de l'Homme, 1963) provide a valuable perspective on Acadian life at the time.

Albert Camus (1913–1960) won the Nobel Prize in Literature in 1957. Among his most important works are *Le Mythe de Sisyphe* and *L'Étranger*.

Jean-Paul Sartre (1905–1980) won the Nobel Prize in Literature in 1964, but refused it. Two of his most important non-fiction works are *L'Existentialisme est un humanisme*, 1946, and *Critique de la raison dialectique*, 1960. *Huis clos*, 1944, was his most important play.

Abbé Pierre had worked with the Resistance, helping Jews escape to Switzerland, and died at the age of ninety-four on January 22, 2007.

Charles Bruneau was a distinguished professor of linguistics at the Sorbonne at this time. He published a popular text *Petite Histoire de la langue française* (Paris: A. Colin, 1955–1958).

Chapter 4 – Teacher to Journalist: Fredericton to Ottawa and Beyond

Pierre Juneau was born in Verdun, Quebec on October 17, 1922. He has held virtually every important position in the Canadian broadcasting hierarchy. He was educated at the Collège Sainte-Marie in Montréal and the Sorbonne in Paris. In 1949, he graduated from the Institut Catholique in Paris with a Licentiate in Philosophy, and the same year he joined the National Film Board of Canada. In 1951, he was chief of international distribution and, in 1954, the secretary of the board. In 1968, with the passage by Parliament of a new *Broadcasting Act*, he became the first Chairman of the Canadian Radio-Television Commission, a position he held until 1975. He was appointed an Officer of the Order of Canada that year.

Dr. Murray Stewart served as principal of New Brunswick Teachers' College from 1967 to 1973. He himself was a graduate of the college, having received an M.A. in education from the University of New Brunswick in 1947, and, in 1949, a doctorate in education from McKinley-Roosevelt University in Chicago.

R.H. Chapman went on to Mount Allison University for both a B.A. (1924) and, later, an M.A. (1930). In 1947, he also acquired a master's degree from Columbia University in New York.

René Lévesque was born on August 22, 1922, in Campbellton, NB, and died on November 1, 1987, in Montreal. In 1944, he went to Europe as a freelance war correspondent and became a broadcaster on the American French-language radio station beamed into Nazi-occupied Europe. He accompanied French troops as they entered Germany, and witnessed the liberation of the Dachau concentration camp. When he returned to Canada, he joined the CBC. In 1960, he joined the Quebec Liberal Party and was one of the most popular and energetic ministers in the Lesage government. In 1967, he left the Liberal Party to sit briefly as an independent. He was one of the founding members of the sovereignty-association movement that became the Parti Québécois. In 1976, this party won the provincial election and Lévesque became premier in the province, a position he held until 1985.

Jacques Languirand, born on May 1, 1931 in Montreal, is a highly productive radio and television journalist and an actor, writer, and producer, as well as a member of the faculty of both the Université de Montréal and McGill University. His program *Par 4 Chemins*, first broadcast by Radio-Canada in 1971, became, in 2006, the longest-running program hosted by a single person and broadcast by the same network. Among his many honours are the Governor General's Award for *Les Insolites* et *Les Violons d'Automne* (1962), appointment as an Officer of the Order of Canada (2003), the *Prix Georges-Émile-Lapalme pour la qualité et le rayonnement de la langue française* (2003) and the Governor General's Award for "les Arts de la scène"(2006).

John George Diefenbaker was born in Neustadt, Ontario, on September 18, 1895, and died on August 16, 1979. He was the son of German immigrants, who, after a number of moves, settled in Saskatoon in 1910. It was this province that profoundly shaped his character. He graduated from the University of Saskatchewan in 1915 with a B.A. and received an M.A. the following year. He served overseas in the First World War, as a lieutenant. On his return, he began to study law and was admitted to the bar in 1919. Diefenbaker was first admitted to the House of Commons in March 1940. In 1956, he was elected leader of the Progressive Conservative Party and became leader of the Official Opposition in 1957. He became prime minister of Canada in 1957, a position he held until 1963. Historian Michael Bliss considered that "he stood for a fascinating and still relevant combination of individual and egalitarian values."

Paul Joseph Martin was born in Ottawa on June 23, 1903. He was elected to the House of Commons in 1935, and was minister of national health and welfare in King's cabinet, a position he continued to hold during St. Laurent's term in office.

Lester Bowles Pearson was born at Newtonbrook, Ontario, on April 23, 1897. He was the son of a Methodist parson. Ontario was a formative influence on his character.

Pierre Sévigny was born on September 13, 1917, in Quebec City. He was the son of a prominent politician and judge. He was an early Quebec supporter of Diefenbaker. Elected to the House of Commons in 1958, he was appointed deputy speaker in May 1958 and associate minister of defence in August 1959. He resigned from the government in February 1963, and was defeated in the federal election of that year.

James Taylor was born in Little Shemogue, NB, in 1928. He was educated at Mount Allison University, where he received a B.A. in 1949 and an M.A. in 1950. In 1950–1951 he studied in London. He worked as a journalist until 1963, when he was seconded to the Royal Commission on Bilingualism and Biculturalism. He obtained a Ph.D. from the University of Pennsylvania in 1978. He was the founder of the Department of Communication at the Université de Montréal, where he is now a Professor Emeritus. He was named a "pioneer of the University" in 2003.

Jean Lesage was born in Montreal on June 10, 1912, and died in Quebec City on December 12, 1980. Elected federal MP for Montmagny–l'Islet in 1945, he was re-elected in 1949, 1953, 1957, and 1958. He became leader of the provincial Liberal Party on May 31, 1958, and not only completely transformed that party, but also oversaw a period of profound change in the collective life of the Québécois.

Joseph-David Réal Caouette was born in Abitibi, Quebec, on September 26, 1917, and died in Ottawa on December 16, 1976. He was first elected to Parliament in 1946, but was unsuccessful in the federal elections of 1953, 1957, and 1958. He returned to Parliament in 1962 as a member of the Social Credit Party for Villeneuve, a seat he retained for the rest of his life.

Marcel Chaput was born on October 14, 1918, and died on January 19, 1991.

Thomas Clement Douglas was born in Scotland on October 20, 1904, and died on February 24, 1986. He came to Canada at the age of six. He became a Baptist minister and was elected leader of the Saskatchewan CCF in 1942. In 1944, he became premier of Saskatchewan, a post he held until 1961. During his tenure, he introduced universal public health care in the province. He was elected to Parliament as leader of the NDP in 1962 and served in that position until 1979.

Chapter 5 – Foreign Correspondent: London and Washington
Ed Higginson is now retired, but he was a freelance cameraman under contract to CBC-TV News in London from 1961 to 1966. The London crews covered England, Ireland, India, Pakistan, Cyprus, Africa, and the Middle East, as well as war zones.

David Halton joined the CBC in 1965 and became the network's Paris-based correspondent a year later. His distinguished career took him to a variety of national and international postings. From 1971 to 1974, he reported for *The National* about Quebec and in Washington as the CBC's senior Washington correspondent. In 2005, he received the Gordon Sinclair Award for Broadcast Journalism.

Charles André Joseph Marie de Gaulle was born on November 22, 1890, and died on November 9, 1970. He was from a well-to-do Catholic family and was educated at the Jesuit Collège Stanislas in Paris. Deciding to make his career in the military, he entered the Academy of St. Cyr. He served with distinction during the First World War and, at the outbreak of the Second World War he commanded a tank brigade attached to the French Fifth Army. In May 1940, he became a brigadier-general and, after the fall of France, he left for England, where he organized the Free French forces. Following the liberation of France in 1944, he became prime minister of the French provisional government, but retired from government politics in 1946. The crisis of 1958 saw his return.

John XXIII was born Angelo Giuseppe Roncalli at Sotto Il Monte, Italy, on November 25, 1881. He died in Rome on June 3, 1963. He was elected Pope on October 28, 1958. His major encyclicals were *Pacem in Terris* and *Mater et Magistra*. He summoned the Second Vatican Council, which he prayed would renew the Christian sense in Catholicism. The faithful called him "the good Pope."

Morley Safer was born on November 8, 1931, in Toronto. He began his journalism career as a reporter for various newspapers in Canada and England. In 1964, he joined CBS News as a London-based correspondent. He is best known for his work as a correspondent during the Vietnam War and for his work on the CBS program *60 Minutes*, which he started in 1970. He and Roméo were lifelong friends.

Alphonse Ouimet was born in Montreal in 1908 and died there in 1988. He graduated with a degree in electrical engineering from the University of McGill in 1932 and was president of the CBC from 1958 to 1967.

Richard O'Hagan was born on March 23, 1928, at Woodstock, NB. He was special assistant to the leader of the Opposition from 1961 to 1963 and press secretary to the prime minister from 1963 to 1966. He was appointed minister-counsellor to the Canadian embassy in Washington in November 1966.

Maurice Sauvé was born in Montreal on September 20, 1923, and died there on April 13, 1992. He graduated with a doctorate from the Sorbonne in 1952 and worked for the Canadian and Catholic Confederation of Labour. In 1962, he was elected to Parliament and served as minister of forestry and rural development from 1964 to 1968.

Erskine Barton Childers was born on March 11, 1929, and died on August 25, 1996. He became an international civil servant, working for the United Nations in 1967, and went on to spend his life, at one time or another, working with most branches of that body and in most regions. At his retirement in 1989, he was senior adviser to the United Nations Director General for Development and International Economic Cooperation.

Jean Marchand was born in December 1918 and died on August 28, 1988. He was a trade unionist, who had been one of the leaders of the 1949 Asbestos Strike in Quebec, being at the time the secretary of the Catholic Workers Confederation of Canada. Pearson appointed him minister of citizenship and immigration.

Pierre Elliott Trudeau was born on October 18, 1919, and died on September 28, 2000. His family had considerable wealth, and he graduated from the Université de Montréal with a law degree in 1943. From 1949 to 1951, he worked in Ottawa in the Privy Council office. From 1961 to 1965, he was an associate professor of law at the Université de Montréal.

Pierre Nadeau was born in Montreal on December 19, 1936. He won the Trophée Méritas for the best French television reporter. *Jean-Marc Poliquin* (1924–1982) was born in Sainte-Angèle-de-Laval He was particularly good at languages, knowing Hebrew and German, as well as English and French. He spent ten years of his life, 1948 to1958, as a translator in the Senate before becoming a journalist. After 1977, he left journalism for life as an academic at the University of Ottawa and, before his early death, he had published five books, including a life of Pearson.

James Minifie (1900–1974) was born in England and came to Saskatchewan with his parents in 1909. He was a Rhodes Scholar and later studied at the Sorbonne. He began his journalistic career in 1929 with the *New York Herald Tribune.* For more than fifteen years, he reported first on radio and then on television for the CBC.

In the early 1970s, *Knowlton Nash* accepted an appointment as the head of news and information programming for the CBC. He became the anchor for the CBC's evening news program *The National* in 1978, a position he held until 1988. Afterwards, he was a freelance contributor to both *The National* and *The Sunday Report.*

Donald Campbell Jamieson was born in St. John's, Newfoundland, on April 30, 1921, and died of a heart attack in 1986. He established a private radio network in Newfoundland and the island's first television station, CJON-TV. He was elected to Parliament as a Liberal in 1968 and was minister of transport (1969–1972), minister of regional economic expansion (1972–1976), and secretary of state for external affairs (1976–1978). He was re-elected in the 1979 election, which brought down the Liberal government. In 1982, he was appointed Canada's High Commissioner to the United Kingdom, and served until 1986.

Doug Fisher (September 19, 1919–September 18, 2009) taught history at Port Arthur Collegiate. He served as a member of Parliament for the CCF from 1957 to 1968 and became a full-time parliamentary columnist, publishing first in the *Telegram* and later in the Toronto *Sun*.

Gerald Cannon Hickey is considered a pre-eminent world expert on the Montagnards, the peoples of the central highlands of Vietnam. He was in Vietnam from 1956 to 1973, and has published nine books on Vietnam. He first went there as a member of the Michigan State University Group in South Vietnam and returned later when he was a research assistant at Yale University. He became thoroughly disenchanted with American policy in the country in the early 1960s.

Chapter 6 – An Unexpected Path to Political Life
Paul Gérin-Lajoie was born in Montreal on February 23, 1920. He was educated at Collège Jean-de-Brébeuf and the Université de Montréal. He went to Oxford University on a Rhodes Scholarship and earned a Doctor of Laws degree. He became minister of education in the Lesage government in 1964. He was made a Companion of the Order of Canada "in recognition of his distinguished services to his country, as President of the Canadian International Development Agency from 1970 to 1977, and as deputy prime minister and minister of education of the government of Quebec from 1960 to 1966."

Jules Léger was born at Saint-Anicet, Quebec, on April 4, 1913, and died in Ottawa on November 24, 1980. He was governor general of Canada from January 1974 until January 1979. He had studied at the Université de Montréal and the Sorbonne, and joined the Department of External Affairs in 1940.

Monique Bégin was born in Rome in 1936 and spent her early childhood in France and Portugal, able to return to Canada only at the conclusion of the Second World War. She received an M.A. from the Université de Montréal and pursued doctoral studies at the Sorbonne. In 1967, she was appointed the executive secretary of the Royal Commission on the Status of Women. Elected in 1972, she became, with Albanie Morin and Jeanne Sauvé, one of the first women ever elected to the House of Commons from Quebec. She was appointed to cabinet as minister of national revenue in 1976, and served as minister of health and welfare from 1977 to 1979 and from 1980 to 1984. In 1986, she was the first appointment to the joint Ottawa-Carleton University Chair of Women Studies. From 1990 to 1995, she served as dean of the Faculty of Health Sciences at the University of Ottawa, and remains a Professor Emeritus of that university. She was elected a fellow of the Royal Society of Canada in 1996, appointed an Officer of the Order of Canada in 1997, holds more than fifteen honorary doctorates, and has continued to serve on both national and international bodies concerned with health matters.

Anthony Westell has had a distinguished career in Canadian journalism, winning three national newspaper awards and being inducted into the Canadian News Hall of Fame in 1992. Born in England in 1926, he began his career there before joining the *Globe and Mail* as a reporter in 1956. He was the Ottawa correspondent for that newspaper from 1964 to 1969. He became the Ottawa editor of the Toronto *Star* in 1969. He joined the school of journalism at Carleton University in 1972. He has published a number of books, including *Paradox: Trudeau as Prime Minister*, *Reinventing Canada*, and his autobiography, *The Inside Story: A Life in Journalism*.

Eugene Alfred Forsey was born in Grand Bank, Newfoundland, on May 29, 1904, and died in Victoria, BC, on February 20, 1991. A Rhodes Scholar, he was a member of the Department of Economics and Politics at McGill University from 1929 to 1941. He was appointed to the Senate in 1970. He was known for his socialist views, but was considered during his lifetime to be Canada's foremost constitutional expert with a conservative bent.

Gordon (Robert) Robertson was born in Davidson, Saskatchewan, in May 1917. He was educated at the University of Saskatchewan, Oxford University, and the University of Toronto. He joined the Department of External Affairs in 1941 and had a distinguished career as a public servant, serving as the commissioner of the Northwest Territories from 1953 to 1963, clerk of the Privy Council and secretary to the Cabinet, 1963–1975, and secretary to the Cabinet for federal-provincial relations, 1975–1979. He was made a Companion of the Order of Canada in 1976.

Robert Lorne Stanfield was born on April 11, 1914, and died on December 16, 2003. He was educated at Dalhousie University and Harvard University. He was premier of Nova Scotia from 1956 to 1967, and leader of the Progressive Conservative Party of Canada from September 9, 1967, to February 21, 1976. He was chairman of the Institute for Research on Public Policy from 1983 to 1987. He was one of the few granted the style "Right Honourable" without having held an office that bestowed this distinction.

Marshall Alexander Crowe was born in Rossburn, Manitoba, in 1921. He graduated from the University of Manitoba in history and economics in 1947. He returned to university in 1992, this time the University of Ottawa, and graduated with a law degree. He was elected as a backbencher in his first year of practice. In between, he had a distinguished career in the Department of

External Affairs (1947–1961), as an economic advisor to the Canadian Imperial Bank of Commerce (1961–1967), and as deputy secretary to the Cabinet (1967–1971). He was chairman of the Canadian Development Corporation (1971–1973) and chairman of the National Energy Board (1973–1978). He returned to the private sector as president of M.A. Crowe Consultants in 1978, and is still phenomenally active today.

Louis Joseph Robichaud was born in St. Anthony, Kent County, NB, on October 21, 1925, and died from cancer on January 6, 2005, at l'Hôpital Stella-Maris-de-Kent. He graduated from the Collège Sacré-Coeur in 1947 and then spent two years at Université Laval, where he was greatly influenced by the Dominican Father Georges-Henri Lévesque. Robichaud then articled with a law firm in Bathurst for three years before being admitted to the bar. He was elected to the New Brunswick legislature in 1952, and became provincial Liberal leader in 1958. He led the party to victory in 1960, 1963, and 1967, before being defeated by Richard Hatfield, the Conservative leader, in 1970. Robichaud was appointed a Companion of the Order of Canada in 1971, and was appointed to the Senate in 1973.

Jean-Robert Bourassa was born in Montreal on July 14, 1933, and died on October 2, 1996. He graduated from the Université de Montréal law school in 1956, later obtaining a degree in political economy from Harvard University, and was elected to the Quebec Legislative Assembly in 1966.

Jacques Parizeau was born in Montreal on August 9, 1930. He was educated at the Collège Stanislas and graduated with a Ph.D. in economics from the London School of Economics. He became an important adviser to the Quebec government in the 1960s. He officially joined the Parti Québécois in September 1969.

Chapter 7 – From Backbencher to Minister

Henry Read Emmerson (November 7, 1883–June 21, 1954) was a member of Parliament for Westmorland County, elected in 1935 and re-elected in 1940 and 1945. In 1949, he was appointed to the Canadian Senate, representing the senatorial division of Dorchester, NB.

Bertin LeBlanc became president of the Westmorland–Kent Liberal Association the same day Roméo was chosen candidate for the 1972 election. He became Roméo's special assistant in 1975, a position he held for four years. In 1978, Bertin LeBlanc was elected MLA for Kent-South. He lost his seat in 1982, and returned to Ottawa to work for Roméo the same year.

Yvon LeBlanc was born in Cap Pelé and received his high school education at St. Joseph's between 1964 and 1968. He took his B.A. at the Université de Moncton, graduating in 1968. He went on to take a law degree from the University of New Brunswick in 1971, before opening a private practice in Bouctouche, NB. He served as deputy minister, justice and consumer affairs, and deputy attorney-general in the Shawn Graham Liberal government, 2006–2010.

Born in Bouctouche, NB, in 1929, *Antonine Maillet* was educated at the Université de Moncton and Université Laval. Her first novel, *Pointe-aux-Coques*, was published in 1958. She was the first francophone writer not living in France to receive the Prix Goncourt. She has received many other honours, and is a Companion of the Order of Canada. She was named a member of the Queen's Privy Council of Canada in 1992 by Prime Minister Brian Mulroney.

Viola Léger became a friend of Antonine Maillet early in her career. Léger was working in Paris when Antonine asked her to take the lead in *La Sagouine*. She accepted and played the part more than 2,000 times, sometimes in French and sometimes in English. She was appointed to the Canadian Senate in 2001, and served until 2005.

Keith Davey was born in Toronto on April 21, 1926. He was educated at the University of Toronto and worked as a journalist before holding a number of positions in the Toronto-area Liberal Party. He became a major architect of Liberal election policy for the elections of 1963 and 1965. He was appointed to the Senate by Pearson in 1966.

Jack Davis was born in Kamloops, BC, on July 31, 1916, and died on March 27, 1991. He was an MP from 1962 to 1974. His riding stretched from North Vancouver to Powell River and Pemberton. He was a former Rhodes Scholar who studied economics at Oxford and had a Ph.D. in chemical engineering from McGill University.

Chapter 8 – Minister of Fishermen

Donald W. Munro was a retired senior Canadian diplomat, first elected to the House of Commons in 1972 as the Conservative member for Equimalt–Saanich, British Columbia.

John Alan Beesley, O.C. (August 17, 1927–January 22, 2009) was born in Smithers, BC. He graduated from the University of British Columbia with arts and law degrees and began work with the Department of External Affairs in 1946. He was part of the permanent Canadian mission to the United Nations Geneva from 1964 to 1967. From 1967 to 1983, he was instrumental in shaping the law of the sea as Canada's ambassador to the Law of the Sea conference, Canadian head of delegation, and chair of the conference drafting committee. He was a member of the International Law Commission from 1986 to 1991.

Mitchell Sharp, P.C., C.C. (May 1911–March 19, 2004) was born in Winnipeg and started his career in public service in 1947. He was elected as a member of Parliament in 1963, and made minister of trade and commerce that same year. From 1964 to 1968, he was minister of finance, then secretary of state for external affairs from 1968 to 1974, then president of the Privy Council from 1974 to 1978, and House leader for the Liberal Party from 1974 to 1978.

Lloyd Roseville Crouse (November 19, 1918–April 28, 2007) was first elected as MP for Queens–Lunenberg, NS, in 1957 and was re-elected on ten successive occasions. He served as the lieutenant-governor of Nova Scotia from 1989 to 1994.

John Cornell Crosbie, P.C., O.C., Q.C., was born in St. John's, Newfoundland, on January 30, 1931. He had a distinguished career in the provincial government before being elected to Parliament in 1976. He served as a minister with the Clark government in 1979 and with the Mulroney government from 1984 to 1993. He was appointed lieutenant-governor of Newfoundland on February 4, 2008.

Donald Tansley (May 19, 1925–July 19, 2007) was born in Regina, Saskatchewan. He worked as a senior civil servant for the province of Saskatchewan and also for the government of New Brunswick. He was vice-president of the Canadian International Development Agency (CIDA) from 1968 to 1973 and, while there, produced an influential report on the International Red Cross. In 1999, he received the highest award given by that body, the Durant Medal. He was made an Officer of the Order of Canada in 1999.

Pierre de Bané, born on August 2, 1938, was, in 1968, the first person of Arab descent to be elected to the House of Commons. His riding was Matane, Quebec. He was appointed to Cabinet as minister of supply and services in 1979 and reappointed as minister of regional economic expansion after the 1980 election. He served as MP for sixteen years, and was named to the Senate by Trudeau in 1984.

Chapter 9 – From Elected to Appointed Office
Peter Michael Pitfield, P.C., C.V., Q.C., was born June 18, 1937, in Montreal. He graduated with a law degree from McGill University and was admitted to the Quebec Bar in 1962. He joined the civil service in 1959, was appointed to the Senate on December 2, 1982, and resigned on June 1, 2010. Pitfield's time in the civil service gave Trudeau a personal friend and political ally at the head of the bureaucracy. Pitfield was dismissed by Clark but reappointed by Trudeau.

William Grenville (Bill) Davis, P.C., C.C., was born on July 30, 1929, in Brampton, Ontario. He was the eighteenth premier of Ontario, serving from 1971 to 1985, and played a pivotal role in the passage of the 1982 *Constitution Act.*

Hon. Paul Jones Cosgrove, P.C., Q.C., was born December 12, 1924, and was elected MP for York–Scarborough in the 1980 election.

Martin Brian Mulroney, P.C., C.C., was born on March 20, 1939, in Baie Comeau, Quebec. He entered St. Francis Xavier University in Antigonish, N.S., in 1955, at the age of 16, and graduated three years later. He graduated from Université Laval with a law degree in 1964 and was admitted to the Quebec Bar in 1965. He entered Parliament in August 1983 as the result of a by-election in Central Nova, after Elmer MacKay stood down in his favour.

John Napier Wyndham Turner was born in Richmond, Surrey, England, on June 7, 1929. His father having died, his mother returned with him to Canada in 1932. She remarried in 1945 to Frank MacKenzie Ross, who later served as lieutenant-governor of British Columbia. Turner enrolled in the University of British Columbia in 1945, at the age of 16, and qualified for the 1948 Olympic team, although a knee injury prevented him from competing. He graduated in 1949 and won a Rhodes Scholarship to Oxford. He was called to the Quebec Bar in 1954. In 1962, he entered Parliament for the riding of Saint-Laurent–Saint-Georges. In 1967, he was minister of consumer and corporate affairs. In 1968, he became minister of justice in Pierre Trudeau's cabinet.

Kenneth Colin (K.C.) Irving, O.C., was born in Bouctouche, NB, on March 14, 1899, and died on December 13, 1992. He became one of Canada's leading entrepreneurs and was ranked among the world's most important industrialists. He was born to J.D. Irving, who owned as small sawmill on the edge of town. By the late 1970s, K.C. Irving had made his father's company, JDI, the fourth-largest private landowner in the United States: his sawmills and pulp-and-paper plants fed his paper, tissue, and diaper factories throughout New Brunswick, Nova Scotia, Maine, Quebec, and Ontario. At the same time, he had diversified the Irving interests by the acquisition of various construction, food-processing, engineering, and oil companies, all of which were privately owned and overseen by family members. He married Harriet L. MacNairn in 1927 and they had three sons, Arthur, James, and Jack. Harriet Irving died in 1976. K.C. Irving married his former secretary, Winnifred Jane Johnston, in 1978.

Elsie Wayne was born on April 20, 1932, in Shediac, N.B. In 1983, she became the first woman mayor of Saint John. In 1993, she ran as the ruling Progressive Conservative Party's candidate in the riding of Saint John. Wayne was one only two Tories elected nationwide, and remained an MP until 2003.

Fernand Robichaud was born on December 2, 1939, in Shippagan, NB. He was a teacher and businessman before entering politics. He was re-elected in the 1988 election, but in 1990 resigned his seat to allow the newly chosen Liberal leader, Jean Chrétien, to enter the House of Commons through a by-election. Robichaud ran again and was elected in 1993 and appointed secretary of state for agriculture and agri-food. He was appointed a senator in 1997.

Richard Clippingdale became a member of the Carleton University History Department in 1967 and obtained his Ph.D. in History from the University of Toronto in 1970. He went on to become the assistant secretary of state, corporate policy and public affairs, from 1987 to 1992, and the associate vice-principal and director, Advanced Management Program, Canadian Centre for Management Development, from 1992 to 1994.

Joseph-Jacques Jean Chrétien was born on January 11, 1934, in Shawinigan, Quebec, the eighteenth of nineteen children (ten of whom died in infancy). He attended the Séminaire de Saint-Joseph de Trois-Rivières and studied law at the Université de Laval. He was first elected to the House of Commons in the riding of Saint-Maurice–Laflèche in 1963 and was re-elected in this riding for all but eight of the next forty-one years. He became a Cabinet minister, being appointed to the Department of National Revenue in 1968 by Lester Pearson. He was moved to the Department of Indian Affairs and Northern Development later that year, where he served until 1976. He then served as minister of industry, trade and commerce from 1976 to 1977, and minister of finance from 1977 to 1979. After the brief months when Joe Clark was prime minister, Chrétien served as minister of justice from 1980 to 1982 and minister of energy, mines and resources from 1982 to 1984. He was briefly a member of the Turner cabinet from June 30 to September 17, 1984. In 1986, he retired briefly from public life and served on the boards of several corporations, including the Power Corporation and the Toronto-Dominion Bank. He returned to the House of Commons after winning a by-election in the riding of Beauséjour in New Brunswick. Having won the 1993 election, Chrétien became prime minister of Canada in November 1993, a position he held until 2003, winning the succeeding election of 1997 and a third majority in 2000.

Chaviva Milada Hošek was born in Czechoslovakia on October 6, 1946, to Holocaust survivors. Raised and educated in Montreal, she earned her B.A. from McGill University and a doctorate from Harvard University. She was a professor of English Literature at the University of Toronto for thirteen years. An active feminist, she served as president of the National Action Committee on the Status of Women from 1984 to 1986. She served in the Ontario legislature from 1987 to 1989 and became director of the Liberal Party of Canada's caucus research bureau in 1990. She was director of policy and research in the Prime Minister's Office from 1993 to 2001, when she became CEO of the Canadian Institute for Advanced Research.

Kim Campbell was born in Port Alberni, British Columbia, in 1947. In 1964, she went to the University of British Columbia, where she majored in political science. After a period of study on a scholarship at the London School of Economics, she returned to UBC to study law. She became involved in Vancouver politics in 1984 and was elected to the Vancouver School Board. In 1988, she won Vancouver Centre as a Progressive Conservative.

In 1989, she became minister of state for Indian and Northern Affairs. She was the minister of justice and attorney-general of Canada from 1990 to 1993. In 1993, she was appointed minister of national defence. She became Canada's first female prime minister when she succeeded Brian Mulroney as leader of the Progressive Conservative Party in June 1993.

Ramon John Hnatyshyn was born on March 16, 1934, and died on December 18, 2002. His father, John Hnatyshyn, was born in the Ukraine and came to Canada when he was two months old. He was a lawyer, and in 1959 he was appointed to the Canadian Senate by Prime Minister Diefenbaker. His son was born in Saskatoon and earned a Bachelor of Arts in 1954 and a Bachelor of Laws from the University of Saskatchewan. He ran for the Progressive Conservatives in 1974 and was elected to represent Saskatoon–Biggar. He remained an MP until the election of 1988. He served in the Cabinet of Brian Mulroney as minister of justice and was named governor general in 1989.

Kananginak Pootoogook was born on January 1, 1935, and died on November 23, 2010. He was born in a traditional Inuit camp called Ikersak, near Cape Dorset, Nunavut. He became a leader in setting up the West Baffin Eskimo Co-operative Ltd., the first Inuit owned co-op. In 1970, he began work as a full-time artist. In 1980, he was elected to the Royal Canadian Academy of Arts.

Lucien Bouchard was born in Saint-Coeur-de-Marie on December 22, 1938. He received both a Bachelor of Arts degree and a law degree from Université Laval in 1971. He always believed in the distinct nature of Quebec society and had worked for the "yes" side in the 1980 referendum. At the same time, he had an appreciation of Canada and at one point served as Canada's ambassador to France. The failure of the Meech Lake Accord led to his founding the Bloc Québécois with seven other former federal MPs—five former Tories and two Liberals. In the 1993 federal election, the new party won 54 of 75 ridings in the province, and Bouchard became the first separatist opposition leader in the history of Canada. The 1995 referendum having rejected secession, Bouchard resigned his federal seat and became provincial premier.

Photographic Sources

The images in this book appear courtesy of the following individuals and institutions:

Peter Bregg: 209
Rita Cadieux: 68
Hector Cormier: 99
Graphics Division Environment Canada: 239
N.E.S. Griffiths: 36
Bertin LeBlanc: 213, 252
Diana Fowler LeBlanc: 15, 144, 276, 278, 282, 288
Dominic LeBlanc: 34, 42, 61, 66, 113, 131, 141, 262, 264, 270, 274, 290, 292
Lyn LeBlanc: 49, 66, 161, 179, 186, 207, 217, 226
Library and Archives Canada: 169
Photo Features Ltd.: 195

Index